Holding
NCLB
Accountable

Holding
NCLB
Accountable

Achieving Accountability, Equity, & School Reform

GAIL L. SUNDERMAN
Editor

CORWIN PRESS
A SAGE Company
Thousand Oaks, CA 91320

For information:

Corwin Press, Inc.
A SAGE Company
2455 Teller Road
Thousand Oaks, California 91320
E-mail: order@corwinpress.com

SAGE Ltd.
6 Bonhill Street
London EC2A 4PU
United Kingdom

SAGE India Pvt. Ltd.
M-32 Market
Greater Kailash I
New Delhi 110 048 India

SAGE Asia-Pacific Pte. Ltd.
33 Pekin Street #02-01
Far East Square
Singapore 048763

Printed in the United States of America

Library of Congress Cataloging-in-Publication Data

Holding NCLB accountable : achieving accountability, equity, & school reform / Gail L. Sunderman, editor.
    p. cm.
ISBN 978-1-4129-5787-8 (cloth)
ISBN 978-1-4129-5788-5 (pbk.)
    1. United States. No Child Left Behind Act of 2001. 2. Educational accountability—United States. 3. Educational change—United States. 4. Educational equalization—United States. I. Sunderman, Gail L. II. Title.

LB2806.22.H656 2008
379.1'580973—dc22

2007040309

This book is printed on acid-free paper.

08 09 10 11 10 9 8 7 6 5 4 3 2 1

Acquisitions Editor:	Elizabeth Brenkus
Managing Editor:	Arnis Burvikovs
Editorial Assistants:	Ena Rosen, Desirée Enayati
Production Editor:	Appingo Publishing Services
Cover Designer:	Michael Dubowe
Graphic Designer:	Karine Hovsepian

Contents

Acknowledgments

The ideas in this book originated from a series of roundtables on the No Child Left Behind Act jointly sponsored by the Chief Justice Earl Warren Institute on Race, Ethnicity, and Diversity at the University of California, Berkeley, School of Law and the Civil Rights Project at Harvard University. The Warren Institute is a multidisciplinary research center devoted to producing research and policy prescriptions on racial and ethnic justice issues. The Civil Rights Project is dedicated to research and policy development on a range of civil rights issues. Both are committed to building bridges between research, policy, and action and to being a source of intellectual capital on civil rights issues of our day. Special thanks go to Christopher Edley, Jr., co-director of the Warren Institute and dean of the law school and to Gary Orfield, director of the Civil Rights Project. They provided guidance and insight into developing the ideas for the roundtables. Jill Morningstar and Albert Kaufman were instrumental in planning and organizing the roundtables and reviewing the author's original manuscripts. Without their collaboration and hard work, the roundtables would remain just an idea. Jennifer Blatz, Marilyn Bryne, Lori Kelly, Karen McCree, Pamela Lomax, Carolyn Peelle, and Guy Johnson provided invaluable assistance with the roundtables and preparation of this book. I am grateful to have worked with the authors who have contributed to this volume and to the editors at Corwin for their invaluable assistance and support. Generous funding from the Bill and Melinda Gates Foundation and the Charles Stewart Mott Foundation is gratefully acknowledged.

Corwin Press gratefully acknowledges the reviews of this material by the following individuals:

Kenneth Arndt, Superintendent
CUSD #300
Carpentersville, IL

About the Editor

Gail L. Sunderman is a senior research associate in K–12 Education for the Civil Rights Project at UCLA. Her research focuses on educational policy and politics, and urban school reform, including the development and implementation of education policy and the impact of policy on the educational opportunities for at-risk students. At the Civil Rights Project, she is project director on a five-year study examining the implementation of the No Child Left Behind Act of 2001 and is coauthor of the book, *NCLB Meets School Realities: Lessons from the Field*. Prior research includes studies on the implementation of Title I schoolwide programs, governance reform in the Chicago Public Schools, and understanding institutional and organizational constraints on implementing school reform initiatives. Her work has appeared in *Harvard Educational Review, Teacher's College Record*, and *Educational Researcher*. She is a former Fulbright scholar and received her PhD in political science from the University of Chicago.

About the Contributors

Robert Balfanz is a research scientist at the Center for Social Organization of Schools, Johns Hopkins University. He is the codirector of the Talent Development Middle and High School Project, which is currently working with over one hundred high-poverty secondary schools to develop, implement, and evaluate comprehensive whole-school reforms. He is also cooperator of the Baltimore Talent Development High School, an Innovation High School run in partnership with the Baltimore City Public School System. He has published widely on secondary school reform, high school dropouts, and instructional interventions in high-poverty schools. Recent work includes *Locating the Dropout Crisis*, with coauthor Nettie Legters, in which they identify the number and location of high schools with high dropout rates. Dr. Balfanz is currently the lead investigator on a Middle School Dropout Prevention project in collaboration with the Philadelphia Education Fund which is funded by the William Penn Foundation. Dr. Balfanz has also been the coauthor of a number of mathematics curriculums including UCSMP Everyday Mathematics and Big Math for Little Kids.

Linda Darling-Hammond is Charles E. Ducommun professor of education at Stanford University School of Education, where she serves as principal investigator for the School Redesign Network and the Stanford Educational Leadership Institute. Her research, teaching, and policy work focus on educational policy, teaching and teacher education, school restructuring, and educational equity. She was the founding executive director of the National Commission on Teaching and America's Future, which produced the 1996 widely cited blueprint for education reform: *What Matters Most: Teaching for America's Future*. Among her more than two hundred publications is *The Right To Learn*, recipient of the 1998 Outstanding Book Award from the American Educational Research Association, and *Teaching as the Learning Profession*, awarded the National Staff Development Council's Outstanding Book Award in 2000. She began her career as a public school teacher and has cofounded several schools, including a charter high school in East Palo Alto, California.

Walter M. Haney is professor of education at Boston College's School Education and senior research associate in the Center for the Study of Testing Evaluation and Educational Policy (CSTEEP). He specializes in educational evaluation and assessment and educational technology. He was born in Texas, and raised in East Lansing, Michigan. After undergraduate school at Michigan State University, he taught in the Royal Kingdom of Laos for three years. He completed his MA and EdD degrees at Harvard University and has been on the faculty of Boston College for more than tweny years.

Willis D. Hawley is professor emeritus of education and public policy at the University of Maryland and scholar-in-residence at the American Association of School Administrators. From 1997 to 1999 he was executive director of the National Partnership for Excellence and Accountability in Teaching. At the University of Maryland, he served as dean of the College of Education. He received his PhD in political science, with distinction, from the University of California, Berkeley. Hawley has published numerous books, articles, and book chapters dealing with the education of teachers, teacher quality, school reform, urban politics, political learning, organizational change, school desegregation, and educational policy, and has developed courseware to facilitate online learning and software to enhance the utilization of research. His book on improving the quality of teaching in schools will be published by Corwin Press in 2007. In 1977–1978 he served as director of education studies, President's Reorganization Project, Executive Office of the President of the United States. He organized and directed the Common Destiny Alliance, a national consortium of organizations and scholars committed to improving intergroup relations.

Michael J. Kieffer is a doctoral student in language and literacy at Harvard Graduate School of Education. A former teacher in an urban middle school, he aims to conduct research that can inform policy and instructional practice to better serve the needs of English language learners. Currently, Kieffer is project coordinator for a study of reading comprehension among adolescent English language learners and their native English-speaking classmates in urban schools. His continuing research includes a meta-analysis on the effectiveness of accommodations for English language learners on large-scale assessments, an analysis of developmental trajectories in reading for students in high- and low-poverty schools, and a study of the role of word-learning strategies in vocabulary and reading comprehension development. He has also worked as a new teacher coach, trained preservice teachers, authored a professional development curriculum on secondary literacy instruction, and published in the peer-reviewed journal, *The Reading Teacher*.

Daniel Koretz is a professor at the Harvard Graduate School of Education whose research focuses on educational assessment and policy. A primary emphasis in his work has been the effects of high-stakes testing, including effects on schooling and the validity of score gains. His research has included studies of the effects of testing programs in several states; the assessment of students with disabilities; international differences in the variability of student performance; alternatives to traditional college admissions testing; and the application of value-added models to educational achievement. His current work focuses on the design and evaluation of test-focused educational accountability systems. His doctorate is in developmental psychology from Cornell University.

Mindy L. Kornhaber is an associate professor in the Department of Education Policy Studies at the Pennsylvania State University. Her research seeks to shed light on how educational policies enhance or impede individual potential and how such policies might enable human potential to be developed both to a high level and on an equitable basis. She has published articles and books on intelligence, school reform, and the educational consequences of high-stakes testing.

Jaekyung Lee is an associate professor in the Graduate School of Education at the State University of New York at Buffalo. He holds a PhD in education from the University of Chicago. His research focuses on educational policy for equity, particularly the issues of closing the achievement gap. He is the recipient of 2007 AERA Early Career Award.

Nettie Legters is a research scientist at the Johns Hopkins University Center for Social Organization of Schools, and co-director of the Center's Talent Development High Schools program. Her research focuses on equity in education, school organization, teachers' work, dropout prevention, and implementation, scale-up, and impact of secondary education reform. Dr. Legters has dedicated her professional career to improving low-performing high schools and advancing the national high school reform movement. She has published extensively and presented to a wide variety of audiences in national, state, regional, and district forums. Her book, *Comprehensive Reform for Urban High Schools: A Talent Development Approach*, is available through Teachers College Press.

Nonie K. Lesaux is assistant professor of human development and psychology at the Harvard Graduate School of Education. Her research focuses primarily on the reading development and difficulties of children from language minority backgrounds. Lesaux was senior research associate for the *National Literacy Panel on Language Minority Youth*, a panel that conducted a comprehensive, evidence-based review of the research on the development of literacy among language minority learners, and is a contributing author to three chapters in that report. Lesaux focuses on conducting research that has implications for practitioners, researchers, and policymakers, and has published her research in several journals including *Journal of Educational Psychology, Developmental Psychology, Reading and Writing: An Interdisciplinary Journal, Teachers College Record, Educational Evaluation and Policy Analysis, Education Policy Analysis Archives*, and *The Reading Teacher*. She is a member of the International Academy for Research in Learning Disabilities, the Society for the Scientific Study of Reading, the International Reading Association, and the Society for Research in Child Development.

Robert L. Linn is distinguished professor emeritus of education at the University of Colorado at Boulder and a director of the National Center for Research on Evaluation, Standards, and Student Testing. He has published over two hundred journal articles and chapters in books dealing with a wide range of theoretical and applied issues in educational measurement. He has received several awards for his contributions to the field, including the ETS Award for Distinguished Service to Measurement, the E. L. Thorndike Award, the E. F. Lindquist Award, the National Council on Measurement in Education Career Award, and the American Educational Research Association Award for Distinguished Contributions to Educational Research. He is past president of the American Educational Research Association, past president of the National Council on Measurement in Education, past president of the Evaluation and Measurement Division of the American Psychological Association, and past vice president for the Research and Measurement Division of the American Educational Research Association. He is a member of the National Academy of Education and a Lifetime National Associate of the National Academies.

Goodwin Liu is a law professor at University of California, Berkeley specializing in constitutional law, education policy, civil rights, and the Supreme Court. He is also co-director (with Christopher Edley, Jr.) of the Chief Justice Earl Warren Institute on Race, Ethnicity, and Diversity, a multidisciplinary research center at University of California Berkeley. Professor Liu has published widely on affirmative action, school desegregation, school finance, and federal education policy. Before joining the Boalt faculty, he served as a law clerk to Justice Ruth Bader Ginsburg at the U.S. Supreme Court and as special assistant to the deputy secretary of education during the Clinton Administration. He is a Stanford alumnus, Rhodes Scholar, and graduate of Yale Law School.

Heinrich Mintrop taught middle school and high school for over a decade in both the United States and Germany before he entered into his academic career. He received a PhD in education from Stanford University in 1996. He is currently an associate professor of education at the University of California, Berkeley. As a researcher, he explores issues of school improvement and accountability in both their academic and civic dimensions. He has recently published the book *Schools on Probation. How Accountability Works (and Doesn't Work)* at Teachers College Press. At University of California Berkeley, he is involved in programs that prepare strong leaders for high-need urban schools.

Gary Orfield is professor of education, law, political science, and urban planning at UCLA and codirector of the Civil Rights Project. He is an author or editor of many books including *Dropouts in America, School Resegregation, Must the South Turn Back,* and *Higher Education and the Color Line.* He received the 2007 Social Justice Award from the American Educational Research Association.

Russell W. Rumberger is professor of education in the Gevirtz Graduate School of Education at the University of California, University of California Santa Barbara and director of the University of California Linguistic Minority Research Institute, a multi-campus research unit established in 1984 to foster interdisciplinary research and to improve academic achievement of children from diverse language backgrounds. He received a PhD in education and an MA in economics from Stanford University in 1978 and a BS in electrical engineering from Carnegie-Mellon University in 1971. A faculty member at University of California, Santa Barbara, since 1987, Rumberger has published widely in several areas of education: education and work; the schooling of disadvantaged students, particularly school dropouts and linguistic minority students; school effectiveness; and education policy. He is currently directing the California Dropout Research Project, which will produce a series of reports and policy briefs about the dropout problem in California and a state policy agenda to improve California's high school graduation rate.

Catherine E. Snow is the Henry Lee Shattuck Professor at the Harvard Graduate School of Education. She studies determinants of literacy development and academic achievement among students in urban schools, with special attention to struggling readers and to English language learners. She is leading the Boston Field Site of the Strategic Education Research Partnership, a practice-research partnership focused on improving literacy in middle schools. She has published widely. Her most recent book, coauthored with Michelle Porche, Patton Tabors, and Stephanie Ross Harris, is called *Is Literacy Enough? Pathways to Academic Success for Adolescents*. It identifies the determinants of literacy success for children from low-income families, but also defines the additional motivational resources and the school and family supports those students need as they enter adolescence if they are to be academically successful.

Introduction

Rethinking the Challenge of NCLB

"Many of the ideas in NCLB are wonderful. You know, when you have kids who are struggling, you want to provide them . . . with different kinds of opportunities to learn. You want to bring in these outside resources because they supposedly have a proven track record. You know, you want to allow kids who are in really the worst performing schools to have an opportunity. The devil is in the details. It's actually implementing this stuff that becomes a nightmare."
Personal interview, Chicago Public Schools, July 28, 2004

"Teachers want to do a good job. The trick is to get them the right kinds of resources and to reward their progress in the right direction."
Personal interview, Chicago Public Schools, July 28, 2004

The words of these teachers articulate both the aspiration of the No Child Left Behind (NCLB) Act of 2001, to provide better educational opportunities to all children, and the challenge that comes with trying to achieve that goal. The goals of the law are compelling and are shared by many Americans who want to see that all children receive a high-quality education. By demanding high standards for all students, NCLB promises to close the achievement gap and bring all students up to proficiency by 2014. And the act proposes specific remedies, from test-based accountability to market-driven reforms, to reach these goals. Yet, as noted, when it comes to attaining those goals with the tools and requirements specified in the law, the devil is in the details.

The language of high standards, accountability, and equity that characterizes the discourse on NCLB often means that the very real challenges of implementing its requirements are downplayed, masked, or simply ignored. NCLB relies on test-based accountability and operates on the theory that measuring performance, identifying schools and districts that fail to meet an expected performance level and applying a series of sanctions is what is needed to induce schools—and teachers—to work harder to improve student achievement. But when considered from the perspective of those charged with implementing the law—educators—the challenge is how to connect the goals of the legislation with real change in the classroom, genuine improvement in educational achievement, and a significant narrowing of the achievement gap. It means developing the capacity of states and districts to implement the law's requirements and designing better accountability systems that will improve the achievement of historically low-scoring groups while generating fewer negative side effects. It requires recognizing that lasting school reform involves intensive capacity building and providing schools with the right mix of incentives, support, and resources if struggling schools are to reach high performance goals.

The book is organized around four themes. Three of these—accountability, capacity, and school reform—provide the framework for the chapters. A fourth theme—the implications of the law for low-income and minority students—is carried throughout the book. The law proclaims its goal is to "close the achievement gap between high- and low-performing children, especially the achievement gap between minority and nonminority students, and between disadvantaged children and their more advantaged peers," and lays out a theory of school reform that is intended to achieve that goal. This book considers the limits of the NCLB performance-based system when it comes to improving the achievement of these targeted groups of students and the capacity requirements necessary for achieving successful school reform.

From a civil rights perspective, the law's emphasis on improving the achievement of low-income and minority students, those learning English, and students with disabilities is crucial. Advocates argue for improving the law rather than dismantling it. Since this will require that the law be changed in ways that support thoughtful and innovative responses to accountability, school improvement, and student achievement that are based on research, the authors in this book propose changes to NCLB that will mitigate the negative aspects of the law and promote the conditions necessary for meaningful student learning.

A CIVIL RIGHTS PERSPECTIVE ON NCLB

For those concerned with educational equity, NCLB represents a shift in the public discourse on how to improve school performance and the causes of the achievement gaps between minority and majority students, and low-income students and their more affluent peers. While the law is framed in the language of educational equity, it rejects any connection between racial isolation, economic inequities, unequal resources, or concentrated poverty and school achievement. Instead it frames the debate as one where all students can learn if the teachers and schools responsible for educating them work harder and are held accountable for results (Kantor & Lowe, 2006; Rothstein, 2004; Sunderman, Kim, & Orfield, 2005). For example, the statement of purpose to the Act says that it aims to identify schools "that have failed to provide a high-quality education to their students" and that resources should be distributed and target to districts and schools "to make a difference" (NCLB, Section 1001). This shift helped generate bipartisan support for the law when it was passed in 2001 because it freed lawmakers on both sides of the aisle from confronting the social context of present-day schooling and its effect on educational opportunities. At the same time, it made education policy the primary vehicle for improving the life chances of poor and minority students, and it removed pressure on policymakers to address broader social policy issues that affect differences in student performance.

For many in the civil rights community, NCLB represented an opportunity to focus on how public education has failed minority students. Skeptical that decisions made by state and local educators would result in tangible benefits for minority students, many civil rights advocates favored a stronger role for the federal government. That federal power had been successfully used to enforce civil rights and expand access to education for minorities, women, and students with disabilities led many to believe that federal power could be used to change educational practices and student learning. The subgroup rules, the reliance on "objective" measures of student achievement, and public reporting requirements would show how minority students were performing and provide the impetus needed to address their concerns.

To achieve its goals, the law's accountability provisions put pressure on schools and teachers to improve school performance. However, as the authors in this book show, the current design of the accountability system has serious limitations that are as likely to harm as to help schools serving low-income and minority students, the very students it was intended to help. These issues are examined in the first two sections of the book.

NCLB is also premised on the theory that school reform can be accomplished quickly, with little additional resources, and that there are known ways to improve schools and student performance. Existing resources are considered to be sufficient to improve poorly performing schools and, rather than needing additional resources, the incentive structure of the accountability system will cause states, districts, and schools to reallocate resources in productive ways. When it comes to how to reform schools, the law is very clear. It outlines a set of initiatives—many of them based on the idea that competition and privatization of schooling will provide the impetus for schools to improve—that schools must implement depending on how long they are identified as underperforming. The idea that the capacity of states charged with helping schools improve would need to be expanded or that poorly performing schools may need additional resources and support that develops their internal capacity, is not part of the NCLB formula. The last two sections of the book address issues about how states are meeting the NCLB requirements and whether they are reallocating resources in the ways envisioned by reformers.

Overview of the Chapters

Part I. NCLB and Accountability. Accountability is at the heart of NCLB, specifically, test-based accountability for specific educational outcomes with very high stakes attached for schools not reaching those goals. This section includes four chapters that examine the NCLB accountability measures, the challenges of measuring progress for accountability purposes, and the complexities of developing tests to assess English language learners.

The section begins with *The Pending Reauthorization of NCLB: An Opportunity to Rethink the Basic Strategy,* in which Daniel Koretz clearly and concisely lays out what we know and don't know about educational accountability and its effects. He moves beyond the debate about the specifics of NCLB (such as the problems with the adequate yearly progress (AYP) provisions) to talk about the broader issue of what we know about holding schools accountable and what empirical evidence is available to support or refute the claims of NCLB and accountability advocates. Rather than ask whether high-stakes testing *works,* Koretz asks what *types* of accountability systems will most improve opportunities for low-performing students while minimizing the negative side effects.

Focusing in on the specifics of the NCLB law, *Toward a More Effective Definition of Adequate Yearly Progress* examines the AYP provisions of the law, which are the primary mechanism used to hold schools and districts accountable under NCLB. Robert L. Linn delineates the limitations of AYP, particularly as they relate to achieving equity, and provides suggestions for improving AYP.

Recognizing the contraints of accountability systems that rely primarily on a single indicator in, *Beyond Standardization in School Accountability* Mindy L. Kornhaber considers whether accountability systems can be developed that combine multiple indicators of student achievement, educational inputs, and other variables of school performance. She argues that any educational accountability system should be informative (allow the public to know the status and progress of students' knowledge, skills, and understanding within and across schools) and be cognitively constructive (advance students' learning and enable educators to improve instruction). Using these two aims, she provides the groundwork for developing a non-standardized system of school review that would lead to a more comprehensive picture of school performance and discusses the implications of this type of system for low-income and minority students.

English language learners are one of the subgroups identified by NCLB for special attention to their achievement and academic needs. The chapter by Michael J. Kieffer, Nonie K. Lesaux, and Catherine E. Snow, *Promises and Pitfalls: Implications of NCLB for Identifying, Assessing, and Educating English Language Learners*, examines how NCLB policies affect this subgroup. They focus on two areas where English language learners experience the impact of NCLB: (1) how the English language learner is identified and categorized for purposes of disaggregation and academic monitoring and (2) how language development and academic progress of language minority students is assessed. They argue that while the NCLB policies raised awareness of the academic needs of language minority learners, they fall short of benefiting this subgroup because they overlook the complexity of second language development.

Part II. Evidence on How NCLB Is Working. Some in the research and policy community argue that it is too early to assess the impact of NCLB on student achievement because the law has only been in effect a short time, and measuring educational change requires a longer time frame. However, the law, by definition, requires schools to make rapid progress towards improving the achievement of low-performing students. Indeed, its 100 percent proficiency requirement by 2013–2014 implies a steep improvement trajectory if the goal is to be met. Since the law attaches very strong sanctions for not reaching state proficiency goals, accessing whether the federal rules are promoting gains in student achievement is essential. The two chapters in this section ask whether NCLB is contributing to increasing student achievement and narrowing the achievement gap and consider the challenges of determining school quality using test scores.

Jaekyung Lee provides evidence that achieving NCLB's aims to increase student achievement and close the racial and socioeconomic achievement gap may prove elusive. *Two Takes on the Impact of NCLB on Academic Improvement: Tracking State Proficiency Trends Through NAEP versus State Assessments* provides a systematic trend analysis of the National Assessment of Educational Progress (NAEP) national and state-level achievement results during pre-NCLB (1990–2001) and post-NCLB (2002–2005) periods. Lee compares post-NCLB trends with pre-NCLB trends to examine whether states and the nation are making progress towards improving student achievement. He also examines the discrepancies between NAEP and state assessment results.

NCLB has brought increased attention to the rating of school quality based on students' performance on state math and reading tests. Because of the uneven quality of state tests, the emphasis of test-based accountability has focused more attention on NAEP as a check on state test results. In *Evidence on Education Under NCLB (and How Florida Boosted NAEP Scores and Reduced the Race Gap)* Walter M. Haney discusses why NAEP results are a dubious basis for reaching summary judgments on school quality. Using data from Florida, he shows how NAEP results are misleading when the progression of students through the grades are examined.

Part III. State Capacity to Implement NCLB. NCLB expanded state authority for education and gave state education agencies primary responsibility for implementing its requirements. This is not surprising given their historic role in governing education, but if the responsibilities are new and broader than they had been before, then understanding the feasibility of that role and the resources necessary to carry it out is vital to the success of NCLB. These three chapters provide insights into understanding state capacity needs under NCLB from different perspectives.

In *Interstate Inequality and the Federal Role in School Finance,* Goodwin Liu takes a detailed look at educational inequality across states. NCLB imposes the same accountability provisions on all states, but allows states to set standards and allocate resources to achieve its goals. Often overlooked in debates about educational inequality is not the inequality *within* states but *between* states. By examining state fiscal capacity and effort, Liu shows that interstate disparities in education resources have more to do with the capacity of states to finance education than with their willingness to do so. He also demonstrates how Title I reinforces rather than reduces interstate inequality in school funding and proposes recommendations for reforming the federal role in school finance to be more responsive to state effort and capacity.

Under NCLB, state education agencies play a crucial role in supporting and monitoring the implementation of the federal mandates. Using data collected from six states, *Massive Responsibilities and Limited Resources: The State Response to NCLB* by Gail L. Sunderman and Gary Orfield examines the state response to meeting the law's requirements. They identify significant changes in NCLB from previous legislation that alter the state role and examine whether states have the resources, knowledge, and organizational capacity to implement the law and intervene in low-performing schools on the scale demanded by NCLB. The authors found that states focused on aspects of the law where they had expertise, but for the more ambitious goals of improving school performance, the law provided few resources and state experience was limited.

Using data from states that began experimenting with outcome-based accountability systems some ten years prior to the passage of NCLB, the chapter by Heinrich Mintrop, *Low-Performing Schools' Programs and State Capacity Requirements: Meeting the NCLB Educational Goals,* gauges the scope of low-performing schools' programs and the required state capacities to implement them. Mintrop shows that while outcome-based accountability systems seem to introduce a greater degree of rationality into school improvement and thus simplify the school improvement task, the successes of these systems are limited and require substantial capacity building. In his research, Mintrop found that the adoption of rigorous performance goals created a huge intervention burden on states, which they sought to minimize by limiting the scope of improvement programs. He discusses the implications of these earlier experiences for school improvement under NCLB.

Part IV. NCLB Impact on School Reform. Undoubtedly, if NCLB is to reach its goals, schools are going to have to improve. Yet there is a huge disconnect between what is known about successful school reform and the mechanisms in the law used to promote school improvement. These four chapters explore what we know about successful school reform and how NCLB might help or hinder those efforts.

Improving High Schools and the Role of NCLB by Linda Darling-Hammond looks at how various aspects of NCLB accountability provisions support or undermine a national movement to reform large, comprehensive high schools. She identifies areas that research suggests are critical elements of high-performing urban high schools and shows how two areas of the law—the definition and development of highly qualified teachers and the design of testing and accountability regulations—have made it more difficult for high schools in low-income neighborhoods to do their work. Darling-Hammond proposes specific amendments to NCLB that would address these concerns.

The theory of reform embedded in NCLB is that holding schools accountable for increased student performance will drive school reform (schools will reallocate resources in ways that will improve student achievement) and create the conditions for continuous improvement (accelerate and sustain school improvement that results in high levels of learning for all students). The chapter by Willis D. Hawley, *NCLB and Continuous School Improvement,* contrasts what is known about implementing school reform initiatives that accomplish meaningful change in schools with the potential of NCLB to develop school and district capacity to foster continuous and meaningful change. Hawley recommends changes in NCLB that would strengthen the law's effects on long-term improvements in student learning.

Robert Balfanz and Nettie Legters examine the relationship between the 12 percent of high schools that produce about half of the nation's dropouts and whether these are the schools being identified for improvement under NCLB in *NCLB and Reforming the Nation's Lowest-Performing High Schools: Help, Hindrance, or Unrealized Potential?* Finding that about 40 percent of these low-performing high schools made AYP, they look at what differentiates these schools from those that failed to make AYP. They identify core weaknesses in the NCLB accountability measures that work against effectively and consistently identifying low-performing high schools and offer proposals to address these shortcomings.

The challenge for many high schools is finding ways to reduce the dropout rate. The chapter by Russell W. Rumberger, *Can NCLB Improve High School Graduation Rates?*, reviews the research on how high schools contribute to students dropping out and effective strategies to reduce dropout rates. Rumberger explores NCLB as a strategy for improving schools in general and graduation rates specifically, and why performance-based accountability systems are limited when it comes to achieving these goals.

CONCLUSION

The chapters in this volume elucidate the challenges of improving NCLB by showing what needs to be changed in order to meet the goals of the law. While the chapters take on different aspects of NCLB and its implementation, they underscore some important and related points, and they offer broad recommendations that could improve the act. These recommendations converge on two key points. To develop a more realistic accountability system, Congress needs to amend the law to lessen its negative impact and support a serious program of research, development, and evaluation to facilitate the design of better educational accountability systems. To give low-performing schools a chance to improve, Congress needs to consider what it will take in human and financial resources to meet the law's requirements, both at the state level and in the schools.

1

The Pending Reauthorization of NCLB

An Opportunity to Rethink the Basic Strategy

Daniel Koretz

The pending reauthorization of No Child Left Behind (NCLB) is generating intense debate about possible modifications of many of its provisions such as the requirements for disaggregated reporting, adequate yearly progress (AYP), the draconian requirements for the assessment of students with disabilities, and the provisions for testing students with limited proficiency in English.

But as important as it is, the debate about the specifics of NCLB obscures three more important problems that we cannot afford to ignore:

- First, we know far too little about how to hold schools accountable for improving student performance. NCLB and its state-level forebears—dating back to the first minimum-competency testing programs more than three decades ago—have been based on a shifting combination of common sense and professional judgment, not on hard evidence.

- Second, some important aspects of NCLB (and its antecedent state programs) are inconsistent with the evidence we do already have.
- Third, much of the apparent progress generated by NCLB and similar programs is spurious, a comforting illusion that we maintain for ourselves—at a great cost to children—by failing to perform appropriate evaluations.

In this chapter, I will elaborate on these three points and will briefly sketch a few of the most important things we know—and don't know—about test-based educational accountability and its effects. I will end with a plea that we use the coming reauthorization as an opportunity to belatedly ramp up the hard work of research, development, and evaluation needed to create effective accountability systems—not as a substitute for alterations to the requirements for AYP, disaggregated reporting, and the like, but as an essential complement to them.

As a former public school teacher, parent, and educational researcher for more than a quarter of a century, I remain convinced that the educational system needs more effective accountability systems and that achievement testing has to be one element of them. But research has shown that we are making a hash of it. It is our obligation to children—particularly to those faring poorly in the current system—to do better.

WHAT THE EVIDENCE DOES AND DOES NOT TELL US

Clues to more productive approaches to educational accountability—in particular, approaches that are most likely to benefit the students in historically low-performing groups—lie both in what research has found and in the questions it has not yet answered.

Does High-Stakes Testing Work?

A modest number of studies argue that high-stakes testing does or doesn't improve student performance in tested subjects. This research tells us little. Much of it is of very low quality, and even the careful studies are hobbled by data that are inadequate for the task. Moreover, this research asks too simple a question. Asking whether test-based accountability *works* is a bit like asking whether medicine works. What medicines? For what medical conditions? Similarly, test-based accountability takes many forms that are likely to have different effects. Its impact is likely to vary among types of schools and students.

Test-based accountability also has diverse effects that go beyond the test scores that serve as outcomes in these studies. A program that succeeds in raising mathematics scores may reduce achievement in other important subjects, for example, if teachers rob Peter to pay Paul, taking time away from science or history to give more time to mathematics. And education has important goals that are not easily measured with standardized tests and remain unevaluated (Rothstein & Jacobsen, 2006).

Thus, the debate about whether high-stakes testing works is a red herring, distracting us from the question we ought to be asking: what *types* of accountability systems will most improve opportunities for students while minimizing the inevitable negative side effects? We need research and evaluation to address this question, because we still lack a well-grounded answer. We need to look at a range of outcomes beyond scores on the tests used for accountability. We need to create opportunities for designing these programs and for rigorously evaluating their positive and negative effects.

Can Score Increases Be Trusted?

Although research does not tell us whether high-stakes testing works, evidence does show us that high-stakes testing does not work nearly as well as it seems to. Just as economic work on incentives predicts, people try—often successfully—to game the system. As a consequence, scores on high-stakes tests can become dramatically inflated. That is, gains in scores can be much larger than the true improvements in student achievement that the scores are intended to signal. This creates an illusion of progress that is comforting to policymakers and educators but of no help whatever to children.

The issue of score inflation remains oddly controversial. Many in the policy world ignore it altogether or treat it as something that we really need not worry about. One superintendent of a large urban district dismissed the entire issue with a single sentence: "That's just a matter of opinion." He was wrong. Score inflation is a matter of evidence, not merely of opinion, and the problem is severe.

The inflation of test scores should not be surprising, since similar corruption of measures occurs in many other fields. Over the years, the press has documented corruption of measures of postal delivery times, airline on-time statistics, computer chip speeds, diesel engine emissions, television program viewership, and cardiac surgery outcomes, as well as scores on achievement tests (e.g., Cushman, 1998; Farhi, 1996; Hickman, Levin, Rupley, & Willmott, 1997; Lewis, 1998; Markoff, 2002; McAllister, 1998; Zuckerman, 2000). If many cardiac surgeons avoid doing procedures on high-risk patients who may benefit for fear of worsening their numbers, as the majority of respondents to a recent survey admitted (Narins, Dozier, Ling, & Zareba, 2005), it is hardly remarkable that some teachers and students will take shortcuts that inflate test scores.

The few relevant studies are of two types: detailed evaluations of scores in specific jurisdictions, and a few broad comparisons of trends on state tests and the National Assessment of Educational Progress (NAEP).

We have far fewer of the former than we should. The reason is not hard to fathom. Imagine yourself as superintendent of a district or state with rapidly increasing test scores. A researcher asks you for permission to evaluate the validity of these gains, to explore whether they are inflated and, if so, whether there are any useful patterns in the amount of inflation. This is not a politically appealing prospect.

The logic of both types of study is the same. The goal of education is to teach students skills and knowledge. A test score, which reflects performance on a very small sample of this material, is valuable only to the extent that it accurately represents students' overall mastery. In this respect, a test is much like a political poll. For example, two months before the 2004 election, a Zogby International poll of 1,018 likely voters showed George W. Bush with a 4 percent lead over John Kerry. This was a good prediction, as two months later Bush's margin was about 2.5 percent. But should we have cared how the specific 1,018 respondents actually voted? In general, the answer is "no." The voters sampled are just a drop in the bucket of millions of voters, and we worry about their opinions only because of what they suggest about the inclinations of the electorate as a whole. Analogously, we should not be too concerned about performance on the few specific items on a given test. Instead, we need to worry about the much larger domain of knowledge and skill that these few items are designed to represent.

For that reason, gains in scores on a high-stakes test, if they represent real gains in achievement, should *generalize*. Higher scores should predict better performance in the real world outside of the students' current schools—whether that is further education or later work. By the same token, score increases should generalize to better performance on other tests designed to measure similar bundles of knowledge and skills. Gains will not be exactly the same from one test to the next, but when tests are designed to support similar inferences about performance, gains ought to generalize reasonably well.

The results of the relatively few relevant studies are both striking and consistent: gains on high-stakes tests often do not generalize well to other measures, and the gap is frequently huge. When students do show improvements on other, lower stakes measures used to audit gains (most often NAEP), the gains on the audit test have generally been one-third to one-fifth the size of the gains shown on the high-stakes test. And in several cases, large gains on high-stakes tests have been accompanied by no improvement whatever on an audit test. For example, when Kentucky instituted a high-stakes testing program in the early 1990s—in several respects, a precursor of NCLB—fourth graders showed an increase of about three-fourths of a standard deviation on the state's high-stakes reading test in the space of only two years. This was a remarkably large increase for such a short time. By way of comparison, the pervasive decline in scores during the 1960s and 1970s that did much to provoke the last several decades of education reform averaged roughly three-tenths of a standard deviation over a span of ten to fifteen years. During the two years that scores on the Kentucky reading test skyrocketed, the scores of Kentucky students on the NAEP reading test showed no increase at all (Hambleton et al., 1995). Other studies have found similar results in Chicago, in Houston, in Texas as a whole, and in an anonymous district I studied (Jacob, 2002; Klein, Hamilton, McCaffrey, & Stecher, 2000; Koretz, Linn, Dunbar, & Shepard, 1991; Schemo & Fessenden, 2003).

These few studies are complemented by a second group that provides a broad overview of the comparability of trends on state tests and NAEP. Studies in this second group show that in many—but not all—states, gains on state tests are larger, often markedly larger, than the same states' gains on NAEP (Fuller, Gesicki, Kang, & Wright, 2006; Fuller, Wright, Gesicki, & Kang, 2007; Ho & Haertel, 2006; Lee, 2006; Linn & Dunbar, 1990).

The implication of this research is inescapable: much of the apparent progress shown by increasing scores on high-stakes tests is simply spurious, an illusion that allows us to proclaim success while students continue to be deprived of opportunity.

Research indicates that score inflation varies markedly from school to school, but it does not yet provide any guidance about which types of schools are usually most affected. Given the current state of our knowledge, we cannot accurately predict which schools have sizable inflation and which do not, and we usually have no means of determining this from available data. This has two unfortunate consequences.

First, it vitiates conclusions about the *relative* effectiveness of schools. If inflation were uniform, overall gains would be exaggerated, but one could still identify the schools with relatively large or relatively small improvements in learning. But given our inability to pin down school-level variations in score inflation, conclusions about relative effectiveness are entirely untrustworthy if they are based only on scores on high-stakes tests, and we can expect to reward or sanction the wrong schools a good bit of the time.

Second, we cannot ascertain the relative impact of test-based accountability programs on the groups of students who are the focus of reform—in particular, groups that currently show low average achievement. Several other researchers and I have hypothesized that score inflation will often be worse in low-achieving schools. Our logic is simple: Systems such as NCLB require teachers in high-achieving schools to make relatively modest gains. (This depends on states' performance standards, of course, but it is also built into the AYP system and the *straight-line* systems many states used before NCLB.) Moreover, many high-achieving schools are in communities that offer relatively substantial out-of-school supports for student achievement, such as well-educated parents who press for high grades and can reteach material at home and buy afterschool tutoring. Teachers in low-achieving schools are required to generate far larger gains, and in many cases, they must do it with weaker community support. Faced with the need to do more with less, teachers in low-achieving schools will face stronger incentives to cut corners in ways that inflate scores. But this remains only a hypothesis, not yet tested by much empirical evidence. Ho and Haertel (2006) found evidence that the disparity between trends in scores on state tests and those on NAEP tended to be larger for students eligible for free and reduced-price lunch, but with few data points, the difference was not statistically significant. We urgently need finer grained studies of this issue.

Some researchers have argued that unrealistically high performance standards are analogous to auto emissions controls: if you require more improvement than manufacturers can provide, you end up with some fraction of what you demand and, thus, are better off than you were before. Whether or not this is true of emissions controls, it is not likely to be true of test-based accountability. Under NCLB, one gets no credit for getting partway to AYP, and the tools for inflating scores are ready at hand. Therefore, one might get *less* real improvement by requiring too much gain, because teachers will have incentives to abandon legitimate instructional improvements that generate slower gains in favor of shortcuts—inappropriate test preparation or simple cheating—that generate faster gains. After more than three decades of high-stakes testing in the United States, we ought to have some hard evidence on this point, but we do not.

When I recently gave a talk on test preparation to a large group of principals, many from inner-city schools, I encountered educators' responses to excessive expectations for score gains. I explained the principle that tests represent very small samples from larger domains of knowledge and skills. Therefore, the good way to prepare students for high-stakes tests is to focus on the knowledge and skills the tests are supposed to represent so that students will have better capabilities when they leave school. The bad way to prepare them is to focus narrowly on the specifics of their own test—that is, to focus on raising scores on that specific test *as an end in itself*—which can lead to spurious gains limited to that one measure. By analogy, they should try to persuade the entire electorate in order to win the election, rather than trying to persuade Zogby's 1,018 respondents to change their votes.

I then gave the principals a dozen real examples of test-preparation activities, ranging from egregiously bad to reasonable by this criterion. I asked them to decide whether each one would teach the underlying knowledge and skills and therefore produce real gains that would generalize to more than one test.

A minority of the principals identified the particularly bad examples, and a few added examples of their own. One said that they are told what parts of the state's standards will be emphasized on the test so that teachers need not spend much time on the others—a sure recipe for score inflation. (There is now a term for this that makes it seem innocuous: *power standards.*)

But many of the principals steadfastly defended every single example of test preparation, even those that were unarguably bad. The most extreme was a case in which a district provided the actual test item in advance, changing only three trivial details, which is no more than simple cheating. That too was fine with many of the administrators. Many of them became hostile as the discussion continued.

In retrospect, these responses may not be surprising, given the incentives and sanctions these principals face under NCLB. For several years, they have been struggling to make AYP, which requires many of them to make far more rapid gains than any of us can tell them how to do by legitimate means. And the consequences of failure are dire. Then I explained to them that many of the methods they have been using in their desperate fight to keep their noses above water are simply inflating test scores. Upton Sinclair's principle applies: "It's difficult to get a man to understand something when his salary depends on his not understanding it." Until we impose a system that creates the right incentives, it is not reasonable to expect educators to ignore the perverse incentives we have already put into place.

How Do Educators Respond to High-Stakes Testing?

A substantial number of studies over the past few decades have investigated teachers' responses to high-stakes testing. These studies show a mix of desirable and undesirable responses (Stecher, 2002), and they help explain the inflation of scores found in the previously noted studies.

On the positive side, research suggests that in some cases, high-stakes testing has motivated teachers to work harder and more effectively. It leads many teachers to align their instruction more closely with the tested content, which—as we will see—can be both good and bad. Some teachers report that the results of high-stakes tests are useful for diagnosis. (However, it is the test—not the high-stakes attached to it—that is useful in this respect; tests designed for diagnostic purposes were widely used in American schools for decades before high-stakes testing became common.) Some studies have found specific instructional effects consistent with the goals of the accountability systems of which they are a part such as an increase in writing instruction when tests require substantial writing.

At the same time, research has shown a variety of negative effects of high-stakes testing on educational practice. Many of these can inflate test scores, and some are undesirable for other reasons as well. It is helpful to distinguish among different types of test preparation in terms of their potential to generate meaningful gains in achievement, score inflation, or both (Koretz & Hamilton, 2006; Koretz, McCaffrey, & Hamilton, 2001). I use "test preparation" to refer to all techniques used to prepare students for tests, whether good or bad, and deliberately avoid terms such as *teaching the test* and *teaching to the test*, which come freighted with inconsistent and often poorly reasoned connotations. The different types of test preparation are as follows:

- Teaching more
- Working harder
- Working more effectively
- Reallocation
- Alignment
- Coaching
- Cheating

The first three are what most proponents of high-stakes testing programs—including NCLB—want and expect. "Working more effectively" (for example, finding better methods for presenting material to students) can only be for the good. "Teaching more" (allocating more time to instruction) and "working harder" (for example, implementing more demanding lessons) can both be carried to excess, to a point at which the marginal effects on learning are negative or they have other negative effects (such as an aversion to schooling or to learning) that offset short-term gains in achievement. But within reason, all three of these forms of test preparation can be expected to lead to meaningful gains in scores that signal higher achievement.

Cheating is the other extreme: it can only produce spurious gains in scores. There are limited systematic data about cheating, but there are enough accounts in newspapers and elsewhere to make it clear that it is hardly rare (see, for example, www.caveon.com/resources_news.htm). It takes all manner of forms: providing inappropriate hints during test administration, changing answer sheets after tests are completed, circulating actual test items (or items that are nearly identical) before a test, and so on. It is not clear that all instances of cheating are intentional, but they inflate scores regardless. The incentive to cheat is strongest in the schools that must make the largest gains—that is, low-scoring schools—but we have no systematic data showing whether it is in fact more common in such schools.

The controversial types of test preparation are the remaining three: reallocation, alignment, and coaching. All three can produce real gains, inflation, or both. The general principle is clear: these forms of test preparation are desirable when they improve students' mastery of the broad domains of achievement—say, eighth-grade mathematics—that the tests are designed to represent. They are undesirable and inflate test scores when they focus unduly on the particulars of the specific test chosen and therefore produce greater gains on that particular test than true improvements in learning warrant. In practice, however, the dividing line between the good and bad forms of reallocation, alignment, and coaching is sufficiently indistinct; keeping educators on the right side will be very hard until we do a better job of creating incentives for them.

Reallocation refers simply to shifting resources—instructional time, students' study time, and so on—to better fit the particulars of a testing program. Research has found that educators report reallocating their instruction in response to high-stakes tests. Reallocation occurs across subject areas, as shown by the reports of districts and schools reducing or eliminating time allocated to untested subject areas to make more time for the subjects that count in the accountability system (e.g., Rothstein & Jacobsen, 2006; Sunderman, Tracey, Kim, & Orfield, 2004). Educators can also reallocate instructional time within subject areas by emphasizing the particular portions that are emphasized by the test. Reallocation *within* subject areas is a key piece of the score-inflation puzzle.

Some amount of reallocation within subjects is desirable and is one of the intended effects of test-based accountability. If a testing program shows that students in a given school are not learning topic A, and topic A is important, the school's teachers should put more effort into teaching topic A.

The problem is that instruction is very nearly a zero-sum game: more resources for topic A necessarily mean fewer for topic B. If topic B is also important for the inference about performance, then taking resources away from it can inflate test scores.

Remember that a test is a small sample of a large domain of achievement, just as a poll is small sample of voters. The key to the success of both is that the small sample has to *represent* the larger domain. If teachers take resources away from relatively unimportant material to make way for emphasizing topic A, then all is fine. But if the material that gets *less* emphasis is an important part of the domain—if it is an important part of what users of the scores think they are measuring—then performance on the tested sample will show improvements when mastery of these other important parts of the domain is stagnant or even declining. This is precisely what studies of score inflation have found.

The more predictable a test is, the easier it becomes for teachers to reallocate in a way that inflates scores. For any number of reasons—the pressure of time, costs, a desire to keep test forms similar to facilitate linking of scores from year to year, the creativity needed to avoid similarities—most tests show a considerable resemblance from year to year. In many programs, much of the specific content is replaced each year, but the types of content and the style and format of test items show noticeable similarities from year to year. Some educators try hard to discern these recurrences, but they need not do it on their own; there is a vibrant industry of test-prep firms that will do it for them, and many districts and states provide help with this as well.

Alignment is a cornerstone of current education policy and is noted repeatedly in NCLB. Instruction is to be aligned with content and performance standards, and assessments must be aligned with both. Up to a point, alignment is clearly a good thing: we want teachers to focus on important material, and no one would want to judge teachers or schools by testing students on content that schools are not expected to teach.

Alignment is often cast as an unmitigated good and is frequently presented as a means of preventing score inflation. Not long ago, for example, a principal well known for achieving high scores in a poor, mostly minority school angrily told a crowd of college students that concerns about teaching to the test are completely unwarranted in her state. We don't have to worry about teaching to the test, she maintained, because her state's test covers important knowledge and skills that the students need.

This is nonsense, even assuming that her state's test does focus on important knowledge and skills. She was mistaking the test for the domain it represents—confusing Zogby's 1,018 respondents with the electorate. Alignment is nothing more than reallocation by another name, albeit with the constraint that the material emphasized must be consistent with standards. But whether alignment or other reallocation inflates scores depends on more than the quality of the material that is given additional emphasis. It also critically depends on the material that is given *less* emphasis. Because tests are such small samples from large domains, it is entirely practical to give more emphasis to some important material while taking it away from other equally important material. There is ample room to take it away from other material aligned with standards (hence test preparation focusing on "power standards") Research confirms this. Studies of Kentucky's assessment program of the 1990s, which was an archetypal standards-based system, found severe score inflation in every comparison examined (Koretz & Barron, 1998).

The final form of test preparation is *coaching*, a term that I use to refer to focusing instruction on fine details of the test such as the format of test items, the particular scoring rubrics, or minor details of content. Encouraging students to use format-dependent, test-taking strategies such as plugging in and process of elimination, is a form of coaching, and these can generate gains that evaporate when students are presented with different tasks—for example, constructed-response tasks that have no choices to eliminate.

Inflation of scores does *not* require that teachers or students focus on unimportant material. It can arise that way, for example, if teachers focus on test-taking tricks rather than important content. But this is not necessary. Inflation can occur from excessive narrowing of instruction, even if the material taught is valuable. One secondary-school mathematics teacher told me that her state's test presented only regular polygons, and therefore, she asked, why would she bother teaching about irregular polygons? What she meant was, "Because my goal is to raise scores, why would I. . .?" If her question had been, "Because my goal is to teach my students plane geometry, why would I. . .?" the answer would have been different and equally obvious.

The lesson is that the incentives we currently give teachers are too crude and simply don't work as advertised. The goal has become raising scores as an end in itself—persuading Zogby's 1,018 respondents—rather than improving learning. The incentives teachers face do not favor the good forms of reallocation, alignment, and coaching over the bad. Many educators take the path of least resistance; by doing so, they inflate scores. The system cheats kids of the education they deserve.

A common but mistaken response is that inappropriate reallocation and coaching arise because we use "bad" tests. The argument is that if we just built better tests, these problems would be solved. This was an argument made for moving from multiple-choice to performance assessments nearly twenty years ago, and for moving from those to today's standards-referenced tests. Neither change solved the problems of inappropriate test preparation or score inflation, and better tests will not solve them now. With enough creativity, time, resources, and evaluation, we could improve tests to *lessen* these problems, for example, by deliberately avoiding un-needed recurrences over time and by building in novel content and forms of presentation for purposes of auditing score gains. But there are numerous factors that limit how much we ameliorate the problem—for example, the need to keep tests sufficiently similar from year to year to allow meaningful linking of scores; resource limitations; the limited and already strained capacity of the testing industry; and the requirement that, when students are given scores, those within a cohort are administered the same or comparable sets of items. Moreover, many important outcomes of education are difficult or impossible to measure with standardized testing.

Finally, there is the problem of incentives for chief state school officers. Under the provisions of NCLB, what would motivate one to spend considerably more money to buy a somewhat inflation-resistant test that would generate smaller observed gains in scores? Better tests—by which I mean tests designed with an eye to the problems caused by test-based accountability—might indeed be an important step, but it will not suffice, and it is no substitute for putting in place a more reasonable set of incentives for teachers.

How Much Gain Is Feasible?

One of the most remarkable and dysfunctional aspects of the test-based accountability systems now in place under NCLB is that performance targets are usually made up from whole cloth, with no basis in experience, historical evidence, or evaluations of previous programs. And for political rather than empirical reasons, the targets are uniform for all schools in a state, regardless of their initial levels of performance and the particular impediments they face to improving scores.

Proponents of standards-based reporting of test scores will bristle at the word *arbitrary*, but that is a reasonable label for performance targets set without empirical evidence of attainable improvements. We do have relevant evidence, but policymakers have generally ignored it. We might start with the data on long-term trends in achievement. For example, the achievement decline of the 1960s and 1970s created great consternation and was a major impetus for the waves of education reform that continue with NCLB. Should we assume that schools could quickly implement reforms that produce gains as rapid as the declines of that era? Or, as Linn (2005) has suggested, we might identify the most rapidly improving schools—perhaps the top 10 percent—and use their gains to set goals. We could also use international comparisons to help us decide what is reasonable. For example, given international differences in factors outside of the control of schools, even ideal policies would presumably only bring us to the level of the highest performing countries over a long period, if at all.

Finally, we could use research, development, and evaluation to help set targets, as we do in policy domains as varied as public health and auto safety. That is, we could design new reforms, implement them on a limited but planned basis, and subject them to rigorous tests to determine their effects before putting them into operation nationwide or even statewide.

Because evidence is not brought to bear, standards are inconsistent and often unrealistic. Linn (2000, this volume) has shown that if states set eighth-grade mathematics standards comparable in difficulty to the NAEP proficient standard, as many critics of state standards suggest they should, we would be setting targets that roughly one-third of the students in Japan and Korea—two of the highest scoring countries in the world—would fail to meet. Is it realistic to expect that virtually all of our students (including most students with disabilities and many students with limited proficiency in English) will exceed such a threshold in a mere twelve years? That is not only unrealistic; it is counterproductive—increasing the incentives to cut corners and inflate scores—and cruel to some lower performing students. Without a basis in historical data and research, we simply assume that educators and students can reach these targets by legitimate means and that we are doing more good than harm by imposing these expectations. Even worse, we rarely have in place credible mechanisms for measuring the good and the harm.

How Much Can the Variability of Achievement Be Shrunk?

One of the most positive aspects of NCLB is its focus on equity. Many of the key aspects of NCLB—disaggregated reporting, the conjunctive AYP system (which classifies a school as failing if any one of the mandated reporting groups fails to make AYP), the uniformity of the ultimate performance targets, and the AYP requirement of greater gains by lower scoring schools—are motivated by a laudable desire to decrease inequities in educational outcomes. These provisions follow in the footsteps of widespread state initiatives that had the same goals, such as the "straight-line" accountability systems that required all schools to continually progress from their initial performance to the uniform statewide goal. They reflect one of the principal policy mantras of the past fifteen years: "All students can learn to high levels." This raises an obvious question that to my knowledge has received almost no attention in the debate about NCLB or other accountability systems: Just how much can we shrink the variability of achievement?

To answer this question, it is essential to separate two distinct issues that are often confounded in the public debate. One issue is variation *among groups*—for example, differences in performance between poor and rich, or between minority and majority children. The second is the *total* variability of performance of individual children, which arises from both the variation among children *within* groups and the differences among the groups.

It might seem reasonable to expect that we can shrink the variability of performance a great deal. We have enormous and well-documented inequities in school quality and in the opportunities afforded to students. Despite intermittent progress for several decades, we still have very large gaps in performance between racial/ethnic groups and between the poor and the well-off. One might expect that if we garnered the political will to combat these inequities—which would take a great deal more than an educational accountability system such as NCLB—the total variation in student achievement would shrink dramatically.

However, this is not the case: in the United States, the mean differences in scores between groups, while very large, contribute little to the total variability of performance among individual students. Most of the variation in the entire population arises from the huge variation in scores *within* groups, not from the differences *between* groups. If one entirely eradicated the mean differences between racial/ethnic groups in the United States, so that scores in every group were distributed just as they now are among non-Hispanic whites, the total variation in student performance would shrink modestly. I calculated this with two nationally representative tests (NAEP and NELS) for reading and mathematics in grade eight. The reductions in the standard deviations—a conventional measure of the spread of scores—ranged from about 0.5 percent to 9 percent.

International data similarly give us reason to dampen our expectations. Most other countries—including those that are more homogeneous, such as Japan and Korea—are roughly similar to the United States in the variability of students' scores (Beaton et al., 1996).

The implication is clear: even if we finally create a more equitable educational system and more equitable community supports for learning, we are going to be stuck with enormous variations in student performance, perhaps appreciably smaller than the variation we have now, but still very large indeed.

Therefore, what we need is a system that will put pressure on underperforming schools and schools serving historically low-achieving students—to increase the equity of educational outcomes between groups—

while still sensibly and realistically acknowledging the large variability that will persist *within* groups. We have at this time no good models for this, in part because the policy community has not seen the need for them. This gap in our knowledge should be especially worrisome to those in the education community—and I include myself—for whom the goal of greater equity of opportunity is particularly important. If between-group equity is not clearly distinguished from variability within groups, a failure to meet unrealistic expectations about the latter—a failure to get all students to achieve to some high standard—might lead cynics to become pessimistic about addressing the former.

What Are the Advantages and Disadvantages of Focusing on "Percent Proficient?"

As one state official said to me recently when discussing how to report performance on his state's test, "Proficiency is the coin of the realm." And NCLB, of course, carries this to an extreme. The accountability apparatus of NCLB hinges largely on a single statistic: the percentage of students above the proficient standard.

While reporting performance in this way does have one substantial merit—it helps to focus attention on expectations—it also has numerous severe disadvantages. Two are particularly relevant here. (For more discussion of these points, see Linn, 2003.)

The first of these disadvantages is that focusing only on percent proficient leaves all other changes in the distribution of performance unmeasured. Perhaps worse, it makes these other changes irrelevant to the accountability system. For example, take a state that has imposed a high standard for proficiency. If one measures only the percent of students above proficient, all progress with students below that cut score, no matter how large, goes unnoted and unrewarded. Conversely, a school that makes very small gains among students just below the proficient standard, just enough to get them over it, will be mistakenly credited with having effected major improvements. Many educators frankly admit that they focus disproportionate attention on students near the standard and give short shrift to students well below or well above it. There is even a common slang term for the students who are near the standard: *bubble kids*. This problem ought to be particularly disquieting to those who are concerned with improving the achievement of students in the poorest and lowest scoring schools.

The second disadvantage of reporting in terms of performance standards is not obvious: It distorts comparisons among groups. To be more precise, it distorts comparisons in trends among groups that differ in their initial level of achievement. This fact is a consequence of the distribution of scores: a great number of students score near the average, and the number becomes progressively fewer as one moves toward high and low extremes of performance. For example, if African American and white students in a given state were making identical progress, measures such as "percent above proficient" would create the misleading appearance of differences in their rate of gain (Koretz, 2003; Koretz & Hamilton, 2006).

WHAT SHOULD WE DO NOW?

The course we are now on is not working well, and over time, as the unrealistic targets we have set draw near, it is likely to become worse. But research has not yet provided us good alternative designs. So what can we do?

First, we should complement in-school programs with out-of-school interventions. There is currently some debate about what proportion of the variance in test scores is attributable to out-of-school factors, but it is clearly large. It is therefore simply unrealistic to expect improved educational services to fully offset the disadvantages faced by historically lower scoring groups. Interventions that go beyond educational accountability could include additional services both in school settings and outside of them—for example, high-intensity preschool services focused on cognitive development and language acquisition. Many of the needed interventions outside of the classroom are much more difficult and expensive than simply holding educators accountable for scores, but if we are serious about equity, they are probably necessary.

Second, we must set targets for improvement that are more realistic. We need more research on performance targets, but we already know enough to recognize that the current system simply is not sensible. We need to rely on the data we do have—international and other normative data, historical data, and program evaluations—to set targets that educators are able to reach by legitimate means.

Third, we need to use better metrics for reporting and rewarding performance on tests. We need measures that reflect improvement across the entire range of performance and that do not create perverse incentives to ignore students in certain ranges. If we persist in using percent proficient as part of our reporting and accountability system, we need to supplement this with other measures, and these other measures must count.

Fourth, we must do all we can to lessen the narrowing of instruction that current test-based accountability systems produce—both the excessive focus on tested subjects at the expense of others and the excessive focus on the content of the test at the expense of other important content within the same subject area. Here too we need more research, but we cannot afford to ignore the problem in the meantime. For example, states and districts should stop disseminating test-preparation materials that focus on test-taking tricks or inappropriate forms of coaching. They can encourage the test vendors to lessen the unintended recurrences (for example, repetition of details of format or content) that facilitate coaching. Professional development activities can focus on the differences between good and bad test preparation. Principals and others can be on the lookout for undesirable reallocation of instruction. In theory, all of these actions might help, although given the incentives NCLB creates to raise scores at any cost, particularly for schools serving historically low-scoring students, it is naïve to expect their effects to be large until we develop a more reasonable accountability system. Most adults in the system, from teachers to chief state school officers, currently have strong incentives to ignore this advice. Principals, for example, are given no incentive to press teachers to avoid inappropriate test preparation that could inflate scores. In fact, their incentive is the reverse.

Fifth, we must stop taking score gains on high-stakes tests at face value. To be clear, research thus far does not suggest that all gains on all high-stakes tests are spurious. But it does unambiguously show that score inflation is not rare and that it can be very large, dwarfing true gains in achievement. And currently, commonly reported data do not allow us to distinguish routinely between the spurious and the real.

To address the fourth and fifth of these issues, we must begin to seriously and routinely evaluate the performance of our accountability systems. This evaluation must include auditing of the gains on high-stakes tests. This auditing and evaluation will have two benefits. First, it will give us better information about student performance. We should not tolerate a situation in which real improvements in equity are slowed by illusory achievement gains. Second, auditing may substantially improve the incentives faced by teachers, thus reducing the gaming of the system that currently inflates scores and cheats children. As of now, teachers who inflate scores stand virtually no chance of getting caught, and admonitions to teach "to the standards" rather than "to the test" are empty rhetoric, particularly when districts and states provide the tools for doing the reverse. But if educators know that auditing will sometimes expose score inflation, they will have more reason to avoid the shortcuts that cause it.

At the moment, NAEP can provide an audit measure in many states, but it is not available in most grades, and over reliance on that one test may lead some people to start gaming NAEP as well. Routine auditing will likely require additional measures, either separate from operational tests or embedded within them. The key is that a good audit test measures the same core knowledge and skills as the accountability test measures, but it differs in many of the particulars—the details of content, format, scoring rubrics, and so on—that individual educators and test preparation firms capitalize on to inflate test scores. While this principle is clear and simple, the practical details of constructing audit tests remain unexplored for the simple reason that the people who buy tests have had no incentive to ask for audit measures. That must change, and the reauthorization of NCLB provides a powerful opportunity to change it.

Finally—and I would argue, most important of all—we need to start, belatedly, on a serious program of research, development, and evaluation to facilitate the design of better educational accountability programs that will do more to improve the achievement of all students (in particular, that of historically low-scoring groups) while generating fewer negative side effects. The list of important unanswered questions remains daunting: How can we best pressure schools to reduce inequities while accommodating the inevitably wide variations in performance within groups? How can we better design assessment systems to reduce the problem of spurious gains in scores? How can we create a better mix of incentives for educators, one that will encourage greater effort with less narrowing of instruction? What types of formative assessments and other test-preparation activities produce the largest gains in learning and the least score inflation? The list goes on.

Some people now argue that we have a solution at hand that circumvents the need for more research and development (R&D): value-added assessments. Such systems measure the gains students make while in a given grade, rather than tracking the improvements of successive cohorts of students in a single grade. Value-added systems indeed have many important advantages over the current system. For example, they are less sensitive to bias from differences in the characteristics of students, and they measure what many people consider a more appropriate variable for accountability: what a teacher or school teaches a group of students while they are in the school's care. Value-added assessments, however, still confront a substantial set of difficulties. For example, if testing is annual, value-added systems work only in subjects in which the curriculum is largely cumulative. They are highly error-prone, so most of the apparent differences among teachers or schools arise from measurement error rather than from real differences in output. They are seriously problematic where there is substantial differentiation of curricula, such as in most middle school mathematics programs. The rankings they provide are not always consistent from one test to another. Their results can be highly sensitive to arcane technical aspects of test construction and scaling. And their results are sometimes sensitive to choices in the statistical models used, many of which are extremely complex and not understood by most users of the data (McCaffrey, Lockwood, Koretz, & Hamilton, 2003). None of these difficulties argues against exploring value-added approaches as a part of educational accountability systems. But they do argue persuasively against accepting this approach as a new silver bullet that would once again free us from the hard but needed work of rigorous research and evaluation.

One of the most serious negative ramifications of NCLB is that it impedes the R&D needed for long-term improvements in policy. This may seem an odd claim, given that NCLB has encouraged the creation of vast databases of test scores. These data, however, generally are not useful for serious evaluation of alternative policies because of the problem of score inflation and because reporting is often limited to percents above standards. And the pressure created by NCLB makes experimentation with alternatives too risky. When everyone is in a race—often a desperate race—to raise scores on the few measures that count under NCLB, and to raise them continually, it is simply unrealistic to expect states, districts, and schools to agree to participate in R&D and experimentation. Experimentation runs the risk of smaller gains over the short term in the service of greater benefits over the long term, and NCLB makes this trade very costly. This constraint is especially severe for schools serving low-achieving groups, because those schools face particularly great pressure to raise scores by a large amount very quickly.

This, then, is my reason for arguing that we should not let concerns about changes to the details of NCLB—even the most important details—blind us to the need for a longer term plan for creating better educational accountability systems. Building those better systems requires more systematic, empirical data, and that, in turn, requires a serious agenda of R&D. Whether this R&D is carried out over the coming years will depend substantially on whether the reauthorization of NCLB makes it more feasible. Because of the frantic race for score increases created by NCLB in its current form, serious R&D will be hindered unless the provisions of NCLB are substantially changed. One option might be to provide waivers from NCLB accountability provisions to jurisdictions willing to do the needed, difficult work of helping to design the programs our children need and deserve. In addition, the incorporation of audit provisions into NCLB might also encourage R&D by reducing the inflated gains of jurisdictions to which the experimenting ones might be compared. And given the costs of the needed R&D—which are too large for many jurisdictions to take on—NCLB could include a mechanism for providing federal support for these efforts.

2

Toward a More Effective Definition of Adequate Yearly Progress

Robert L. Linn

The Elementary and Secondary Education Act (ESEA) of 1965 was the main educational component of President Johnson's "Great Society" program. The central aim of ESEA is to provide aid to schools for the education of economically disadvantaged children. It is the principal federal law affecting elementary and secondary education throughout the country (Hess & Petrilli, 2006, p. 9). During the first three decades, the focus of ESEA was on the distribution of funds and on educational inputs. That began to change with the 1994 reauthorization of ESEA by the Improving America's Schools Act (IASA) of 1994, when a shift started to take place to give greater attention to student achievement outcomes. Under IASA, however,

The work herein was partially supported under the Educational Research and Development Center Program PR/Award R305B960002, as administered by the Institute of Education Sciences, U.S. Department of Education. The findings and opinions expressed in this chapter are those of the author and do not necessarily reflect the positions or polices of the National Center for Education Research, the Institute of Education Sciences (IES), or the U.S. Department of Education.

the shift in focus from inputs to outcomes did not have real teeth. IASA held schools accountable for student achievement, but the penalties for schools that fell short of expectations were less severe than they are under the most recent reauthorization of ESEA, the No Child Left Behind (NCLB) Act of 2001. NCLB not only strengthened the focus on student achievement, but it added the teeth by strengthening the consequences for school failure and by holding schools and school districts accountable for the specific achievement of poor, minority, and limited English proficient students and students with disabilities.

Accountability is a central feature of NCLB. Adequate yearly progress (AYP) is the measure that is used to hold schools and school districts accountable under NCLB. "The law's fundamental dictate is that all schools and districts 'make AYP'" (Hess & Petrilli, 2006, p. 33). Schools that meet AYP requirements are assumed to be functioning well and enhancing student academic achievement. Schools that fail to make AYP are presumed to be falling short of expectations. Schools that do not make AYP for two years in a row are identified as "needs improvement" and are subject to sanctions. The schools must develop a school improvement plan, offer supplemental services such as tutoring, and must allow students the option of transferring to another public school within the district that is not in the needs improvement category. The sanctions become increasingly severe for schools that continue to fall short of AYP targets for a third, fourth, or fifth consecutive year.

To make AYP, schools and districts must meet or exceed AYP targets that are set in terms of the percentage of students who are proficient or above in mathematics and reading or English language arts. Those targets are set annually at levels that increase over the years and at rates that lead to the 100 percent proficiency goal by 2013–2014. States must set the proficient academic achievement level as well as at least two other levels (basic and advanced) on their reading or English language arts and mathematics assessments. NCLB provides a general description of proficient academic achievement and encourages setting the standard at a high level. In practice, however, states have set the proficient achievement bar at levels that vary widely in stringency (Linn, 2003b, in press). For example, in 2005 only 35 percent of the grade four students in Missouri were at the proficient level or above according to the Missouri definition of proficient achievement in reading whereas 89 percent of the grade four students in Mississippi were found to be proficient or above according to the Mississippi definition of proficient achievement in reading (Olson, 2005). Such a huge discrepancy can only be explained by the difference in the stringency of the definitions of the proficient achievement level in Missouri and Mississippi.

LIMITATIONS OF AYP

The definition of AYP has several serious limitations. First, the expectation of universal proficiency by 2013–2014 is not a goal that can be achieved unless proficiency is watered down to correspond to a low level of achievement (Linn, 2003a). Second, as was previously mentioned, the definition of proficient achievement varies wildly from state to state. Indeed, the variation is so large that "proficient" achievement lacks any semblance of a common meaning across states. Consequently, it is not meaningful to talk about universal proficiency as though it implied a common high level of student achievement. Third, AYP is limited by the almost exclusive focus on current achievement in a given year in comparison to a fixed target rather than attending to gains in achievement. Fourth, because there are many hurdles to clear to make AYP, states have introduced a number of different conditions for subgroup reporting that make it easier for schools to make AYP, and those conditions have undermined the fundamental concept. Finally, the narrow focus on state assessments of achievement in mathematics and reading or English language arts has potentially negative consequences. The chapter will consider each of these five limitations in greater detail and offer suggestions for changing the determination of AYP in ways that will address each of the limitations.

The Unrealistic Expectation of Universal Proficiency

On the National Assessment of Educational Progress (NAEP) in both 2003 and 2005, 29 percent of the nation's eighth-grade students performed at the proficient level or above in mathematics (Braswell, Dion, Daane, & Jin, 2005; Perie, Grigg, & Dion, 2005). In other words, the grade eight NAEP mathematics proficient score was at the 71st percentile of the U.S. eighth graders in 2003. In 2005, proficient achievement was also at the 71st percentile (29 percent proficient or above; Perie, Grigg, & Dion, 2005). The percentage of students at the proficient level or above was up from 26 percent in 2000 and from 23 percent in 1996 (Braswell et al., 2005). The lack of progress in the percentage of eighth-grade students who were proficient in mathematics between 2003 and 2005 does not bode well for reaching 100 percent proficiency by 2013–2014. Nor is the 6 percentage point increase between 1996 and 2003 encouraging. Even if the rate of increase were to double from an average of just under 1 percent per year between 1996 and 2003 to an average of 2 percent per year, less than half (47 percent) of the eighth-grade students would be proficient in mathematics in 2013–2014, according to NAEP.

The picture is somewhat brighter for fourth-grade mathematics because fourth-grade students have made greater gains in percent proficient or above according to the NAEP definition of proficient achievement than eighth-grade students have. The percentage of fourth graders who were proficient or above was 21 percent in 1996, 24 percent in 2000, 32 percent in 2003 (Braswell et al., 2005) and 35 percent of fourth graders in public schools were proficient or above in 2005 (Perie, Grigg, & Dion, 2005). Although the improvement in the mathematics achievement of fourth-grade students has been substantial and fairly steady with increases in the percentage of students who were proficient or above averaging approximately 1.6 percent per year, a continuation at that rate would still leave half (51 percent) of the fourth graders performing below the proficient level in mathematics in 2014.

The NAEP mathematics assessment results make the 100 percent proficiency goal appear to be out of reach despite the fact that the gains in mathematics achievement have been substantially greater than the gains in reading. The prospects for reading are even more discouraging than they are for mathematics. The trend lines for NAEP reading assessments are best described as essentially flat. Thirty percent of the fourth-grade public school students and 29 percent of the eighth-grade public school students were proficient or above on the 2005 NAEP reading assessments (Perie, Grigg, & Donahue, 2005). The corresponding 1998 results for all students were 29 percent at grade four and 32 percent at grade eight (Donahue, Daane, & Jin, 2005). That is, there was only a single percentage point increase in the percentage of students who were proficient or above in reading at grade four from 1998 to 2005, and the corresponding percentage for eighth-grade students was slightly lower in 2005 than it was in 1998.

Trends on NAEP over the past several years provide ample reasons to doubt that the 100 percent proficiency goal is obtainable even with the best of efforts or the belief that the rate of improvement would be twice as great in the future as it has been in recent years (Linn, 2003a; see also Lee, 2006). NAEP's definition of proficient achievement is admittedly ambitious, but ambitious academic achievement standards are exactly what are called for by NCLB. Even if the NAEP basic achievement were used, the goal of 100 percent by 2014 is not realistic. The percentage of public school students who performed at the basic level or above in reading increased by only 4 points (from 58 percent to 62 percent) from 1998 to 2005 at grade four and was unchanged at grade eight (Perie, Grigg, & Donahue, 2005). Gains in the percentage of students performing at the basic level or above were greater in mathematics, but not large enough to make 100 percent a reasonable goal by 2014. At grade eight, the percentage of public school students at the basic level or above went from 62 percent in 2000 to 67 percent in 2003 and to 68 percent in 2005. The corresponding percentages at grade four were 64 percent in 2000, 76 percent in 2003, and 79 percent in 2005 (Perie, Grigg, & Dion, 2005).

For another perspective on the idea of universal proficiency, it is useful to consider international assessments such as the international assessment of mathematics achievement conducted by the International Association for Evaluation of Educational Achievement (IEA). IEA's 2003 Third International Mathematics and Science Study (TIMSS) assessment of mathematics included forty-six countries at grade eight and twenty-five countries at grade four (Mullis, Martin, & Foy, 2005). Although U.S. students performed above the international average at both grade levels, they did not perform nearly as well as students from some of the other participating countries did. At grade eight, students from the Republic of Korea had an average level of mathematics achievement in the "knowing cognitive domain" that was higher than that of any other country. Singapore had the highest average at grade four (Korea did not participate at that grade level). In every country, however, there was considerable variability in student achievement.

Percentiles of achievement in mathematics at grade eight are shown in Table 2.1 for four selected countries, Korea, Japan, the Netherlands, and the United States which had average achievement scores that ranked first, fifth, ninth, and fourteenth, respectively, among the forty-six participating countries. The mathematics achievement of students from Korea, Japan, and the Netherlands is clearly better than that of U.S. students. A score of 557 is at the 75th percentile in the United States and might be used as a rough proxy to define proficient achievement. (This means that 75 percent of American students scored below proficient.) Note that a score of 557 is above the 50th percentile in the Netherlands and substantially above the 25th percentile for students in Japan and Korea. In other words, no country had even three-fourths—much less all—of their students at the proficient level or above when that level is defined by the 75th percentile in the United States.

Table 2.1   Percentiles of Achievement in Knowing Cognitive Domain for the 2003 TIMSS Mathematics Assessment at Grade Eight

	Country			
Percentile	Korea Rep of	Japan	Netherlands	United States
95	717	677	611	623
75	650	611	563	557
50	599	567	522	509
25	539	519	480	462
5	444	443	422	397
International Rank Among 46 Countries				
	1	5	9	14

Source: Mullis, Martin, & Foy, 2005.

Comparative international results for grade four are shown in Table 2.2 in a manner that parallels the grade eight results in Table 2.1. The medians for the Netherlands and the United States are quite similar, as would be expected given the proximity of their international ranks. The distribution of performance is more spread out in the United States than it is in the Netherlands. Thus, the 95th percentile is lower and the 5th percentile is higher in the Netherlands than it is in the United States. The averages for Japan and Singapore are considerably higher than the U.S. average. Nonetheless, as can be seen, more than one-quarter of the students in Singapore score below the U.S. 75th percentile and more half the students in Japan score below that level. As was true at the eighth grade, no country is even close to having all of its students at the proficient level or above when proficient performance is defined to be equal to the 75th percentile in the United States. If a small country such as Singapore with a relatively homogeneous population and a strong emphasis on education still has more than one-quarter of its students below a reasonable proxy for proficient performance corresponding to the U.S. 75th percentile, then it is hard to imagine that the goal of 100 percent proficiency is at all realistic. Tying AYP targets to this unrealistic goal for 2013–2014 will make the annual targets less and less obtainable as we approach that date.

Table 2.2   Percentiles of Achievement in Knowing Cognitive Domain for the 2003 TIMSS Mathematics Assessment at Grade Four

	Country			
Percentile	Singapore	Japan	Netherlands	United States
95	784	696	617	657
75	697	620	566	584
50	633	566	531	529
25	563	512	494	474
5	442	424	440	396
	International Rank Among 25 Countries			
	1	4	7	8

Source: Mullis, Martin, & Foy, 2005.

Definitions of Proficient Achievement

As has already been noted, NCLB encourages states to set the proficient academic achievement standard at a high level. This is consistent with the standards-based reforms of the last fifteen or twenty years that have consistently encouraged standards to be set at ambitious levels. That is the context in which the basic, proficient, and advanced academic achievement standards (called *achievement levels*) were set on NAEP in the early 1990s and for many states that set their achievement standards before the enactment of

NCLB. Given the context in which academic achievement standards were being set prior to NCLB, it is not surprising that, as was done for NAEP, a number of states also set their standards at ambitious levels. Of course, there are no consequences for students or schools for performance that is below the proficient level on NAEP, and prior to NCLB there were few, if any, consequences for students or schools that performed below the proficient level on most state assessments. The context suddenly changed when President Bush signed NCLB into law in January of 2002.

As has already been discussed, NCLB introduced clear consequences for schools where the percentage of students who scored at or above the proficient level on a state assessment was less than the target percentage required to make AYP. The consequences for failing to make AYP—together with the knowledge that the annual targets for the percentage of students who are proficient or above has to increase from year to year on a trajectory that would reach 100 percent by February 13, 2014—led a few states to reconsider their academic achievement standards. In addition, states that had to introduce new assessments and set new academic achievement standards post-NCLB were operating in a radically different context than existed before law was enacted. Not surprisingly, states that set academic achievement standards since 2002 have generally set them at more lenient levels than states that set their standards before 2002 have. There was little comparability in the definitions of proficient achievement prior to 2002, but the variation is greater now than it was then. It makes no sense when states such as Massachusetts, which is known to do well on other indicators such as NAEP, have a smaller percentage of students meeting the proficient standard than states such as Mississippi, which fares poorly on other indicators of achievement, have.

The effect of the change in context is clearly illustrated by the actions in Colorado following the enactment of NCLB. Colorado had established academic achievement standards before NCLB became law. Four levels of achievement called *advanced, proficient, partially proficient,* and *unsatisfactory* were set on the Colorado Student Assessment Program (CSAP). The four performance levels are still used to report on student achievement to schools, districts, and parents. For purposes of NCLB, however, Colorado uses only three levels of achievement. The four CSAP levels used for state purposes are collapsed into three levels for determining AYP. The state's unsatisfactory level is relabeled *basic*, the partially proficient and proficient levels are collapsed into a single level called *proficient*, while the highest level of achievement retains its label of *advanced*.

The lower level of achievement required for a student to be called *proficient* for purposes of NCLB than for state purposes makes a substantial difference in the percentage of students who are identified as proficient in Colorado. In reading in 2006, for example, 90 percent of fourth-grade students reached the proficient level or above for purposes of NCLB, but 22 percent had CSAP scores in the partially proficient category. Thus, 68 percent—rather than 90 percent—of the grade four students were reported to be proficient or above in reading on state reports to schools, districts, and parents. Similar differences were obtained for other grade levels and for mathematics. For example, 75 percent of the eighth-grade students were reported to be proficient or above in mathematics in 2006 using the NCLB performance levels, but only 45 percent reached the proficient level or above when the partially proficient level was reported separately to schools, districts, and parents.

States that introduced new assessments after 2002, on which academic performance standards had to be set, did not have to collapse levels of achievement to have standards that were more lenient post NCLB than they were before that time. Recognizing that the definition of proficient achievement has real consequences for schools and is not merely an aspiration, states established academic achievement standards that were less stringent than the ones that states had established before NCLB was enacted.

The stringency of academic achievement standards depends on a number of factors, including the context in which the standards are set, the uses that are to be made of the standards, the method that is used to set standards, and the judges who participate in the standard-setting process (Glass, 1978; Jaeger, 1989; Linn, 2003b, in press). Consistent with the uncertainties surrounding standard setting, there is a broad professional consensus that "there is NO true standard that the application of the right method, in the right way, with enough people will find" (Zieky, 1995, p. 29).

Because standard setting is subject to the many sources of variability, such as the influence of context and the fact that states set their standards at different times, there is tremendous variability in the stringency of the standards from state to state. Olson (2005) reported the percentage of students who scored at the proficient level on the individual state assessments and on NAEP at grades four and eight in 2005 for forty-seven states. (The closest grade was used for the few states that did not have assessments in place at either grade four or eight in 2005.) The average percent proficient or above on the state assessments in reading and mathematics at grades four and eight were more than twice as large as the average percent proficient or above on NAEP (Linn, in press).

Not only were the state proficient standards less stringent on average than the NAEP standards, but the percentages of students reported to be proficient or above on the state assessments also were considerably more variable from state to state than the corresponding percentages on state NAEP. The ratios of the variances for the percentage of students who were proficient or above according to the forty-seven state assessments to the variances of the corresponding percentages for state-by-state NAEP results in 2005 were 6.61, 6.67, 5.36, and 6.02 for grade four reading, grade eight reading, grade four mathematics, and grade eight mathematics, respectively. The differences in variances between NAEP and state assessments are not due to actual differences in achievement between states, but are due instead to differences in the stringency of proficiency standards between states. Furthermore, there is little relationship between the percentages proficient or above on the state assessments and the corresponding percentages proficient or above on NAEP (Linn, in press).

The percentages proficient or above for a number of individual states on their own assessments make no sense when compared to other things that are known about education and student achievement in those states. On the grade eight NAEP 2005 mathematics assessment, for example, the percentage of public school students performing at the proficient level or above was somewhat higher in Missouri (26 percent) than in Tennessee (21 percent; Perie, Grigg, & Dion, 2005, p. 16). On their own grade eight state mathematics assessments, however, a whopping 87 percent of Tennessee students were reported to be proficient or above, whereas only 16 percent of Missouri's students were reported to have performed at the proficient level or above (Olson, 2005, p. S2). The large discrepancy in percentages on the state assessments for Missouri and Tennessee cannot reasonably be explained by differences in student achievement in mathematics at grade eight. The most obvious explanation of the discrepancy is that the proficient academic achievement standard is much more stringent for the Missouri grade eight mathematics assessment than it is in Tennessee. Other examples could be presented to reinforce the conclusion that the stringency of state academic achievement standards varies greatly from state to state. A consequence of the variability in stringency is that "proficient" achievement has no common meaning across states. Thus, even if the unrealistic goal of 100 percent proficient or above could be achieved, it would mean radically different things in different states.

Current Status Versus Improvement

The "adequate yearly progress" label seems to imply that student achievement has improved during the course of a year. However, with the exception of the Safe Harbor provision, which allows schools that would not have done so otherwise to make AYP if the percentage of students scoring below the proficient level is reduced by 10 percent or more from the previous year, the determination of AYP does not depend on improvement from one year to the next. In practice, the Safe Harbor provision saves few schools because a reduction of the percentage of students who perform below the proficient level by 10 percent is much larger than gains that are normally realized from one year to the next. In the last couple of years, however, states have begun using confidence intervals around the reductions in the percentage of students below the proficient level, thereby effectively lowering the 10 percent figure and increasing the number of schools that are saved by the Safe Harbor provision. Nonetheless, for most schools, AYP depends on a comparison of the percentage of students who are at the proficient level or above in a given year to a target percentage known as the *annual measurable objective* (AMO) for that year.

The comparison of current student performance to the AMO makes it relatively easy for schools in which students who are already achieving at high levels to exceed the AMO and make AYP. Indeed, a school in which students have been achieving at high levels can have a decline in achievement from one year to the next and still make AYP. Schools serving students who start the school year with achievement that is far below the AMO for a given year, on the other hand, must have dramatic gains in achievement in a given year to make AYP. Most of the latter schools will fail to meet AYP, even if they show rather sizeable year-to-year gains in student achievement because they start the year so far below the AMO. Thus, the current AYP system provides an advantage to schools serving students who are already achieving at high levels and puts schools serving initially low achieving students at a substantial disadvantage.

In contrast to the NCLB accountability system that, with rare exceptions, relies on a comparison of current status to a fixed annual target, most state accountability systems give substantially more weight to year-to-year improvement in student achievement. The measurement of improvement is done in two ways. Some states (e.g., North Carolina and Tennessee) track individual student achievement longitudinally and use gains in achievement to hold schools accountable. Other states (e.g., California and Kentucky) compare the performance of successive cohorts of students (e.g., fourth graders in 2005 and fourth graders in 2006) to measure improvement, and some states (e.g., Colorado and Florida) use a combination of current performance and improvement in performance to hold schools accountable. Giving schools credit for year-to-year improvement in student achievement puts schools that start the year with quite different levels of student achievement on a more equal footing than a system that relies almost exclusively on current achievement.

In response to concerns about the current approach to AYP, Secretary of Education Spellings (2005) announced a pilot program that let states propose ways of using a growth model to make AYP determinations. Growth models take a variety of forms, but share the characteristic that student performance in one year is compared to the performance of those same students the previous year. Several "core principles" that must be met for a proposal to be approved were specified by Secretary Spellings in a letter to the chief state school officers. The first principle stated that the growth model "must ensure that all students are proficient by 2013–2014 and set annual goals to ensure that the achievement gap is closing for all groups" (Spellings, 2005, para. 6, core principle 1). Because, as was previously discussed, the 100 percent proficient goal is unrealistic, this principle severely limits the utility of growth models for determining AYP.

The pilot program proposals submitted by North Carolina and Tennessee were approved for implementation of growth model pilots in

2005–2006 (Spellings, 2006). Six other states (Alaska, Arkansas, Arizona, Delaware, Florida, and Oregon) that submitted proposals were told that they would get early consideration for possible implementation in 2006–2007 if they submitted revised proposals.

Although the pilot program is a step toward the inclusion of improvement in student achievement in the determination of AYP, it is currently limited to only a few states. It is also severely limited by the maintenance of the 100 percent proficient goal in 2013–2014 that is both unrealistic and unequal from state to state due to the lack of a common definition proficient academic achievement. The constraints imposed by the 100 percent proficiency requirement may be the reason that the implementation of the growth models to determine AYP in North Carolina and Tennessee did not result in major changes in the AYP status of schools in 2006 (Olson, 2006).

Multiple Hurdles

Unlike accountability systems in most states, which use a compensatory approach that allows superior achievement in one content area to make up for subpar performance in another content area, NCLB uses a conjunctive approach whereby schools must have achievement that meets or exceeds percentage proficient or above targets in both reading or English language arts and in mathematics. Actually, more than just the two achievement hurdles must be cleared in order to make AYP. At a minimum, a school must clear five hurdles. In addition to the two percentage proficient or above targets, a school must assess at least 95 percent of their eligible students in each subject area and exceed the performance target for the other academic indicator selected by the state (typically, attendance for elementary and middle schools and graduation rate for high schools).

For large schools with diverse student bodies, the number of hurdles that must be cleared to make AYP can be substantially greater than the minimum of five. Marion et al. (2002) have shown that the number of hurdles to be cleared could be as large as thirty-seven. The larger number of hurdles is due to the requirements for disaggregated reporting of subgroup performance. Four hurdles (two for subgroup participation rates and two for subgroup achievement in reading/English language arts and mathematics) are added to the five, for the school as a whole, for each subgroup that is large enough to require disaggregated reporting. Thus, if there are eight subgroups of sufficient size, the school would have to clear a total of thirty-seven hurdles. Although few schools are large and diverse enough to reach the maximum, many large schools have to clear twenty-one or twenty-five hurdles because they have four or five subgroups that are large enough to require disaggregated reporting.

Making schools accountable for the achievement of subgroups identified by NCLB is clearly consistent with the NCLB goal of closing gaps in achievement for the identified subgroups. It is also clear, however, that

NCLB's multiple-hurdle approach makes it considerably more difficult for large schools with diverse student bodies to meet AYP requirements than it is for small schools or schools with homogenous student bodies to meet them (Kim & Sunderman, 2005; Linn, 2005; Novak & Fuller, 2003).

States have responded to the challenges schools face in making AYP in a number of ways. They have increased the minimum number of students in a subgroup that is required for disaggregated reporting. They have introduced the use of confidence intervals for the percentage of students who are proficient or above and for determining the year-to-year change in the percentage of students who score below the proficient level for purposes of Safe Harbor calculations (N. Chudowski & V. Chudowski, 2005; Sunderman, 2006). These changes make it easier for a school to make AYP, but they also make the definition of AYP more complicated and less transparent.

Narrow Focus on State Reading and Mathematics Assessments

There is no question that reading and mathematics are critically important. The narrow focus on these two subjects as measured by state assessments, however, can lead to distortions in the curriculum and instruction that students receive. As was evident from responses at recent public hearings on NCLB (Public Education Network, 2007), there is widespread concern that the focus of the NCLB accountability system is too narrow. A substantial proportion of the public believes that there is too much emphasis on a single assessment as the determining factor for AYP. Opinions expressed at the hearing favored a reduction in the emphasis on state reading and mathematics assessments, coupled with an increased reliance on information from formative assessments and evaluations.

The focus on reading and mathematics, together with the high stakes attached to making AYP, has led schools to increase the time spent on these subjects at the expense of other subjects such as science and social studies, which are also important parts of education. Although states will be required to have science assessments in place starting in 2007–2008, no clear use of the science assessment has been specified. Moreover, they are only required at one grade level in each grade-level span (elementary, middle, and high school). Thus, it is not clear that the addition of science assessments will lead to any real changes in the NCLB accountability system.

Most of the districts (71 percent) that participated in a survey conducted by the Center on Education Policy (CEP; 2006) reported a reduction in the time devoted to at least one other subject to allow more time to be devoted to reading and mathematics (p. 89). Although the additional time spent on reading and mathematics instruction may enhance achievement in those subjects, it comes at the expense of other important subjects. The report of reduced time spent on nontested subjects is consistent with results reported in other studies. Sunderman, Tracey, Kim, and Orfield (2004), for example, found that a substantial majority of teachers in the two districts that they surveyed reported that AYP requirements caused some teachers to de-emphasize or neglect content in untested topics and to increase the amount of time spent on classroom activities specifically designed to prepare students for state-mandated assessments.

The great emphasis on performance on just two assessments, one in reading or English language arts and one in mathematics, coupled with the sanctions for schools that fail to make AYP, can not only narrow instruction to those subjects, but can also distort the teaching of reading and mathematics. Drill and practice on topics covered on the tests in a predictable manner and frequent practice on benchmark tests consisting of items with the formats that mirror the items on the state assessment can lead to score inflation, that is, "a gain in scores that substantially overstates the improvement in learning it implies" (Koretz, 2005, p. 99).

SUGGESTIONS FOR IMPROVING THE DETERMINATION OF AYP

The determination of AYP could be improved by addressing the five limitations of the current approach that were previously discussed. First, the unrealistic expectation of 100 percent proficiency should be replaced by a goal that is still ambitious, but realistically obtainable with sufficient effort on the part of educators and students (Linn, 2003a). One way to select a goal that is both ambitious and realistically obtainable is to look at accomplishments of schools that have shown substantial gains in student achievement in the past. For example, schools that rank among the top, say 20 percent, of all schools in terms of the gains their students have made over a period of four or five years could establish the goal for all schools. The goal would be more realistic than the 100 percent proficiency goal, since 20 percent of the schools have already managed to make those gains. The goal also would be ambitious for the majority of schools that had not realized such large gains in student achievement in the past.

Second, the notion of proficient academic achievement should either be modified so that it is defined to have a common meaning from state to state, or it should be replaced by another marker of achievement. An achievement target that would be reasonably comparable from one state to the next could be defined starting with a cutscore on each state assessment that was equal to the median achievement of students in a base year (e.g., 2002). Although there would be a small variation in the stringency of the median due to differences in the achievement of students in different states and due to the differences in the state assessments, the variation would be tiny in comparison to the state-to-state variation in the definitions of proficient achievement. Using the average annual gains made by the top 20 percent of the schools, the annual target could then be established for the percentage of students scoring above the median performance in the 2002 base year. This might lead to an annual target increase of, say, 3 percent. With a 3 percent gain per year, the proportion of students scoring above the 2002 base year median would need to increase from 50 percent in 2002 to 86 percent in 2014. Such a goal is clearly ambitious, but it is also much more realistic than the current 100 percent proficient goal. Moreover, it would provide a reasonably uniform definition of target achievement across states.

Of course, not all schools would start with half of their students scoring above the state median. Schools where only one-quarter or less of their students score above the state median would have to have extraordinary improvement to meet the targets set for all schools. Hence, there would also need to be a Safe Harbor type of provision. Instead of meeting the absolute target of the percentage of students above the base year median, schools could qualify as making AYP if they showed substantial improvement each year (e.g., an increase of 4 or 5 percent of their students scoring above the base year median for the state).

Third, the way in which AYP is determined should be expanded to allow schools that show substantial increases in student achievement to meet the requirements rather than relying almost entirely on a comparison of current achievement to an annual target. Improvement could be evaluated either by computing growth for individual students with a longitudinal data system such as allowed for states approved for the NCLB pilot program, or by comparing achievement of successive cohorts of students. Growth models based on longitudinal student data could take a variety of forms. This is evident from a consideration of the various approaches for which states have received approval under the current pilot program. The impact of such models will have little positive effect, however, unless the unrealistic requirement of reaching 100 percent proficiency by 2014 is relaxed.

Allowing schools to make AYP either by meeting an absolute target or by making substantial gains in student achievement from the previous year does not give up on the same goals for students. Such a system would not dilute the goals for some groups of students, rather, by allowing improvement as well as current status as ways of making AYP, it would make it more realistic for schools with a large percentage of students with low achievement initially to get credit for demonstrating substantial gains in student achievement that would eventually lead to high levels of performance.

Fourth, the conjunctive, multiple-hurdle approach to determining AYP should be replaced by a compensatory system that would allow superior achievement in one subject to make up for achievement that is somewhat below a target level in another subject. States generally use some form of a compensatory system in their own accountability systems and a move in that direction by NCLB would make the federal and state accountability systems more compatible. Monitoring the achievement of subgroups should continue and superior achievement for one subgroup should not make up for below-par achievement for another subgroup. However, the volatility due to small numbers of students in particular subgroups should be addressed by allowing schools to aggregate subgroup results over two or three years rather than requiring results to meet targets every year.

Finally, the measures used for accountability should be broadened to include more subjects and assessment information obtained from sources other than state assessments. Where statewide assessments in content areas other than reading and mathematics are available, they could be used along with reading and mathematics assessment results to form composites for accountability. Composites would have at least two advantages over the separate requirements in reading and mathematics. First, by including more content areas, there would be less pressure to focus on just reading and mathematics at the expense of other subjects. Second, composite scores by design allow for superior performance in one content area to compensate for lower performance in another area.

Formative assessments and professional judgments of student achievement by educators could be used to supplement the information that is provided by state assessments. The additional measures could be easily accommodated in a compensatory system. The additional measures in a composite index would be likely to reduce the use of practices that result in inflated test scores, such as narrow teaching to the specific content and formats used on state assessments.

Combining teacher produced ratings of student achievement with state assessments and other assessment results would require that the teacher scores be reported in a common metric such as a one to five scale. Concerns that teachers might report inflated ratings would need to be addressed. Admittedly, grade inflation poses a serious obstacle to incorporating teacher judgments of student achievement, but the potential gain in information would be worth the added effort needed to obtain and use teacher-produced scores. One approach that has been used in some state assessments where teachers rate the work of students in their own schools is to introduce a system of outside auditing of a sample of the student work. Auditing increases the expense, but provides protection against inflated scores, and it has the added benefit of providing teachers with feedback on the appropriateness of their judgments of student work.

A common set of district-selected benchmark assessments, formative classroom assessments selected by teachers, and systematic teacher ratings of student accomplishments could also supplement the information about student achievement that is provided by state assessments. Students who may not do well on a standardized state assessment would have other ways of demonstrating what they know and are able to do. With a broader array of measures, teachers would not have the same pressure to devote so much time to narrow test preparation for poor and minority students, but could instead spend the time on broader instructional goals.

3

Beyond Standardization in School Accountability

Mindy L. Kornhaber

Any system of educational accountability in the United States should be guided by two essential and equally important aims. First, it should be informative—it should allow the public to know the status and progress of students' knowledge, skills, and understanding within and across schools. Second, the system should be cognitively constructive—it should advance all students' learning and enable educators to improve instruction.

Neither of these aims is being met under the No Child Left Behind (NCLB) Act of 2001, as the first section of this chapter explains. The second section uses the groundwork of informative and cognitively constructive aims to eliminate ambiguities in the meaning of multiple measures. These ambiguities have impeded substantive uses of such measures. The third section describes the components of a system of multiple measures. This system would not be simple or easy to build. Yet, relative to systems that rely on a single high-stakes test, it stands a far greater chance of producing genuine benefits across a wide range of students. The fourth section provides policy recommendations that may be useful in revising NCLB, so that it can begin to address informative and cognitively constructive aims.

The author wishes to thank Edward Fierros, Jill Morningstar, Robert Rothman, Hoi Suen, and Gail Sunderman for their helpful comments on earlier drafts of this chapter.

FAILURE TO MEET INFORMATIVE AND CONSTRUCTIVE AIMS UNDER NCLB

Deficiencies in Meeting Informative Aims

Our ability to obtain reasonable information from standardized testing rests on several assumptions. One assumption is that the tests have been administered under the same or similar conditions. Given standardized test materials and procedures, it becomes possible to say that test scores shed light on the tested topic rather than matters extraneous to it. Of course, standardization is never perfect. The question is, how far from that ideal is it possible to roam and still claim that scores illuminate the tested topic?

Standardization of testing conditions is a substantial challenge given the greatly varying contexts and populations of American public schools. For example, some 15–20 percent of all students have learning disabilities, are English language learners, or both (Hoffman, 2003). To test students with disabilities, varied accommodations are necessary and required by federal law. However, research reveals little agreement on what types of accommodations yield scores that are valid for these students (Thurlow, et al., 2006). Accommodation policies and practices have also been frequently revised, in part because it is often unclear which accommodations are suitable for different learning disabilities (Thurlow, et al., 2006). English language learners are also given varying accommodations, depending in part on state law. The assessments these students take and the accommodations they are given may not take adequate account of the language demands needed in academic settings. This makes it difficult to know whether their scores signal the level of proficiency needed for school success (see Kieffer, Lesaux, & Snow, this volume).

Including students with disabilities and English language learners in accountability systems is intended to make schools attend to the students' needs. Yet, given the great variability of these populations and the absence of standardization in their assessment processes, it is exceedingly difficult to draw reasonable inferences from these students' scores about their learning (Heubert & Hauser, 1999; McDonnell, McLaughlin, & Morison, 1997; Pellegrino, et al., 2001). Because such scores are inadequately informative, they are also a very problematic foundation on which to base consequences.

A second deficiency in NCLB's informative powers stems from the wide variations in procedures used to prepare students for testing. The *Standards for Educational and Psychological Testing* (the "Joint Standards") call for examinees to have an "equal opportunity to become familiar with the test format, practice materials, and so forth" and that "[i]deally, examinees would also be afforded equal opportunity to prepare for a test" (American Educational

Research Association, [AERA] American Psychological Association [APA], & National Council on Measurement in Education [NCME], 1999, p. 74).

There is no agreement, however, on what such equal opportunities entail (AERA, et al., 1999). Promulgating the same state standards and tests may meet a legal threshold for equal preparation in some jurisdictions (GI Forum, 2000). Yet, these do not actually yield equivalent opportunities to learn the tested content—schools with markedly different student populations and neighborhood conditions are markedly different environments for teaching and learning (Darling-Hammond, 2000, 2004; Lee, 2006; Natriello & Pallas, 2001). Because of this, similar scores may say very different things about the quality of teaching and learning within any given school (Stake, 1998). Thus, using scores as the primary basis for sanctioning schools is deeply problematic.

A third serious flaw in standardization pertains to NCLB's goal of universal proficiency. The Joint Standards hold that when a score is used to support a criterion-referenced interpretation (such as "proficiency"), "the rationale and empirical basis should be clearly presented" (AERA, et al., 1999, p. 56). Yet, the meaning of proficiency and how that is established varies considerably across the states (Olson, 2005). Therefore, should NCLB's stated goal actually be achieved by 2014, this information would be worthless. All students cannot possess proficiency in reading, math, and science and yet potentially lose proficiency simply by crossing state lines.

Deficiencies in Meeting Constructive Aims

Educators and state policymakers who are told to increase test scores and decrease score gaps do so in varied ways. Many of their means constitute work-arounds, which improve scores without attendant improvements in learning. Some work-arounds may even undermine learning.

Work-arounds operate at all levels of the education system under NCLB. For example, NCLB requires states to help build local education agencies' capacity to produce learning. However, typically, states lack the resources and knowledge to do so (Center on Education Policy, 2006; see also Sunderman & Orfield, this volume). Given NCLB's largely unattainable goals and the likelihood of sanctions for not meeting them, state actors have creatively redefined "learning" by adjusting confidence intervals, subgroup sizes, and even what counts as "two years in a row" (Center on Education Policy, 2005; Sunderman, 2006). None of this is cognitively constructive; it does not advance students' learning or improve instruction.

Work-arounds at the district and school level include widely reported cheating during NCLB testing (Axtman, 2005; Nichols & Berliner, 2007). Changing the pool of test takers by retaining students before they reach tested grades also improves scores without improving learning. This can also be done by ramping up test preparation for students nearest the passing score, while diminishing attention to other students (Booher-Jennings, 2005).

Another common work-around entails narrowing of the curriculum. About 25 percent of schools report reducing social studies, science, arts, and music in response to NCLB (Center on Education Policy, 2005). While this tends to raise scores, the higher scores do not prove that students are mastering the tested disciplines; increased scores on a given state's high-stakes assessment are often not mirrored on other tests of the same content (Klein, Hamilton, McCaffrey, & Stecher, 2000; Koretz & Barron, 1998). This pattern holds true under NCLB (Fuller, Gesicki, Kang, & Wright, 2006; Lee, 2006). Clearly, if this practice does not enable students to apply knowledge across tests, it is not preparing them to tackle complex problems found in the world beyond school (Suen & Yu, 2006).

Although work-arounds are pervasive, they are probably more commonly found in schools that are at greater risk of sanctions (McNeil, 1988; von Zastrow, 2004). These include schools serving higher percentages of traditionally lower scoring students who are supposed to be NCLB's key beneficiaries. They also include schools with diverse student populations, in which a single errant subgroup will sink the whole ship (Kim & Sunderman, 2005; Lee & Wong, 2004; Popham, 2004). In contrast, students in affluent, homogenous schools will continue to have better access to school and classroom practices that are cognitively constructive. Thus, one logical consequence of NCLB's accountability system will be that substantive opportunities to learn will continue to diverge—and may increasingly diverge—on the basis of wealth, race, and ethnicity.

TOWARD A BETTER ACCOUNTABILITY SYSTEM: CLARIFYING THE MEANING OF MULTIPLE MEASURES

Businesspeople have long urged educators to take lessons from their sector. One key business lesson that education policymakers need to grasp is that an overemphasis on the bottom line corrupts the processes above it. When this occurs, improvements in the bottom line no longer clearly signal actual profits or gains.

A sound educational accountability system thus necessarily employs varied and multiple indicators. Multiple indicators make it harder to rely on work-arounds, and they are more likely to encourage constructive educational practices. In turn, they generate more trustworthy information about the status and growth of learning and teaching practices.

Specifying that an educational accountability system must be informative and cognitively constructive eliminates some of the current ambiguities in the meaning of multiple measures. Given these two fundamental aims, the repeated administration of the same type of state test *does not* constitute an acceptable system of multiple measures. This practice improves statistical accuracy by diminishing the chances of "false negatives." However, it also encourages work-arounds (McNeil & Valenzuela, 2001; Shepard, 2000) and thus fails to be cognitively constructive. Score gains associated with repeated use of a state's test do not permit clear inferences about learning. Thus, repeated administration of the same type of test is also not an adequate system of multiple measures, because it fails to be informative.

Reliance on a content-related test together with nontest indicators, such as attendance or graduation rates allowed under NCLB, also *does not* constitute a workable system of multiple measures. Such a system allows other important outcomes of schooling to be monitored (Stake, 1998), and it may reduce perverse incentives to alter the pool of test takers in order to improve scores (Koretz, 2003). Even so, it cannot prevent gaming and the warping of instructional practices associated with excessive emphasis on a single test. Thus, it fails to be constructive or truly informative.

BEYOND STANDARDIZATION IN SCHOOL ACCOUNTABILITY: COMPONENTS OF A CONSTRUCTIVE AND INFORMATIVE SYSTEM OF MULTIPLE MEASURES

Section 1111 of NCLB repeatedly calls for each state to use the same technically adequate assessments, standards, and accountability system for all its students. Yet, these demands for uniformity have not yielded a cognitively constructive or informative system. As outlined below, a sound educational accountability system can incorporate, but must move beyond, standardization.

Standardized Tests

Standardized tests are a favored accountability tool because of their strengths: they efficiently gather large amounts of data broadly, quickly, and relatively cheaply on a per-pupil basis. These data facilitate comparisons across students, schools, districts, and states. Standardized tests linked to stakes readily enable policymakers to send and collect signals about school systems.

Standardized tests' strengths in conveying information tend to marginalize their weaknesses in being cognitively constructive. Such tests tend to probe disjointed facts and rote skills far more so than the rich problem solving used in mathematics, writing, and other disciplines (Pellegrino, et al., 2001). They rely on contexts that lack the resources (e.g., other people, reference materials, tools) that are commonly required to do good disciplinary work. For these and other reasons, it is difficult to infer that test results are valid representations of actual performance (e.g., "proficiency" in writing or mathematical reasoning). The results' utility is also attenuated by the many months it often takes for test results to reach schools (Pellegrino, et al., 2001).

Rebalancing the position of standardized tests. There are at least two ways to maximize standardized tests' strengths and minimize their weaknesses within a system of multiple indicators. The first is to sharply reduce the blanket, census testing of all students (Pellegrino, et al., 2001). Testing is by nature a sampling enterprise. Therefore, it is costly and inefficient to generate system wide information by testing every student each year. Since high-stakes census testing also has harmful effects on educational practice, reducing such testing, and giving its results a minority role in an accountability system, can benefit instruction. This, in turn, can improve the system's informative function.

This approach may be politically difficult. Sampling would increase opportunities for gaming the pool of test takers. It could well be seen as a retreat from NCLB's concerns with standards, low-achievers, and disaggregated data. In addition, using one test for measuring multiple purposes (e.g., growth and achievement) may increase its political importance and the temptation to employ work-arounds.

A second—and perhaps surprising—option would be to adopt many, varied standardized tests, administer each in a census fashion, and assign all test results together a minority role in the accountability system. A multiplicity of varied tests could undo efforts to teach to the test and thus allow for a more constructive system. In addition, using tests to illuminate different indicators could also make this approach more informative: one test could monitor criterion-referenced achievement on the state standards; another, criterion-referenced achievement pegged elsewhere; another, growth; and another, national norms. Under NCLB, the latter two are increasingly opaque.

Either of these two approaches could improve learning for those traditionally left behind and reduce the achievement gap. Either should reduce the excessive test preparation now visited disproportionately upon traditionally low-scoring groups. In turn, this might redirect resources from test-prep materials to more worthwhile materials. Second, using test data to monitor growth, not just status, makes the learning needs of students across a broad range of achievement much more likely to matter. In contrast, under NCLB, it makes the most sense to attend to those students whose improvement is likeliest to put the school over the bar (Booher-Jennings, 2005). Under NCLB, it also makes sense to retain students in untested grades, even though retention increases the chance of dropping out (Hauser, 2001; Holmes, 1989). Third, by eliminating excessive test preparation for a single, "same test," the accountability system will be more likely to send signals about what matters (e.g., achievement, growth, real disciplinary knowledge and skills). It should also receive more accurate signals about learning and teaching.

Ultimately, our education system must abandon the push for equal and gap-free scores and should instead strive to produce cognitive equity (Kornhaber, 1998). That is, it should enable people, regardless of their ascriptive characteristics, to understand, use, and contribute to an array of disciplinary knowledge in the wider world. Accountability systems that rely almost exclusively on high-stakes tests cannot produce this outcome; such systems invariably work to advance scores more so than actual disciplinary competence, and in the process, they undermine instruction. Thus, improving disciplinary competence requires moving beyond standardized tests to other forms of assessment.

Classroom-Based Assessment/Formative Assessments

Classroom assessment ranges widely from teacher-made tests, to spot checks of cell illustrations or student graphs, to the evaluation of each step in the production of a polished essay. Such assessments guide teachers in their ongoing instruction of individual students, groups, and the entire class. Thus, they continue to be a mainstay of educational practice.

Classroom assessment can mirror the types of activities and products actually used in the practice of the discipline outside of school and can engage resources commonly employed in such work. (Such assessments are sometimes called "authentic.") Relative to standardized tests, this provides more direct evidence of domain-relevant competence (Wiliam, 2001; Shepard, 2000). Thus, a smaller inferential leap is needed to claim that a given assessed performance represents a given degree of disciplinary mastery. Furthermore, classroom assessment can improve actual disciplinary learning (Black & Wiliam, 1998a, 1998b; Stiggins, 2001; Wiggins, 1998).

Yet, just as standardized testing does not in practice fulfill its theoretical promise, neither does classroom assessment. Unlike standardized testing, however, classroom assessment's problems have overshadowed its potential strengths. For example, classroom assessment, reinforced by high-stakes testing, tends to emphasize rote knowledge and skills (Black & Wiliam 1998a, 1998b; Shepard, 2000). Though classroom assessment has been used in large-scale accountability systems (Bandalos, 2004; Koretz, 1998), it is cumbersome to do so. Such assessment must also draw on informed judgment. Judgments made by different raters of student work have often been inconsistent (Koretz, 1998; Linn & Baker, 1996).

All told, compared to standardized tests, classroom assessment can advance cognitively constructive aims relatively better than informative aims (Wiggins, 1998). Nevertheless, classroom assessment must be developed and valued within an accountability system (Pellegrino, et al., 2001; Stiggins, 2001). Unless this is done, work-arounds and gaming will infiltrate educational practice. Then, neither the informative nor the constructive aims of an accountability system will be met, as is now true under NCLB.

Rebalancing the Position of Classroom Assessment

Building teacher capacity. The potential strengths of classroom assessment lie in the development of teachers' capacity to use it formatively (Black & Wiliam, 1998a; Shepard, 2000; Stiggins, 2001). Formative assessment entails a clear understanding of what good work is; the ability to help students to develop this understanding; and the capacity to give students specific, discipline-relevant feedback that fosters good work (Black & Wiliam, 1998a). Teachers can use formative assessment in reviewing and grading exams. For example, a teacher can point out that, although students' answers on an algebra exam were correct, their solutions relied more on arithmetic—rather than algebraic—problem solving. The teacher can then point out the difference between these approaches and work with students to develop algebraic approaches. Teachers can also use formative assessment during instructional time—for example, when they highlight for the class how a given student's essay has incorporated figurative language that is valued in the discipline of writing

When formative assessment is employed, students' learning increases (Black & Wiliam, 1998a, 1998b; Chappius & Stiggins, 2002; Crooks, 1988; Wiliam, 2001, 2004). In a meta-analysis of over two hundred studies, formative assessment was found to produce overall gains in learning, and gains that were larger than existing educational interventions for students with low achievement levels (Black & Wiliam, 1998a, 1998b).

There is good evidence that regular classroom teachers can carry out sound formative assessment. For example, Wiliam (2004) has found that teachers can learn formative assessment practices, given interest and brief opportunities to discuss their efforts. Furthermore, many ordinary teachers, including coaches (Wiggins, 1998) and teachers of music and other arts disciplines, have long used formative assessment. While teachers can learn formative assessment practices, and many already use them, there are still substantial challenges to their widespread adoption. Teachers commonly develop tests to mirror standardized assessments, a practice that is reinforced by external high-stakes testing policies (McNeil, 1988; Shepard, 2000). Classroom teachers are also rarely trained to use formative assessment (Shepard, 2000; Stake, 1998; Stiggins, 2001). Not surprisingly, enacting formative assessment is stressful to teachers (Bandalos, 2004; Stecher, 1998). To meet these challenges, states could require educators to obtain assessment competence (Shepard, 2000), a policy that is now rare even though teachers may spend one-third of their time engaged in assessment activities (Stiggins, 2001). Markedly reducing the role of high-stakes testing in the wider accountability system would also allow formative assessment practices to take hold.

Creating public audiences. A key question concerning formative assessment is whether it is technically adequate for accountability purposes. For example, ratings of portfolios of student work vary widely and for multiple reasons, making it difficult to use such ratings to support inferences about the quality of students' performances (Koretz, 1998; Linn & Baker, 1996). A holistic rating of the portfolio, rather than a rating based on different dimensions of the work, yields more consistent scoring (Koretz, 1998; Pellegrino, et al., 2001). However, it is still hard to draw appropriate inferences from this. For example, in holistic scoring, chance alone would increase consistency in ratings because there are fewer possible scores to assign (Koretz, 1998). Furthermore, efforts to achieve scoring consistency by reducing criteria or score ranges could erode teachers' and students' consideration of the multiple processes and dimensions of strong disciplinary work, which is central to good formative assessment.

One way through this dilemma is to consider that across the disciplines in which formative assessment is widely used in school (e.g., arts, sports), there is a public audience for the work. Thus, the lack of spectators for most classroom work may allow formative assessment to fall prey to low standards. There are several solutions to this threat.

One solution might be to adopt a system of external evaluators. Britain's former school inspectorate was staffed by highly regarded retired teachers and administrators who produced reports that were seen as valid representations of the strengths and needs of the schools they visited (Bolton, 1998; Smith, 2000). These reports provided more specific and fine-grained information for the schools and the public than that provided by school report cards focused on high-stakes tests. Another approach would be to organize consortia of schools or districts to develop formative assessment practices and to align these with state or other external standards. This has been done in Nebraska's Student-Based Teacher-Led Assessment and Reporting System (STARS), in which formative assessments, developed by teachers at the district level, are given a central role (Bandalos, 2004). Networking schools involved in formative assessment with colleges or universities can also build a public audience. This would enable institutions of higher education to address all parts of their mission: service, teaching, and research. In addition, such consortia could improve the articulation of standards between K–12 and higher education. In turn, this might keep at bay calls for test-based accountability at the college level and the downward spiral in teaching and learning that might ensue.

In essence, policy solutions can be put in place to enable educators to acquire skill in formative assessment and to minimize threats to formative assessment from low or idiosyncratic standards. Given this, formative assessment, like standardized tests, can play a minority role in an accountability system.

Other Indicators

If formative and standardized assessments are given balanced roles, it is more likely that the informative and cognitively constructive aims of an accountability system can be met. However, as Stake (1998) has noted, "Schooling includes many performances, provisions, and relationships which could be assessed" (p. 1). Incorporating some of these in an accountability system is crucial to the overall functioning of teaching, learning, and the system itself.

Inputs

Clearly, there are a great range of inputs—including family income and access to good healthcare and preschools—that would foster higher and more equal student achievement. This chapter focuses on only those inputs related to developing a constructive and informative system of school accountability.

One essential input would be that states require substantial coursework in formative assessment for the certification of teachers and administrators. In turn, this would require colleges to develop such courses. As Stiggins (2001) has noted, this could be accomplished by having content-area specialists in colleges of education collaborate with measurement specialists to develop formative assessments for diverse curricular areas.

States should also be required to engage in public-education efforts to help parents and the wider community to understand the strengths and weaknesses of different forms of assessment. This information could be made available on state education department Web sites and distributed within schools. Doing so would help to create the public space needed to develop and adopt sound formative-assessment practices.

Processes

Professional development is an essential component of cognitively constructive—and therefore informative—accountability systems. The accountability systems of schools, districts, and states ought to be evaluated on the quality and accessibility of professional development programs aimed at enhancing formative-assessment practices in classrooms.

Outputs

Graduation rates. State accountability systems should be required to report accurate and disaggregated data on student attainment of a standard high-school diploma in four years (Losen, 2004; Swanson, 2004). Districts and high schools should be held accountable for collecting accurate information about standard diplomas and for making efforts to increase four-year graduation rates. This requirement addresses the perverse incentive to encourage weaker students to leave so that their potentially lower scores do not influence school ratings. Relatedly, retention is often practiced to give students an extra year to prepare for exams. However, since retention is strongly associated with dropping out (Hauser, 2001; Holmes, 1989), an accountability system should require schools and districts to report retention rates and efforts to reduce retention.

Compensatory Combinations

No Child Left Behind requires the conjunctive use of test scores, high-school graduation rates, and at least one other indicator of the state's choosing to determine whether schools and districts are succeeding. That is, schools face sanctions unless they attain adequate performance on all three indicators. In a system of multiple indicators, it would be more useful if ranges of acceptable performance were established for standardized tests, formative assessments, and other indicators and then allow these indicators to be used in a compensatory fashion. That is, somewhat higher performances on some indicators could offset somewhat lower performances on other indicators. This would enable schools and districts to address their local situations. For example, some schools or districts may want to emphasize improving graduation rates and formative-assessment practices more so than improving test scores. Others may decide to give equal weight to test scores, formative assessment, and other indicators. Such an approach would deliver flexibility in meeting important educational goals that NCLB has only promised.

MODIFYING NCLB

It may not be possible to enact a system of genuine multiple measures while NCLB remains in effect. Yet, some modification of the existing legislation may pave the way for an accountability system that is informative and cognitively constructive.

1. NCLB calls for the "same accountability system" (Sec. 1111(b)(2) (A)(ii)) to be used within states. However, any potential for such a system to include formative assessment is undermined by Section 1111(b)(3)(C), which requires assessments that are consistent with professional and technical standards of reliability and validity to serve as "the primary means of determining yearly performance of the State." Given the problems with exclusive reliance on any single type of assessment, this section should be modified so that assessments whose use is consistent with professional and technical standards for reliability and validity should be one—but not necessarily

the primary—means of assessing schools and districts. Ideally, the definition of "same" should be that both tests that meet psychometric standards as well as publicly monitored formative assessment should be included in the determination of school, district, and state adequacy.

2. NCLB Section 1111(b)(2)(C)(vii) allows states to include at least one other indicator besides high-school graduation rates—for example, retention, attendance, and students in advanced placement courses. Section 1111(2)(D) requires, however, that those indicators are employed in ways that are consistent with professional and technical standards for validity and reliability. Further, Section 1111(2)(D)(ii) does not allow additional indicators to modify the categorization of a school as needing improvement, corrective action, or restructuring that results from test scores. This means that additional indicators serve as window dressing: the substance of accountability remains focused on standardized test scores.

These paragraphs need to be modified to require other indicators to be included (e.g., those mentioned in section three of this chapter). Some parameter-driven compensatory combination of these indicators should be allowed to count substantively toward improvement of a school's categorization; otherwise, little attention will be given to other important aspects of schooling. In addition, including some of these other indicators may help to limit work-arounds (Koretz, 2003).

3. Section 1111(b)(2)(A)(iii) requires sanctions and rewards to hold schools and local education authorities accountable for student achievement and for making adequate yearly progress. This should be modified to include not just sanctions and punishments primarily on the basis of test results, but also on the basis of the other important education indicators.

4. NCLB Section 1111(b)(2)(C)(v) requires disaggregation of data except when subgroups are too small to be statistically reliable or when disaggregation will lead to the identification of individual students. In the latter case, subgroup scores should not be released. In the former, information about subgroup performance should nevertheless be made public to encourage attention to these students' learning.

5. Finally, sections of NCLB that address the provision of highly qualified teachers should require states to set in motion the development of certification and professional development programs that enable teachers to acquire and use formative assessment competently within the classroom.

CONCLUSION

Principles of reliability and validity have long been central to systems of educational accountability, and NCLB explicitly calls for tests that meet such technical standards. This chapter indicates that such standards must be complemented by—indeed, framed within—an educational accountability system that strives to be informative and cognitively constructive. Such a system would incorporate multiple types of assessments, including formative classroom assessments, as well as other indicators. It would also attend to inputs, such as the preparation of teachers; to processes, such as professional development; and to outputs, including standard, four-year graduation rates.

With considerable effort, it is possible to build a system of assessment and accountability that can diminish the corruption of learning and information that exists under NCLB. However, no system can do what NCLB has promised: create universal proficiency as measured against high standards. No society has ever achieved that. Furthermore, variability in achievement among individual students and across groups in the United States has multiple sources, most of which originate in processes, policies, and practices beyond K–12 education. However, education can still benefit from a good accountability system, one that is cognitively constructive for teachers and students and that generates accurate information about the status and development of student learning.

4

Promises and Pitfalls

Implications of NCLB for Identifying, Assessing, and Educating English Language Learners

Michael J. Kieffer, Nonie K. Lesaux, and Catherine E. Snow

The fundamental principles of the No Child Left Behind (NCLB) Act of 2001 prescribe holding *all* learners to high standards and raising the academic achievement of all identified subgroups in the K–12 population. One of these subgroups is the growing population of language minority learners, those students for whom English is not the primary language of the home (see below for technical definitions). One of the significant benefits of NCLB has been an increase in awareness of the academic needs and achievement of this historically neglected population; schools are now accountable for teaching English and content knowledge to them. There is little disagreement about the spirit of the law as it relates to language minority learners—that is, to ensure that states and districts meet these students' academic needs. However, finding an approach to implementation that ensures that the law's intended benefits are achieved can be difficult. In the specific case of NCLB, with its presumption that test-based accountability (across subgroups of learners who differ in important ways) is the motor for educational change, the issues of valid and equitable implementation are particularly challenging.

The policies imposed by NCLB have raised awareness of the needs of language minority learners and the challenges of teaching English and content knowledge to them. However, they fall short of ensuring that all language minority students benefit, and they risk both disadvantaging language minority students and misleading schools and districts about their accomplishments and needs. There are at least two specific ways in which NCLB has had an impact on the education of language minority learners: (a) through the procedures for categorizing language minority students for purposes of disaggregation and achievement monitoring, and for identifying the proportion who will receive specialized support for language development, and (b) through the instruments that are used to assess and monitor both language development and academic progress in content areas such as mathematics, science, and English language arts. Underlying these two issues is the basic problem of how to define the population.

MONITORING THE LANGUAGE MINORITY LEARNER POPULATION WHILE ACKNOWLEDGING ITS HETEROGENEITY

We define language minority students as those who come from a home where a language other than English is the primary language spoken. Many of these students are fully bilingual in the home language and English; some are more proficient in English than they are in the home language; and some speak no English at all upon school entry (August & Hakuta, 1997; August & Shanahan, 2006). It is important to note that in most educational policy contexts, only a subset of language minority learners are categorized as English language learners (ELLs; previously called *Limited English Proficient* or *LEP*), who are attended to because civil rights provisions require that they be provided access to meaningful learning experiences (Development Associates, 2003). Evidence suggests, though, that many language minority students who do not qualify as LEP may have urgent educational needs (de Jong, 2004; Gándara, Rumberger, Maxwell-Jolly, & Callahan, 2003).

Although the exact terminology may vary, there are typically three classifications used for language minority learners at various stages in their schooling. One classification is that of initially fluent English proficient (I-FEP). Students with an I-FEP designation are those who enroll in school with sufficient English proficiency to participate meaningfully in mainstream classrooms without support. The second classification—that which receives the most attention in school districts—is that of English language learner (ELL; sometimes referred to as LEP). Students classified as

ELL are those considered to have an English proficiency level that compromises meaningful participation in mainstream classrooms, and thus, they receive support for language learning. The majority of ELLs are subsequently redesignated as fluent English proficient (R-FEP) and are no longer considered in need of such support. A student is never designated R-FEP upon initial assessment; this designation is only assigned to a student who has qualified for reclassification from a specific ELL program to a mainstream classroom.

Originally, under NCLB, no R-FEP students were included in the ELL subgroup for accountability purposes. However, in February of 2004, the U.S. Department of Education gave states the option of including R-FEP students for up to two years after redesignation within the "ELL" subgroup (U.S. Department of Education, 2004). All other R-FEP students, as well as I-FEP students, are represented in the disaggregation system only to the extent that they also qualify under racial/ethnic or socioeconomic categories; they are not represented in the ELL subgroup.

Identifying individual language minority students as ELL, I-FEP, or R-FEP is an art practiced quite differently in different states and districts, leading to widely different proportions of the language minority population classified as ELL. Whereas 65 percent of language minority learners are identified as ELL in New Mexico, only 14 percent of these learners are so identified in New Jersey (Ragan & Lesaux, 2006). Although states differ in their patterns of immigration, differences in classification criteria no doubt account for much of this variability across states. Equal rights to appropriate services and monitoring, requires that language minority students identified for ELL services in New Jersey should also be so identified in New Mexico, and vice versa. Currently, this is demonstrably not the case.

We argue that the entire range of language minority students deserves the opportunity to be considered for special educational attention, and that the language minority population's academic achievement should be monitored over the long term. Like minority racial groups and economically disadvantaged students, the language minority learner group is at elevated educational risk, though, of course, many individuals in the group are academically successful. Attending to the entire population of language minority students would have at least three advantages over the current practice of targeting only students classified as ELL. First, it would allow for a rational approach to monitoring progress over time by identifying a stable group of students rather than a group with constantly shifting membership. Second, it would provide a uniform standard across states and districts for defining the population to be served. Third, it would promote the idea that all students at risk for school failure on the basis of their language minority status must be served, rather than simply those who fall below an arbitrary (and often low) standard for English proficiency.

Disaggregation categories. We argue that identifying the whole population of language minority students as a disaggregation category when calculating adequate yearly progress (AYP) would contribute to improved achievement for language minority students in general, as well as for the ELL tail of the language minority population. This policy would provide a more complete picture of progress toward proficiency for the ELL subgroup, given the comparison to the entire population of language minority learners, and would increase instructional attention to language minority students who are not considered ELL, but who still lack skills needed for academic success.

As noted above, NCLB implements a minimally nuanced system of categorizing language minority learners, distinguishing only those limited in English proficiency, those fully proficient, or a third, intermediate category of formerly limited but now redesignated. The ELL classification is designed to be temporary, unlike all the other disaggregation categories (gender, race, limited income, and special education identification) for which results are reported. Furthermore, exit from the ELL category is premised on performance on tests that are part of or very like the accountability assessments themselves. Thus, it is impossible to estimate the size of this population, monitor its academic achievement, and determine the factors that influence its progress toward academic success.

A specific irony inheres in the use of mainstream accountability assessments with ELLs. The expectation is that the ELL subgroup within schools will achieve the level of performance that defines AYP, just like the other subgroups. However, as soon as an individual ELL student gets to a point of scoring pretty well on the assessment, that student is likely to be reclassified as FEP. This contributes to the public perception that ELL students are subject to widespread failure, and it leads to negative views of schools with many ELLs. Schools with a constant influx of new immigrants—even those that succeed in moving many students toward English proficiency in two or three years—are at a particular disadvantage because they consistently have a substantial ELL subgroup. Furthermore, while Title I puts pressure on schools to keep students classified as ELL to improve that subgroup's performance, Title III generates incentives to reclassify as soon as possible. NCLB's Title III—the lesser discussed cousin to Title I that provides much of the funding for programs to serve ELLs—requires that states establish and enforce goals for ELLs' progress in English, including increasing the percentage who reach proficiency.

The basic flaw in logic is treating—for purposes of monitoring academic progress—a temporary category of ELLs just like a fixed category such as African American. Membership in racially and ethnically defined subgroups is not temporary; thus, it is entirely possible for the subgroup in a school or district to show AYP, and the performance of the subgroup is informative to policymakers and practitioners whether it shows progress or not. But because ELLs get reclassified on the basis of assessments like those used for mainstream accountability purposes, the schools that are most successful at moving ELLs quickly out of special programs are punished the most severely by losing the most successful learners from that subgroup. From the perspective of serving the individual learner, of most concern is the incentive for districts to reclassify ELLs as quickly as possible, with little assurance or explicit evidence that these learners are capable of thriving without support in mainstream classrooms. Some research (de Jong, 2004; Gándara et al., 2003) suggests that many R-FEP students have difficulty accessing grade-level material.

Alternately, those schools that improve ELLs' academic skills without reclassifying them may show AYP, but they may also face consequences under their state's implementation of Title III. Similarly, districts with good preschool and kindergarten programs that produce students classified as FEP early in their school careers are, in effect, punished by losing those high achievers from their ELL category. Thus, using ELL rather than language minority as the designator almost certainly underestimates the achievement outcomes of the overall population of language minority learners, contributes to the public perception that immigrant groups are not learning English, and distorts the information available to districts, states, and the federal government.

Policymakers have—to some extent—acknowledged this irony, as indicated by the 2004 rule to allow the inclusion of R-FEP students for up to two years after redesignation. Although such a stopgap measure may allow some schools to avoid a failing label (if they happen to have a large population of these recently redesignated students performing well), it does little to address the fundamental problem of treating a temporary category as if it were fixed. Similarly, Senator Mike Crapo's (R-ID) 2006 proposal to improve NCLB would make the 2004 provision permanent and would add an additional year in which R-FEP students can be counted. The Crapo cutoff point is no less arbitrary than previous ones. The reality of language minority learners is that they gradually approach the proficiency of English-only learners, that they constitute a subgroup of importance, and that their academic development should be supported and monitored over the full span of time from initial exposure to English until full proficiency is achieved.

A fixed language minority learner category would not only address this irony but would also be coherent with the underlying logic of disaggregated reporting: that schools must meet the needs of students at elevated risk for educational failure on the basis of their demographic characteristics. Just as students of color and students coming from economically disadvantaged homes are at elevated risk, the entire population of language minority learners is at elevated educational risk for reading difficulties and for school failure, more generally (August & Hakuta, 1997; August & Shanahan, 2006). Some might argue that a fixed language minority learner category is inappropriate because educational risk is not equal for all language minority learners. It is certainly greater for students with less proficiency in English. Although it is undoubtedly true that language minority learners' level of educational risk varies, this is equally true for the subgroup of African American students or students receiving free/reduced-priced lunch. Because we define those subgroups based on their existence as populations with elevated risk *on average*, we do not limit these subgroups to those students most at risk (e.g., by excluding from the economically disadvantaged category students whose parents are pursuing graduate degrees or by limiting the African American category to students with a history of low achievement). A rational extension of this logic would include all language minority learners, including those at very high risk due to their very limited conversational English skills, those at medium risk due to limited academic English, and those at only slight risk due to previous success in acquiring basic and academic English skills.

Some might also worry that the permanent language minority label would promote a deficit model of bilingualism, in which the potential benefits of learning two languages are ignored, or that students will be tracked beyond the time when they need support for language learning. However, a fixed language minority learner category would be no more pejorative than a permanent African American category, and it would lead to no more segregated classrooms than already exist. (Does including racial subgroups in NCLB reporting promote racial segregation?) Educators recognize that growing up as an African American in the United States not only limits access to certain resources (namely, economic and social capital of particular kinds) but also provides access to resources (especially cultural and social capital of other kinds). As we raise awareness of the needs of language minority learners, we should help educators recognize that language minority learners enter school not only having had limited access to certain linguistic resources (e.g., academic English) but also having had special access to linguistic resources (the first language). We argue that including the entire population of language minority learners would in fact dispel deficit notions by allowing us to track the success of language minority learners, not just document the struggles of a subgroup defined by their low test scores.

Moreover, a fixed language minority learner category would allow for greater attention to those language minority learners who may not have held the ELL designation for many years but continue to struggle with the academic demands of school. There is little, if any, evidence to suggest that redesignation as fully English proficient is a reliable and valid predictor of ability to succeed in mainstream classrooms without any language support (Linquanti, 2001). There is pressure to reclassify students as soon as possible, and in California, Arizona, and Massachusetts, special educational settings for ELL students are available for only one year. If redesignated students' scores are reported for only two additional years, the entire span of time during which support is available and academic achievement is monitored may be as little as three years. For many children, this is too short. Furthermore, the learning challenges on which redesignation decisions are based may not adequately represent the actual demands of the curriculum—in particular, the demands for understanding and producing academic language. For a large proportion of the language minority population, the three years of language support are kindergarten, first, and second grades, when exposure to academic language—in the classroom and in print—is severely limited.

Academic language for academic success. Many skills are wrapped up in the notion of academic language. Vocabulary knowledge (including the multiple meanings of many English words), the ability to handle increasing word complexity and length, understanding complex sentence structures, and extended discourse structures are all aspects of academic language (Scarcella, 2003). For example, among second graders being read a storybook, several language minority students missed the meaning of a paragraph because of the sentence: *The mother made him get out and he ran off.* In this case, *made* carried its less common causative meaning *to force.* Aspects of academic language relate to the language of text, including the organization of paragraphs, the function of transitions such as *therefore* and *in contrast,* and a wide range of vocabulary that appears far more often in text than it does in oral conversation. Consider this sentence: *John was very hungry, despite having just eaten a large plate of beans and rice.* The term *despite* is key to the meaning of the sentence, yet is not typically used in everyday conversation with children.

Academic vocabulary plays an especially prominent role in the upper elementary, middle, and high school years as students read to learn about concepts, ideas, and facts in math, science, and social studies classes. In these classrooms, language minority learners encounter many words that are not part of everyday classroom conversation (e.g., *analyze, sustain*), yet are key to comprehension and the acquisition of knowledge. Language minority learners with the ELL designation reclassified at first grade may indeed be "proficient" enough for the language demands of the primary grade classrooms and texts. But if those learners lack quality classroom experiences to learn the academic language needed for later grades (as is too often the case), they will never catch up with English-only classmates. Thus, learners classified as fully proficient in the primary grades may lack the proficiency needed to participate meaningfully in mainstream middle-grade classrooms without specialized language support.

Several studies of elementary and middle-grade language minority learners—whether formally designated ELL or not—have revealed vocabulary levels between the 20th and 30th percentiles (Carlo et al., 2004; Francis et al., 2006; Kieffer & Lesaux, 2008; Proctor, Carlo, August, & Snow, 2005; Tabors, Páez, & Lopez, 2003). Lack of proficiency in academic vocabulary affects language minority learners' ability to comprehend and analyze texts in the years beyond the primary grades, limits their ability to write and express themselves effectively, and can hinder their acquisition of academic content in all academic areas, including mathematics.

Reading comprehension and content area learning are challenges for a large proportion of the language minority population. However, at this time, there is no mechanism in place to systematically monitor the population's progress; the only mechanism in place monitors an ever-changing subgroup of language minority learners: those designated as ELL, or as R-FEP, for up two years. If the progress of all students who were ever designated as ELL were monitored, then the oxymoronic nature of the current system would be reduced. But the problems of state-to-state variation in designation criteria and the increased academic risk of many language minority students never designated as ELL would only be addressed by defining the disaggregation category as language minority. We argue that this would be the optimal approach to ensuring both attention to and equity for students who, as a group, show heightened risk of academic failure.

We do not argue that the importance of English proficiency for language minority learners should be downplayed, nor do we argue that the temporary ELL designation should be abolished. The careful identification of those students most in need of additional language support for accessing the curriculum at any given grade level is essential for ensuring equal opportunities to learn. In fact, a uniform and psychometrically valid standard for classifying students as ELL imposed nationally would have enormous benefits for ensuring that learners are provided with more equitable support services across states and districts. However, for the reasons described above, such a standard should *not* define the category by which a school's success in promoting the learning of the language minority population is judged.

ASSESSING THE LANGUAGE DEVELOPMENT AND ACADEMIC PROGRESS OF LANGUAGE MINORITY LEARNERS

Language proficiency assessments. NCLB had the beneficial effect of stimulating the development of language proficiency assessments for use in the required monitoring of ELL students nationwide. Although many states were already assessing some language minority learners' proficiency and academic progress, at various levels and for varying purposes, NCLB has ensured that these data are systematically collected and reported using valid instruments. The tests now being used to evaluate and monitor the development of language minority students' English proficiency have improved psychometric properties and the potential to shift instruction for ELLs so it reflects standards for English language development. However, the language proficiency assessments fail to adequately emphasize the complex academic language needed for success in content area classes, with the risk that this key domain will be neglected in instruction for ELL students.

Though U.S. schools have been classifying incoming students as LEP since the early 1970s, the criteria for those decisions and the tools available to make them were generally unsatisfactory. Among many problems and ambiguities in this process, most pressing was the absence of well-designed and rigorous tests of the skills that would be a sensible basis for sending students to mainstream classrooms. Probably the most widely used assessment between 1980 and 2000 was the Language Assessment Scales (LAS; de Avila & Duncan, 2005); although appropriate for assessing basic proficiencies, the LAS is not linked to any particular academic outcomes, and it has insufficient alternate forms or psychometric sensitivity for use in monitoring progress (e.g., Pray, 2005; Del Vecchio & Guerrero, 1995). Given its emphasis on reading and writing, as well as on oral proficiency, the LAS itself represented a vast improvement on the Bilingual Syntax Measure (Burt, Dulay, & Hernández Chávez, 1976), the instrument most widely used previously, which focused exclusively on oral proficiency, and primarily in conversational contexts.

In the wake of NCLB's requirement that all ELLs be tested annually on English speaking, listening, reading, and writing skills, several proficiency tests have been developed. (Some states have developed their own tests, while other states have formed themselves into consortia to reduce development costs). Presumably, these new tests will be used as part of the system for classifying students as ELL or formerly ELL, as well as to meet the accountability requirements of NCLB's Title III (which emphasize monitoring growth in English proficiency, not just redesignation). As more attention is paid to the process of operationalizing English proficiency in each of the four domains and the psychometric properties of these tests, they will likely represent an improvement. Preliminary evidence suggests that this is indeed the case (Ferrara, 2006; Abedi, 2005).

Furthermore, whereas the previously used tests lacked any connection to academic content, the state-developed tests are typically aligned with state standards for second language development. In addition, the NCLB guidelines for these proficiency assessments specify reading and writing as well as listening and speaking, which may help educators to conceptualize language proficiency as more than basic oral conversational skills, and promote instructional emphasis on academic language and content. However, the guidelines do not specify testing academic language or predicting performance in content area classrooms; after about third grade, it is performance in content areas—not just proficiency in English—that constitutes academic success. Thus, the likelihood of being able to do the work in math, science, social studies, and literature study ought to be the criterion against which language minority learners' progress is monitored. To the extent that *academic performance* is included in current tests, it is typically operationalized as alignment with English Language Arts standards, rather than as the full range of skills needed for achievement across the content areas. Some districts and states include grades or performance on achievement tests as additional criteria for exiting ELL programs (Ragan & Lesaux, 2006), but again, ELA performance is the most likely to be the focus.

Figures 4.1a and 4.1b provide two examples drawn from Grade 6–8 Texas' Reading Proficiency Test in English (TRPT), one of the older state tests of English proficiency. Although it is a reading test with some content-based items, the TRPT shows a strong emphasis on basic vocabulary and everyday uses of language, such as telling time or reading a calendar, even in this version of the test for middle school students. These items are useful for measuring students' status and growth in basic English proficiency. English proficiency tests *should* be sensitive to differences in students' proficiency at the low ranges, to inform instruction and to monitor the growth of new arrivals. However, tests used to make decisions about transitioning students to mainstream instruction or to determine whether schools are serving the needs of all ELLs *must* measure challenging academic language skills. Francis' (2006) comparison of ELLs' performance on Title I and Title III assessments makes clear that growth on the ELP assessment was faster and better predicted by time in the United States than scores on the math or English Language Arts assessment, confirming the disjunction of the skills needed for the two types of assessment.

Without attention to the full range of meaningful indicators of academic performance, the use of the proficiency tests for accountability purposes and reclassification of ELLs may result in the skills covered on these tests setting the instructional agenda for bilingual and Structured English Immersion classrooms. If these language proficiency tests do not include complex academic material and text, the danger is that these classrooms will focus primarily on conversational English and reading of simple narrative texts without preparing students for the complexity of grade-level material to which they will subsequently be exposed.

Of course, the different language proficiency tests vary enormously in the degree to which they attend to higher level academic performance. Even the format of the listening and speaking components of the assessments vary widely. California and Arizona use individually administered tests with standardized listening and speaking prompts, whereas Massachusetts and Texas train teachers to assess language proficiency by applying a rubric to observations of students performing academic and social tasks in the classroom. It is an open question as to which of the two approaches will have the greatest benefits for students. Although there is very little empirical evidence comparing these two approaches, the standardized test approach will likely yield more comparable scores, whereas the rubric approach might offer a more valid measure of students' performance and the potential to raise teachers' awareness of academic language skills.

Figure 4.1a Items from the Texas Reading Proficiency Test in English for Grades Six to Eight.

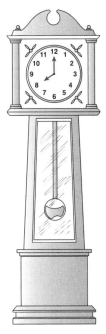

5. **What time is it?**

   A It is eight o'clock.

   B The clock is old.

   C It is early in the afternoon.

   D It is time for lunch.

By permission: Texas Educational Agency. Copyright © and trademark ™ 2000. All rights reserved.

The range of skills associated with reading and writing proficiency, successful use of academic language, and adequate oral English are difficult to characterize (e.g., Scarcella, 2003; Bailey & Butler, 2003). However, in most states, the expectations for language minority learners are derived from English Language Arts standards developed for native speakers, and thus, may well be quite irrelevant to success in reading and writing for purposes of learning math, science, or social studies. As previously noted, it is important to distinguish academic from conversational language skills, because many of the language minority learners who struggle academically have well-developed conversational English skills.

Figure 4.1b Items from the Texas Reading Proficiency Test in English for Grades Six to Eight.

School Vacation

1. Jack gets a letter from his cousin Ted. Ted lives in the mountains. It is cold there in winter There is a lot of snow.

2. Jack wants to visit Ted. Jack checks his school calender to see when he can go to Tedís house.

February School Calendar						
Sunday	**Monday**	**Tuesday**	**Wednesday**	**Thursday**	**Friday**	**Saturday**
	1 Game Day	2	3	4	5 Bake Sale	6
7	8	9	10	11	12 Report Cards	13
14	15	16	17	18	19	20
	Winter Break—No School					
21	22	23	24	25	26 Parents' Day	27
28						

22. What event will take place on February 26?
F School Play
G Game Day
H Parents' Day
J Bake Sale

24. This story is mostly about a boy who—
F wants to visit his cousin
G likes to read
H plays in the snow
J likes cold weather

Finally, the shift to an assessment-based system raises concerns about how assessment results will be used. Although the proficiency tests have been—and will continue to be—designed for the purposes of evaluating schools' success in moving ELLs toward English proficiency, states and districts undoubtedly use these assessments for other purposes for which they are not designed. For instance, California districts routinely use the California English Language Development Test for initial placement, annual monitoring, and reclassification of students, as well as to inform decisions about interventions for struggling learners. Given the psychometric properties of the test and the complexity of the language proficiency construct, this single measure cannot possibly serve all of these four purposes well. A test designed strictly to identify whether a learner is above or below the redesignation threshold is likely to be insensitive to fine distinctions such as those between beginning and early intermediate students. This same test will provide little or no information on which to base interventions for individual children who are struggling. Such practices are examples of inappropriate and unethical test use (Sattler, 2001); in these instances, the benefits of tracking the academic achievement of the population are, in fact, outweighed by the costs of using the tests in inappropriate ways.

Mainstream accountability assessments. Under NCLB guidelines, students classified as ELLs must be included in the state accountability assessments after one year in U.S. schools. Tracking the academic achievement of these learners and ensuring that districts, schools, and teachers incorporate this population in their instructional plans and efforts is beneficial. However, because any test is to some degree a language test, language minority students' scores reflect degree of understanding of the test items and the academic language needed for content area success as much as pure academic ability.

It might seem that ELL students are not particularly disadvantaged in performance on some content area tests. For example, math is thought of as a rather language-free zone. However, math learning is verbally mediated to a large extent; the association of verbal labels to mathematical forms and expressions is common even in the elementary grades (e.g., Lager, 2006). Mathematics language is often a specialized form of natural, conventional language, and it requires a reinterpretation of the way language is used in everyday settings (Cuevas, 1984). Much instruction and assessment in mathematics curriculum occurs via discourse and text that is characterized by academic language (Cazden, 1986).

A careful look at math items—in particular, on the more challenging state tests—reveals that they make enormous language and reading comprehension demands on students. Some of these demands derive from linguistic complexity that is construct irrelevant and thus calls into question the validity of inferences based on the scores (Abedi, Lord, & Hofstetter, 1998). However, some of these demands are intricately related to the conceptual understanding and application involved in the domain. Figure 4.2 shows two items from the California Standards Test for grade six. Notice that each uses unnecessarily rare vocabulary that may be unknown to some ELLs, such as *orchard*, *harvested*, *acre*, and *band* of a hat, as well as unnecessarily complex sentence structure, such as the verb phrases *could be solved* and *is shaped*. However, each item also presents linguistic complexity that is central to the mathematical concepts being assessed, including the math vocabulary *proportion, cylinder, measure,* and *diameter*.

Figure 4.2 Items from the California Math Standards Test for Grade Six.

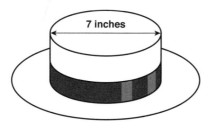

A farmer harvested 14,000 pounds of almonds from an 8-acre orchard. Which proportion could be solved to find *x*, the expected harvest from a 30-acre orchard?

A $\dfrac{8}{14,000} = \dfrac{x}{30}$

B $\dfrac{8}{14,000} = \dfrac{30}{x}$

C $\dfrac{30}{14,000} = \dfrac{x}{8}$

D $\dfrac{30}{14,000} = \dfrac{8}{x}$

The top part of this hat is shaped like a cylinder with a diameter of 7 inches.

7 inches

Which measure is *closest* to the length of the band that goes around the outside of the hat?

A 10.1 inches

B 11.0 inches

C 22.0 inches

D 38.5 inches

By permission: California Department of Education.

There is substantial evidence that the size of the math achievement gap between ELLs and native English speakers differs as a function of the language demands of the items (e.g., Abedi et al., 1998; Abedi, 2003). Even when unnecessary linguistic complexity (e.g., complex syntax) is removed from math test items, ELLs often perform no better than they did on the original items, and they continue to perform substantially worse than native English speakers do (Abedi, Courtney, & Leon, 2003; Abedi, Courtney, Mirocha, Leon, & Goldberg, 2005; Abedi, Hofstetter, Baker, & Lord, 2001; Abedi et al., 1998). This suggests that ELLs in the U. S. are not being taught the *necessary* academic language involved in doing sophisticated mathematical problem solving.

. As a way to address some of concerns about the language demands of content area assessments, NCLB requires that states provide testing accommodations for ELLs, such as English dictionaries, bilingual dictionaries, extra time, and native language versions of the test. However, in the absence of guidance about appropriate accommodations, some states have adopted accommodations for ELLs that have no theoretical justification, such as preferred seating or testing in small groups (Rivera & Collum, 2006). To date, there is little evidence supporting the efficacy of even those accommodations that directly address ELLs' language difficulties without changing the construct being measured; a recent review and meta-analysis found the most commonly used accommodations to be largely ineffective (Francis, Lesaux, Rivera, Kieffer, & Rivera, 2006). Providing bilingual dictionaries or native language versions of the test, although often touted as the most fair treatment, does not necessarily yield higher test scores for ELLs. There is some evidence that ELLs perform no differently when provided bilingual dictionaries, and that they even perform worse when tested in their native language, though the efficacy of these depend on the students' opportunities to learn the content in their native language. Francis et al. (2006) found that providing English dictionaries had a very small, if significant, effect on narrowing the substantial gap in content area performance between ELLs and native English speakers.

Although test makers must ensure that they do not introduce unnecessary linguistic complexity, educators must also realize that better assessments will not eliminate the real differences in content area achievement between ELLs and their native English-speaking peers. Academic language is indispensable in presenting higher grade-level material in every content area and in providing all students with the skills they need to function at higher levels in those subjects. Having tests that reduce the use of complex, academic language is in fact a disservice to these learners if those tests are also omitting crucial content needed for academic success. Ultimately, the language minority population must receive high-quality instruction—which includes an emphasis on the language of the domain—in content areas, and in doing so, must be held to the same academic standards as their English-only peers.

SUMMARY

Transcending the historic lack of emphasis on tracking achievement patterns and ensuring academic growth for all language minority learners, one of the significant benefits of NCLB has been an increased awareness of the academic needs of students from non-English-speaking homes; schools are now accountable for teaching English and content knowledge to these learners. There is little disagreement that the spirit of the law is to improve how schools educate language minority learners by holding them accountable for meeting their special academic needs. However, a prerequisite for tests administered on a large scale is that they be valid and capable of ensuring equitable outcomes. This is a particular challenge for tests administered to language minority learners, given the complexity of second language acquisition, the differences in language proficiency within the population, and the difficulties in designing tests in which language proficiency is *not* one of the primary skills measured.

Although we are not opposed to the use of a test-based system to hold schools and districts accountable for educating language minority students, to be successful, such a system requires a rational approach to defining the population and careful attention to the valid assessment of their skills. This growing and historically underserved population deserves to be part of the accountability system if, in fact, accountability procedures result in more systematic delivery of educational services to meet their needs. However, the current design of the system under NCLB fails to serve the purposes of the law in several ways. To lessen the negative and increase the positive impact, and to be consistent with the spirit of the law, subsequent attention must focus on the following:

- A national definition and operationalization of the constructs of language minority learner and English language learner.

  1. Language minority: students from homes where the primary language of use, as reported by parents, is not English. Language minority learners would then constitute a fixed category for the purposes of data reporting under NCLB. Conclusions about the achievement of language minority learners would not be based on only on a small subgroup which represents the tail end of the language and literacy distribution.

  2. English language learner: the subset of the language minority population who need intensive language support services in order to participate meaningfully in mainstream classrooms, based on English language proficiency measures that reflect academic language skills and provide valid inferences for students' future success. A uniform set of measures and procedures to identify

this subset of the language minority population should be introduced across states and districts. An ELL student redesignated as fluent English proficient (R-FEP) no longer receives language support because he or she has attained proficiency in English; such students, however, remain in the language minority group for the purposes of accountability and progress monitoring.

- The need for academic language to play a well-defined role in the assessment of language proficiency. Different language proficiency assessments place very different degrees of emphasis on academic language. A systematic study of the progress of ELLs (both progress in getting reclassified and in concomitant performance on state accountability and NAEP assessments) could exploit this natural experiment to explore the impact of different test designs on long-term student performance and to investigate the validity of reclassification as an indicator of ability to thrive in mainstream content area classrooms. Results of this research would address basic policy questions: On what grounds should ELLs be reclassified? Do lax or stringent criteria for reclassification make a difference in long-term outcomes? How much support do reclassified ELLs need to access classroom learning?

- The need for content area assessments to reflect the academic language demands of accessing the content. While we are not arguing for unnecessary complexity in the tests, instruction for language minority students must reflect high academic standards and provide the opportunity for them to develop the academic language of content areas.

- The need for tests and measures to be used in an appropriate and ethical manner. Currently, many tests are being used for multiple, competing purposes, despite designs and psychometric properties that do not support such use. The implementation of the Reading First provisions of NCLB included recommendations concerning assessments to be used, as well as guidelines for preparing teachers to use the information derived from assessment. A similar set of policies should be introduced for those teaching the language minority population: a set of assessments together with guidelines for their use, and guidance to teachers about interpreting test results as a basis for planning instruction. Furthermore, incentives for the development of multiple measures of language and content for language minority students would help ensure the availability of tests to serve different functions (e.g., diagnosis, placement, progress monitoring) appropriately. The development of multiple measures would also increase opportunities to establish validity of the measures for language minority learners.

Although a rational accountability system that validly assesses the skills of language minority learners is far from sufficient for ensuring the civil rights of these learners, history suggests that it is a necessary condition. Providing a high-quality education to language minority learners in the United States will require a concerted, multifaceted effort that goes far beyond identifications and tests, yet one essential step forward in that effort would be to improve how we identify these learners and how we assess their progress toward high levels of academic proficiency.

PART II

5

Two Takes on the Impact of NCLB on Academic Improvement

Tracking State Proficiency Trends Through NAEP Versus State Assessments

Jaekyung Lee

The No Child Left Behind (NCLB) Act of 2001 requires yearly progress of all groups of students toward the goal of 100 percent proficiency by 2014. To understand whether NCLB is working as intended to improve student achievement in reading and math, this chapter compares pre-NCLB

This chapter builds upon the author's earlier report (Lee, 2006)—"Tracking Achievement Gaps and Assessing the Impact of NCLB on the Gaps: An In-Depth Look Into National and State Reading and Math Outcome Trends," published in Cambridge, Massachusetts by the Civil Rights Project at Harvard University. Here, the study focuses on the state-level trends of overall reading and math proficiency rates with updates from extended comparisons of NAEP and state assessment data. I am grateful for feedback on this study from 2007 AERA symposium participants including Gail Sunderman, Gary Orfield, Bruce Fuller, Doug Harris, Lauren Resnick, and other anonymous reviewers.

trends in student achievement with post-NCLB trends. Further, it compares the achievement trends on state assessments with trends on the National Assessment of Educational Progress (NAEP), the so-called nation's report card. It is possible that, once NCLB was enacted, reading and math achievement trends on NAEP and states' own assessments may have changed. It pays attention to how discrepancies between NAEP and state assessment results may lead to different views and conclusions regarding states' progress toward the goal of 100 percent proficiency and the impact of NCLB on their academic improvement.

WEIGHING NEW TEST RESULTS FOR DEBATES ON THE IMPACT OF NCLB

NAEP results that came out in 2005 report national and state-by-state reading and math performance from testing nationally representative samples of more than 300,000 fourth and eighth graders (see Perie, Grigg, & Donahue, 2005 for reading; Perie, Grigg, & Dion, 2005 for math). Since the U.S. Department of Education released the NAEP 2005 reports on October 19, 2005, reactions to these reports varied. The U.S. Department of Education (2005) newsletter *The Achiever* noted, "[O]verall math scores for both groups (fourth and eighth graders) rose to all-time highs, and fourth-grade reading scores matched the all-time record" (p. 2). The U.S. Secretary of Education attributed credit for such gains to NCLB, who claimed, "These results...confirm that we are on the right track with No Child Left Behind, particularly with younger students who have benefited from the core principles of annual assessment and disaggregation of data" (p. 2). Critics of standardized testing interpreted the 2005 NAEP results more negatively. The National Center for Fair and Open Testing (FairTest, 2005) commented on the NAEP 2005 report in its press release: "Flatline NAEP scores show the failure of test-driven school reform. No Child Left Behind has not improved academic performance." FairTest claimed, "NAEP reading scores were essentially unchanged from 2002 to 2005 at grade four and declined markedly at grade eight." FairTest also pointed out, "[M]ath scores did not increase at a significantly faster rate than in the 1990s, well before most high-stakes exams for elementary and middle school were put in place."

The different interpretations of the same results may be attributed partly to differences in the time frame used to analyze changes in the test results and different ways of evaluating the policy impact. To understand whether short-term improvements in NAEP scores can be attributed to NCLB, we need to assess any short-term changes in scores within a longer term time frame. This will allow us to determine whether NCLB had a significant effect on academic growth or if the changes were the continuation of a growth pattern that began before NCLB and continued after its passage.

No matter what the NAEP results tell us about fifty states' academic performances, there is another source of information that states can use to determine the status and progress of their students' academic proficiency—their own state tests. Under NCLB, states can decide which tests to use for accountability and proficiency. In turn, states are required to look at their results and sanction low-performing schools. Since state assessments are the basis for states' educational accountability decision making under NCLB, it raises the question of what states' own assessment results tell us about the impact of NCLB. Previous comparisons of NAEP and state assessment results showed significant discrepancies in the level of student achievement, as well as in the size of statewide achievement gains (Fuller, Gesicki, Kang, & Wright, 2006; Klein, Hamilton, McCaffrey, & Stecher, 2000; Koretz & Barron, 1998; Lee, 2007; Linn, Baker, & Betebenner, 2002). The percentages of students reaching the proficient level tend to be generally lower on NAEP than on state assessments. These results suggest that, for many states, NAEP proficiency levels are more challenging than the states' own (National Education Goals Panel, 1996). Since state standards vary widely in relationship to NAEP standards, questions arise about the generalizability of gains reported on a state's own assessment, and hence, about the validity of claims regarding student achievement (Linn, 2000).

While several studies have attempted to examine the impact of NCLB on student achievement, they are limited because they use a single measure of achievement only "after" NCLB was adopted. Any change we see after NCLB may reflect a continuing trend that occurred before NCLB and that should not be credited to the new law. While it is important to maintain the pace of improvement, it is inappropriate to credit NCLB for improving achievement if the law did not accelerate the pace. States tend to show progress on their own standards regardless of whether or not it transfers into progress independently measured by NAEP. For example, a report by the Education Trust (2004) on post-NCLB achievement trends relied solely on states' own assessment results. The report examined short-term changes in average achievement in state reading and math assessment results as well as changes in racial and economic achievement gaps after NCLB (from 2002 to 2004). The findings of this report suggest that the improvements in performance were positive but that narrowing either the racial or economic achievement gap was slow. A follow-up report by the Education Trust (2006) takes a more comprehensive look into post-NCLB changes across grade levels (from 2003 to 2005) and finds more positive results at the elementary education level than at the secondary level. According to a report by the Center on Education Policy (2006), national survey results show that scores on state tests have risen in a large majority of states and school districts. That report credited school district policies and programs as more important contributors to these gains than the NCLB adequate yearly progress (AYP) requirements. Despite these earlier findings, real, full-scale impact of NCLB on student achievement remains to be examined.

TRACKING PRE- AND POST-NCLB PROFICIENCY TRENDS ON NAEP AND STATE ASSESSMENTS

One way to explore the effects of NCLB accountability policy on student achievement outcomes is tracking achievement before and after NCLB. Trend analysis involves estimating both pre-NCLB and post-NCLB reading and math achievement trends. It enables the evaluator to interpret the pre- to post-NCLB changes by showing whether the achievement gains after NCLB are a continuation of earlier trends or whether they mark a decisive change. With currently available NAEP and state assessment data for the period of 1990 to 2005, we can compare the pre-NCLB period (1990 to 2001) with the post-NCLB period (2002 to 2005).

When NCLB has a significant positive effect, the state performance trajectory will shift upward with a marked increase in the growth rate. In this case, we expect sustained positive gain after NCLB so that post-NCLB growth rate is significantly greater than the pre-NCLB growth rate. However, these achievement trends may also vary according to the kind of tests used to assess reading and math proficiency. It is well known that (1) the level of statewide proficiency (status) is higher on state assessments than on NAEP and (2) the improvement of statewide proficiency (gain) is greater on state assessments than on NAEP. Figure 5.1 illustrates these discrepancies between NAEP and state assessments.

However, it is not known whether these trends changed after NCLB and whether the post-NCLB changes on NAEP and state assessments, relative to the pre-NCLB trends, converge or diverge. On one hand, states may have aligned their own state assessments with NAEP so that the discrepancy between the two assessments narrowed after NCLB (Lee, 2007). On the other hand, under increasing pressure from NCLB, more and more schools may have adopted practices that raise student performance on their own state assessment as opposed to any other assessments so that the discrepancy widened. Therefore, a new question is whether post-NCLB changes, if any, in states' academic proficiency trends differ between state assessments and NAEP. Figure 5.1 illustrates the NAEP and state assessment trajectories for the pre-NCLB and post-NCLB periods. The figure shows hypothetical cases of positive NCLB impact in which pre-NCLB growth accelerated after NCLB and the acceleration of growth occurred more on state assessments than on NAEP. These possible differences between NAEP and state assessments in terms of the acceleration of pre-NCLB growth rates may lead to different conclusions about the impact of NCLB. In light of these concerns, the study explores discrepancies between NAEP and state assessment trends before and after NCLB.

Figure 5.1 Hypothetical Post-NCLB Changes in State Academic Proficiency
Trends on NAEP Versus State Assessment

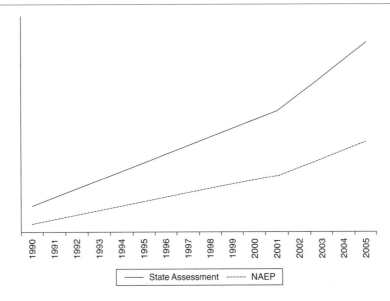

The NAEP results are reported in two ways: (1) scale scores and (2) the percentages of students scoring at or above three benchmarks called *achievement levels* (see Perie, Grigg, & Donahue, 2005 for reading; Perie, Grigg, & Dion, 2005 for math). NAEP reading and math scores are on a 0 to 500 scale. Interpretation of the NAEP scale scores is made with reference to performance standards for each subject and grade, using corresponding cut scores for three achievement levels: basic, proficient, and advanced. This study used state-level aggregate measures of performance in the percentages of students scoring at or above the proficient level that were drawn from 1990 to 2005 NAEP public school sample for grade four and grade eight reading and math assessments (see http://www.nces.ed.gov/nationsreportcard). The NAEP national grade four and eight data were drawn from the NAEP database for the following years: 1992, 1994, 1998, 2000 (grade four only), 2002, 2003, and 2005 in reading; and 1990, 1992, 1996, 2000, 2003, and 2005 in math. The NAEP state grade four and eight data were drawn from the NAEP database for the following years: 1992 (grade four only), 1994 (grade four only), 1998, 2002, 2003, and 2005 in reading; and 1990 (grade eight only), 1992, 1996, 2000, 2003, and 2005 in math.

Since 1998 in reading and 1996 in math, testing accommodations (e.g., extended testing time, and individual test administration) were provided for students with disabilities and/or for English language learners (ELLs). Therefore, the NAEP results included accommodations for these two groups of students for the 1998 to 2005 years in reading and for the 1996 to 2005 years in math. All prior assessment results did not include accommodations. For the sake of keeping track of achievement throughout the 1990s prior to NCLB, all available NAEP data points, including results with and without accommodation, were used.

The NAEP assessment results for individual states were compared with states' own assessment results in fourth- and eighth-grade reading and math. The state assessment results were available in the form of the percentage of students who meet a desired standard (typically at or above a proficient level). The statewide proficiency rate data were obtained from each of the forty-three states (excluding Alabama, Arkansas, Minnesota, Nebraska, New Hampshire, Tennessee, and West Virginia) at grade eight level or forty-five states (excluding Alabama, Arkansas, Nebraska, Tennessee, and West Virginia) at grade four level, where state education departments made at least two years of data available on their Web sites.

When all the available NAEP and state assessment data were matched by state and stacked across years, the number of observations are as follows: $N = 199$ for NAEP and $N = 239$ for state assessments in grade four math; $N = 115$ for NAEP and $N = 244$ for state assessments in grade four reading; $N = 153$ for NAEP and $N = 216$ for state assessments in grade eight reading; and $N = 218$ for NAEP and $N = 215$ for state assessments in grade eight math. The number of states with available data varies by year.

In order to test for the statistical significance of the trends on NAEP and state assessments for each subject and grade, hierarchical linear modeling (HLM) method, growth curve modeling, was used (for detailed information on this statistical modeling, see Lee, 2006). Both pre-NCLB and post-NCLB growth patterns for each assessment are classified by the significance and direction of changes. The pre-NCLB growth dimension tells how the outcome measures for each group changed before NCLB: up (significantly upward trend), down (significantly downward trend), and flat (no significant trend). The post-NCLB change dimension tells how the pre-NCLB growth pattern changed after NCLB: increment (significant post-NCLB gain), decrement (significant post-NCLB loss), and same (no significant change).

This study's framework for assessing the impact of NCLB on state performance is based on the assumption of continuous improvement at varying rates of growth before and after the intervention. Therefore, the key criterion for success was whether there was significant acceleration of the pre-NCLB growth rate after NCLB. This study found that there was not. In addition, if the pre-NCLB trend is ignored, NAEP and state assessments may lead to quite different answers to the simpler question of whether there was any academic improvement after NCLB and if so, how much. Even when the pre-NCLB trend is considered, questions as to whether or not it is reasonable to expect test scores to continue to increase at their pre-NCLB rate or to accelerate the growth rate remain. Arguing that this is an unreasonable assumption would necessitate finding reasons that the rate of growth would have leveled off or dropped without NCLB. For these reasons, future studies of the impact of NCLB on student achievement should make the underlying assumptions of their evaluation approach should explicit and provide rationales for the criteria used for judging the success or failure of the policy, since those criteria would affect the interpretations of the results.

One should interpret the findings from this study cautiously. Since there are only a few years of NAEP or state assessment data available for post-NCLB trend analysis, it may be premature to evaluate the full impact of NCLB, as the policy sets 2014 as the deadline for states to meet its performance targets. Second, this analysis of repeated cross-sectional data confounds the policy effect and the cohort effect. With these caveats in mind, the findings of this study still have implications for NCLB, and test-driven external accountability policy in particular, as we approach the debate about reauthorization.

RESULTS

Trend analyses of NAEP versus state assessment reading and math proficiency data from 1990 to 2005 revealed changes in the percentage of students reaching the NAEP proficiency level—that is, the percentage of students in each state that meet or exceed the national standard (i.e., NAEP proficiency level common to all states) or state standard (i.e., proficiency level on state assessments as determined by each state). The results are summarized in Table 5.1.

Figures 5.2 through 5.5 also show individual states' proficiency trends based on NAEP and state assessments in reading and math at grades four and eight. Across all grades and subjects examined in this study, states tend to show significantly higher proficiency rates on state assessments than on NAEP. The percentage of students performing at or above the proficiency level based on state assessments is about two times larger than the corresponding percentage based on NAEP. This discrepancy between the two assessment results tends to persist throughout the period.

Table 5.1   States' Reading and Math Proficiency Trends on NAEP Versus State Assessments Before and After NCLB

Grade	Subject	Period	Assessment	
			NAEP	*State*
4	Reading	Pre-NCLB	Up	Up
		Post-NCLB	Same	Same
	Math	Pre-NCLB	Up	Up
		Post-NCLB	Increment	Same
8	Reading	Pre-NCLB	Up	Up
		Post-NCLB	Decrement	Same
	Math	Pre-NCLB	Up	Up
		Post-NCLB	Same	Same

Figure 5.2   State Proficiency Trends on NAEP and State Assessments in Grade Four Reading

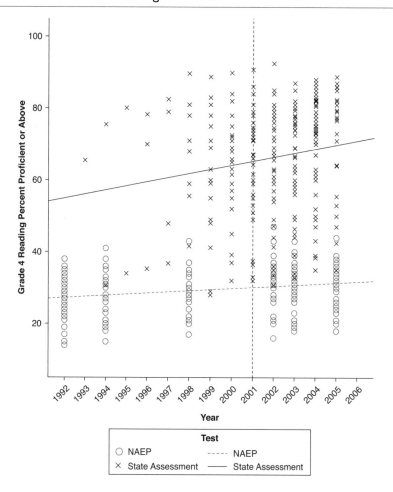

Figure 5.3   State Proficiency Trends on NAEP and State Assessments in
Grade Four Math

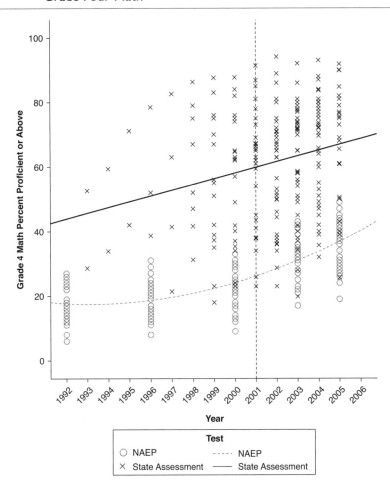

Figure 5.4 State Proficiency Trends on NAEP and State Assessments in Grade Eight Reading

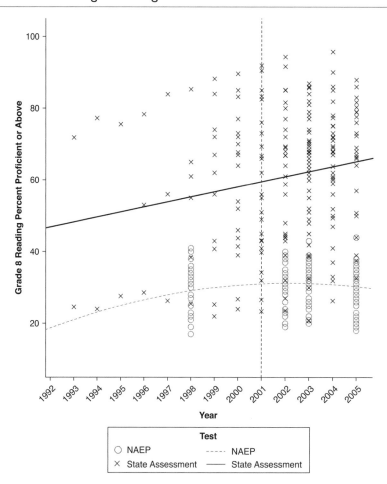

Further, states tend to show faster growth on state assessments than on NAEP. In grade four reading, it appears that the discrepancy between NAEP and state assessments has widened to some extent over time, as the state proficiency rate improved more on the state assessments than on NAEP (see Figure 5.2). The two regression lines in Figure 5.2 that capture the average growth patterns of all states on NAEP and state assessments diverge over time. However, it needs to be noted that states showed significant pre-NCLB growth on both NAEP and state assessments, and they do not reveal any significant changes in the growth rate after NCLB; this pattern is shown in the grade four reading part of Table 5.1 where the pre-NCLB trend was "up" and the post-NCLB change was "same" on both NAEP and state assessments. In other words, states tend to maintain the same pace of academic improvement in grade four reading after NCLB that they exhibited before NCLB.

Figure 5.5 State Proficiency Trends on NAEP and State Assessments in Grade Eight Math

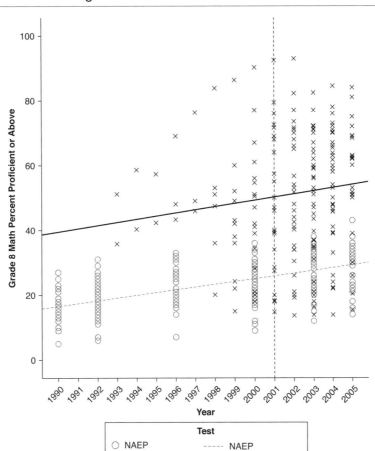

In grade four mathematics, states showed linear growth trajectories on state assessments but curvilinear trajectories on NAEP (see Figure 5.3). Before NCLB, states had showed a significant "upward" trend on both assessments. After NCLB, states showed acceleration of their growth rate on NAEP with significant "increment" to the pre-NCLB trend of math improvement, while they maintained the "same" pace of math improvement on state assessments (see Table 5.1).

In grade eight reading, states also showed linear growth trajectories on state assessments but curvilinear trajectories on NAEP (see Figure 5.4). Before NCLB, states had showed a significant "upward" trend on both assessments. After NCLB, states showed a deceleration of their growth rate on NAEP with significant "decrement" to the pre-NCLB trend of reading improvement, while they maintained the "same" pace of reading improvement on state assessments (see Table 5.1).

In grade eight math, states showed the same pace of academic improvement on both NAEP and state assessments throughout the period (see Figure 5.5). Although the proficiency rate was much higher on state assessments than on NAEP, the discrepancy between the two assessments has remained pretty constant over time. States showed a significant "upward" trend before NCLB and they maintained the "same" trend after NCLB (see Table 5.1).

The key question here is whether and how NCLB had a systematic impact on state performance trends. By and large, the percentage of students scoring at or above proficient on the NAEP or state assessment did not change significantly across states after NCLB. In both NAEP reading and math, there were significant gains before NCLB at grade four and eight. However, there were no significant changes after NCLB in fourth-grade reading and eighth-grade math. These results are consistent with state assessment trends that reveal no post-NCLB changes. Although the progress tends to continue in math after NCLB, it was mixed. The trend in fourth graders' math achievement has accelerated since NCLB. In contrast, state assessment results show a continuing pattern of growth. At the same time, the growth rate in NAEP eighth-grade reading after NCLB decelerated. This post-NCLB setback in the NAEP eighth-grade reading proficiency also stands in marked contrast to the continuing pattern of growth found on the corresponding state assessments.

If we assume that the states stay on the current trajectory of academic improvement, the results of the NAEP-based trend analysis project that by 2014, only 34 percent of fourth graders and 25 percent of eighth graders would meet the reading proficiency target and about 70 percent of fourth graders and 40 percent of eighth graders would meet the math proficiency target. In contrast, the results of the trend analysis based on state assessment results project much higher estimates of the percentage of students meeting the state standard by 2014: 87 percent of fourth graders and 78 percent of eighth graders would meet the reading proficiency target, and similarly, 87 percent of fourth graders and 79 percent of eighth graders would meet the math proficiency target. While neither of the two assessments would lead to 100 percent proficiency target by 2014, the discrepancy between NAEP and state assessment results in the projected proficiency rate could be large enough to question the success of the NCLB policy in raising student achievement.

Further, substantial gaps exist among racial and socioeconomic groups. If current trends in the racial and socioeconomic achievement gaps continue, substantial disparities in proficiency rates between advantaged white and disadvantaged minority groups will persist. However, the achievement gap will appear relatively smaller on state assessments than on NAEP. Under the assumption that the current trajectories of state performance on NAEP and state assessments will continue, it is projected that by 2014, about 90 percent of whites versus 74 percent of blacks will meet or exceed the standard (proficient) on state assessments on average across grades and subjects, whereas about 53 percent of whites versus 19 percent of blacks will do so on NAEP. Consequently, the percentage of whites who will reach the NAEP reading or math proficiency target in 2014 will be about three times larger than the percentage of blacks who will reach the same target. In contrast, the ratio of whites to blacks who will achieve reading or math proficiency targets on state assessments will be only 1.4. Similar discrepancies—albeit to a lesser degree, are found between NAEP and state assessments that estimate the achievement gap between whites and Hispanics. The percentage of whites who will reach the reading or math proficiency target in 2014 will be about two times larger than the percentage of Hispanics who will reach the same target. In contrast, the ratio of whites to Hispanics who will achieve reading or math proficiency targets on state assessments will be 1.3.

CONCLUSION

The goal of NCLB, which requires that states have all students accomplish high standards of learning in core subject areas (i.e., 100 percent of students become proficient in reading and math by 2014), is laudable. If the law can facilitate the systemic efforts of state education systems to close pernicious achievement gaps, this would be noteworthy. Past and current NAEP reading and math achievement trends, however, raise serious concerns about the unrealistic performance goal and timeline and the possible consequences for schools that repeatedly fail to meet their performance targets. If the nation continues to make the same amount of achievement gains as it did over the past fifteen years, less than one-half of the nation's students will reach the reading proficiency targets and less than two-thirds will reach the math proficiency targets by 2014. These projections improve when we switch to state assessment results, which signify that more than three-fourths of the student population will meet reading and math proficiency targets by 2014. Further, the achievement gap between racial groups appears smaller on state assessments than on NAEP. Obviously, the prospect of closing the achievement gap—particularly for disadvantaged minority students—appears to be much more unrealistic when relying on NAEP as opposed to state assessments for future projections.

By and large, the results of both NAEP and state assessment trend analyses in this chapter suggest that NCLB did not have significant impact on improving reading and math achievement across the states so far. The NAEP proficiency rate remains flat or declines in reading and grows at the same pace in math after NCLB that it did prior to NCLB. The only exception is NAEP grade four math, which shows accelerated growth after NCLB. In contrast, the state assessment proficiency rate grows at the same pace in both reading and math after NCLB.

Sustained growth under NCLB is good news, but it is not a testament to a positive effect of NCLB because the post-NCLB growth simply extends the past trend. It is misleading to claim that NCLB has a positive effect on academic achievement simply because the NAEP or state test scores continue to rise after NCLB. This inference is flawed since the increase in overall proficiency rates was most likely part of a trend that began before NCLB and does not reflect any significant acceleration in the pace of academic improvement after NCLB.

The comparison of post-NCLB trends relative to pre-NCLB trends across states reveals that NAEP versus state assessment results diverge in some cases (i.e., grade four math and grade eight reading). In none of the cases, however, do the analyses of state proficiency trends from the two assessments consistently reveal significant effects of NCLB on academic improvement. Thus, the argument that NAEP understates the effects of accountability because NAEP is not well aligned with the curriculum is not supported.

If we continue the current policy course, academic proficiency is unlikely to improve significantly on NAEP, and it is possible that the state assessment will continue to give a false impression of progress, short-changing our children and encouraging more investment in high-stakes testing policy. Despite the increasing importance of NAEP as a tool to confirm states' own assessment results, the discrepancies between NAEP and state assessment results requires us to investigate the adequacy and utility of both assessments. In comparison with NAEP, state assessments tend to inflate the overall proficiency level, and in some cases, inflate the level of improvement as well. This poses a threat to the validity of the current practice that relies solely on states' own standards and assessment results for school accountability decision making. While there are debates about the content of NAEP as a gold standard to judge the validity of state assessments and about the use of NAEP as an instrument for monitoring versus accountability, NAEP remains the only tool for cross-checking different states' test results (see Lee, 2007; Loveless, 2006; Resnick, 1999). As Congress moves to reauthorize the NCLB in 2007, it is poised to discuss the topic of increasing the rigor of state standards and tests by linking them to those set at the national level (Olson, 2007). Although this policy movement toward national standards and testing could help alleviate the problem, it could raise the risk of mandating a level of learning measured by national tests such as NAEP and transforming NAEP into a new layer of high-stakes testing.

Further, a more complex issue of comparability may arise when we attempt to use both NAEP and state assessment results to evaluate NCLB in terms of its policy impact on academic improvement. While it is debatable which assessment, NAEP or state test, is more appropriate for evaluating the effect of test-driven accountability policy, cross-examining the evidence from both measures should help. In order to determine whether test-driven external accountability policy, the hallmark of NCLB, works, we need to know how well the nation and states have improved the percentage of students meeting the standard before NCLB as well as after NCLB.

6

Evidence on Education Under NCLB (and How Florida Boosted NAEP Scores and Reduced the Race Gap)

Walter M. Haney

The No Child Left Behind (NCLB) Act of 2001 has brought increased attention to the rating of school quality in terms of student performance on state math and reading tests. However, many observers have noted the weakness of rating school quality simply in terms of such measures. Doubts arise not just because of the noncomparability of state reading and math tests and ratings based on them (Linn & Baker, 2002), but for the more fundamental reason that the goals of public education in the United States clearly extend beyond the teaching of reading and math skills. To address the former problem, many observers have suggested reliance on the state National Assessment of Education Progress (NAEP) results as providing a common metric of student performance in grades four and eight in reading and math (and occasionally other subjects) across the states. The broader question of how school quality might be judged has been raised at the 2006 convention of the National Education Association (NEA). The NEA endorsed a system of accountability "based on multiple benchmarks, including teacher-designed classroom assessments, student portfolios, graduation statistics, and college enrollment rates, among other measures" (Honawar, 2006, p. 8).

The problem of reaching summary judgments on school quality based on multiple valued attributes raises intractable problems, however. It is, of course, always possible to come up with some sort of bureaucratic scheme, as now exists in many states, for weighing various sorts of data about schools and reaching some kind of summary judgment about their quality. But anyone who believes in the rationality of such approaches has forgotten the old paradox of value from the field of economics. The paradox refers to the fact that many obviously useful commodities, such as air and water, have very low if any exchange values, whereas much less useful ones, such as diamonds and gold, have extremely high values. According to Schumpeter's (1954) *History of Economic Analysis*, "scholastic doctors" and natural philosophers recognized as early as the sixteenth century that the exchange value or price of commodities derived not from any inherent characteristics of the commodities themselves but from their utility or "desiredness" and relative scarcity. Without going into a digression on the field of economic theory, let me simply mention how this paradox was resolved by Kenneth Arrow. In 1950, Arrow published what has come to be known as his "impossibility theorem" in an article modestly titled "A Difficulty in the Concept of Social Welfare." In this article, Arrow proved mathematically that if there are at least three alternative attributes which members of society are free to order in any way, any social welfare function yielding an ordering based on those preferences violates one of three rational conditions (as long as trivial and dictatorial methods of aggregation are excluded). In short, Arrow's "impossibility theorem" extended Pareto's finding about the immeasurability of general social welfare. If there are at least three alternative attributes of schools that are valued, it may be impossible to derive any rational way to rank them on a single scale.

Rather than going into these general matters here, however, I discuss the illusion of progress in Florida's 2005 grade four NAEP results, and the value of examining rates of student progress through the K–12 grade span as evidence of school-system quality. In conclusion, I suggest how the upcoming reauthorization of the NCLB Act might be shaped.

HOW FLORIDA BOOSTED NAEP SCORES AND "REDUCED THE RACE GAP"

When results of NAEP for 2005 were released, the state of Florida seemed to have made remarkable progress. The national and Florida results on grade four math NAEP are summarized in Table 6.1.

Table 6.1   NAEP Grade 4 Math 2003 and 2005 Results, National and Florida

	2003	2005	Increase
National			
Total	235	237	2
White	243	246	3
Black	216	220	4
Florida			
Total	234	239	5
White	243	247	4
Black	215	224	9

Sources: Perie, Grigg, & Dion, 2005; Braswell, Dion, Daane, & Yin, 2005.

These results seemed quite remarkable. Florida's fourth graders seemed to have moved slightly ahead of fourth graders nationwide on the NAEP 2005 math results. But even more startlingly, Florida seemed to have made dramatic progress in reducing the "race gap" in achievement. While the black-white race gap in grade four math NAEP scores nationwide remained about the same between 2003 and 2005 (26–27 points), Florida seemed to have made dramatic progress in reducing the race gap from 28 points in 2003 (243-215=28) to 23 points in 2005 (247-224=23). Black grade four students in Florida appeared to have improved nearly ten points on average in just two years, from an average of 215 in 2003 to 224 in 2005. Given that the standard deviation on 2005 NAEP grade four math scores was 29, the increase in Florida results was almost one-third of a standard deviation (9/29 = 0.31). Anyone familiar with the literature on meta-analysis and effect sizes (e.g., Cohen, 1977; Wolf, 1986; Cooper & Hedges, 1994) will realize how stupendous an increase Florida seemed to have made in just two years.

Florida's apparent success on NAEP, not surprisingly, has been touted by that state's governor, Jeb Bush. In an August 13, 2006 essay in the *Washington Post* (with coauthor Michael Bloomberg, mayor of New York City), the Florida governor wrote:

> The No Child Left Behind Act of 2001 sent an enormously important message to politicians and educators across America: Stop making excuses for low student achievement and start holding your schools accountable for results.

Florida and New York City are leaders when it comes to accountability in education. We have set high expectations for all students, and in key grades we have eliminated social promotion, the harmful practice of pushing unprepared students ahead. We grade schools based on student performance and growth so that parents and the public, as well as school administrators, know which schools are working well and which are not. Our emphasis on accountability is a big reason our schools are improving, our students are performing at higher levels and we're closing the achievement gap between poor and minority students and their peers. (Bush & Bloomberg, 2006, p. B7).

The Bush-Bloomberg duo went on to say, "The well-respected National Assessment of Educational Progress (NAEP), which is administered in every state, should become an official benchmark for evaluating states' standards" (p. B7).

But what had really happened in Florida? It turns out that the apparent dramatic gains in grade four NAEP math results are simply an indirect reflection of the fact that in 2003–2004, Florida started flunking many more students—including disproportionately high numbers of minority students—and requiring them to repeat grade three. To help explain what happened, let me start with some national enrollment statistics. Before doing so, I note that these data are from the Common Core of Data (CCD), an NCES repository of education statistics. Colleagues and I at Boston College have been analyzing CCD and other enrollment statistics, as part of our *Education Pipeline* project (see, for example, Haney, Madaus, Abrams, Wheelock, & Gruia, 2004; Miao & Haney, 2004).

Table 6.2 shows for 1995–1996 through 2000–2001 the total number of students enrolled in grades K–12 in public schools nationwide (in the top panel) and grade-transition ratios (in the bottom panel)—that is, the number enrolled in one grade one year divided by the number enrolled in the previous grade the previous year.

Let me note one key pattern in these results. The grade-transition ratios for grade three, four, and five are almost all *exactly* 1.00. This means simply that from grade two to five, the national pattern for these years has been for 100 percent of students to be promoted from grade to grade.

Table 6.2   U.S. Public School Enrollment By Grade 1995–1996 to 2000–2001 (in thousands)

	1995–1996	1996–1997	1997–1998	1998–1999	1999–2000	2000–2001
K	3,536	3,532	3,503	3,443	3,397	3,382
1	3,671	3,770	3,755	3,727	3,684	3,635
2	3,507	3,600	3,689	3,681	3,656	3,633
3	3,445	3,524	3,597	3,696	3,690	3,673
4	3,431	3,454	3,507	3,592	3,686	3,708
5	3,438	3,453	3,458	3,520	3,604	3,703
6	3,395	3,494	3,492	3,497	3,564	3,658
7	3,422	3,464	3,520	3,530	3,541	3,624
8	3,356	3,403	3,415	3,480	3,497	3,532
9	3,704	3,801	3,819	3,856	3,935	3,958
10	3,237	3,323	3,376	3,382	3,415	3,487
11	2,826	2,930	2,972	3,021	3,034	3,080
12	2,487	2,586	2,673	2,722	2,782	2,799

Grade Transition Ratio
(number in grade / number in previous grade previous year)

	1995–1996	1996–1997	1997–1998	1998–1999	1999–2000	2000–2001
K						
1		1.07	1.06	1.06	1.07	1.07
2		0.98	0.98	0.98	0.98	0.99
3		1.00	1.00	1.00	1.00	1.00
4		1.00	1.00	1.00	1.00	1.00
5		1.01	1.00	1.00	1.00	1.00
6		1.02	1.01	1.01	1.01	1.01
7		1.02	1.01	1.01	1.01	1.02
8		0.99	0.99	0.99	0.99	1.00
9		1.13	1.12	1.13	1.13	1.13
10		0.90	0.89	0.89	0.89	0.89
11		0.91	0.89	0.89	0.90	0.90
12		0.92	0.91	0.92	0.92	0.92

Source: CCD and Digest of Education Statistics

Now let us consider analogous grade-transition ratios for the state of Florida for the period 1999–2000 to 2004–2005 (Table 6.3).

Table 6.3   Florida Grade-Transition Ratios 1999–2000 to 2004–2005

Grade Transition Ratios 1999–2000 to 2004–2005	*2000– 2001*	*2001– 2002*	*2002– 2003*	*2003– 2004*	*2004 2005*
K					
1	1.07	1.07	1.05	1.06	1.05
2	1.01	1.01	1.00	1.01	0.99
3	1.03	1.03	1.02	1.12	1.10
4	1.03	1.03	1.03	0.92	0.94
5	1.01	1.02	1.00	1.01	1.03
6	1.05	1.05	1.04	1.04	1.05
7	1.03	1.02	1.02	1.02	1.02
8	1.00	1.00	1.00	0.99	1.00
9	1.32	1.34	1.29	1.26	1.22
10	0.76	0.72	0.74	0.77	0.80
11	0.82	0.88	0.92	0.90	0.93
12	0.84	0.90	0.92	0.91	0.91

Source: Boston College Education Pipeline project, based on CCD data

There are a number of interesting contrasts between these results for Florida and the national results presented in Table 6.2. First note that, for the elementary grades, most Florida transition ratios are above 1.00. This is an indirect reflection of the fact that the public school population has been increasing in Florida. The total K–12 public school population in Florida was 2.328 million in 1999–2000 and 2.538 million in 2003–2004. This amounts to about a 2.1 percent annual increase in public school enrollments in Florida over this interval.

A second notable feature of results shown in Table 6.3 is for grades nine and ten. These results indicate a large bulge in enrollments in grade nine and correspondingly large attrition in student enrollments between grades nine and ten. Since such changes in patterns of progress in the United States K–12 system are discussed at more length in our *Education Pipeline* report, I do not elaborate further here, except to note that the grade-nine bulge and attrition between grades nine and ten are larger in Florida than they are nationally. But particularly notable regarding how Florida boosted NAEP grade four results in 2005 are the grade three and four results for 2003–2004 and 2004–2005. What these results indicate is that in the 2003–2004 school year Florida started flunking far more children—on the order of 10 to 12 percent overall—to repeat grade three in 2003–2004 and 2004–2005. Hence it is clear what caused the dramatic jump in grade four NAEP results for 2005. Florida had started flunking more children before they reached grade four.

What caused the dramatic decrease in the race gap in NAEP results in Florida? Grade-transition analyses of enrollment data make the answer abundantly clear. Analyses of grade enrollments in Florida by race (black, Hispanic, and white) make it clear that when Florida started in 2003–2004 to flunk more children to repeat grade three, there were disproportionately more black and Hispanic children (15 to 20 percent of whom were flunked) than white ones (about 4 to 6 percent of whom were flunked in grade three). Thus it is clear that the NAEP grade four results for 2005 reflected no dramatic improvements in elementary education in the state. Rather they were an indirect reflection of Florida policy that resulted in two to three times larger percentages of minority than white children being flunked to repeat grade three.

This is, regrettably, a tragedy in the making. Research now makes it abundantly clear that flunking children to repeat grades in school is not only ineffective in boosting their achievement, but also dramatically increases the probability that they will leave school before high school graduation (see, for example, Edley & Wald, 2002; Heubert & Hauser, 1999; Jimerson, 2001; Jimerson, Anderson, & Whipple, 2002; and Shepard & Smith, 1989). I do not try to summarize here the abundant evidence on these two points, except to note that considerable research has found that among children who are overage for grade nine (regardless of whether they were flunked in grade nine or earlier grades), 65 to 90 percent will not persist in high school to graduation.

EVIDENCE ON EDUCATION UNDER NCLB

The Florida case—what might be called the Florida fraud—helps to illustrate a fundamental point about interpretation of test results in general and NAEP results in particular. Before trying to make meaningful interpretations of test results, one should always pay close attention to who is tested and who is not. Regarding state NAEP results, it is far too often overlooked that since state NAEP testing is based on samples of students enrolled in particular grades, namely grades four and eight, NAEP results are inevitably confounded with patterns by which children are flunked to repeat grades before the grade tested.

Since this is so, what other evidence is available to help us judge the condition of education in the United States? I would argue that a much more robust indicator of the condition of education in the United States, in each state, and in local education agencies (LEAs), are rates of student progress through the elementary and secondary educational system—as pointed out by Ayres (1909) nearly a century ago. Rates of student progress through the grades represent a more robust measure of school quality than test results, for the simple reason that they reflect a host of factors including not just test results, but also grades in courses, attendance, and citizenship. And as we have shown repeatedly, as far back as *The Myth of the Texas Miracle in Education* (Haney, 2000, 2001), if policymakers focus only on grade-level test results, without paying attention to who is *not* tested (such as dropouts and students flunked in grade), they can be badly misled about what is happening in school systems.

So what do we know about rates of student progress through the grades before and after passage of the NCLB Act? Colleagues and I have been analyzing enrollment data at national, state, and LEA levels for some time, and results are far more voluminous than can be presented here. Hence, let me present only evidence concerning two of the most worrisome trends we have identified, namely the increasing bulge of students in grade nine and the corresponding increase in attrition of students between grades nine and ten.

Figure 6.1 shows results on the grade nine bulge and attrition between grade nine and ten for the last thirty years. As may be seen, during the 1970s there were only 5 percent more students enrolled in grade nine than in grade eight the previous year. The grade nine bulge started increasing during the 1980s and has increased even more during the 1990s. These results indicate that the bulge of students in grade nine has roughly tripled in size over the last three decades.

Figure 6.1 Grade Nine Bulge and Attrition Between Grades Nine and Ten, U.S. Public School Enrollment, 1969–1970 to 2003–2004

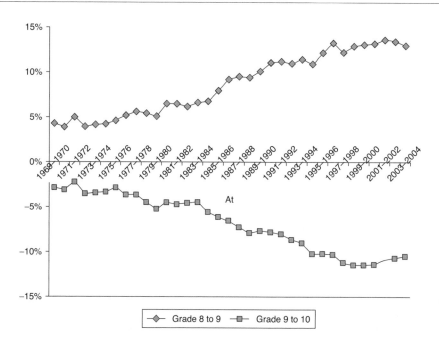

Correspondingly, the rate of attrition of students between grades nine and ten has increased dramatically over this interval. During the 1970s there were about only 3.5 percent fewer students enrolled in grade ten than in grade nine the previous year. The rate of attrition of students between grades nine and ten increased a bit in the late 1970s and more sharply during the 1980s and 1990s. Since 1999–2000 there have been more than 10 percent fewer students enrolled in grade ten than in grade nine the previous year. These results show that attrition of students between grades nine and ten has roughly tripled over the last thirty years.

The causes for these long-term changes in grade-transition ratios are probably several. Given that these changes go back at least two decades, they obviously cannot have been caused by the NCLB Act of 2001 (actually not signed into law until January 2002). But as we discussed in our *Education Pipeline* report, "increases in attrition between grades 9 and 10 have been associated with the minimum competency testing movement in the 1970s, the academic standards movement in the 1980s, and so-called standards-based reform and high stakes testing in the 1990s" (Haney et al., 2004, p. 60).

Other analyses make it clear that attrition between grades nine and ten is far worse for black and Hispanic students than for white students. For the majority of states for which grade-enrollment data are available by race, results show that grade nine to ten attrition for blacks and Hispanics is on the order of 20 percent whereas for whites it is less than 7 percent. These findings indicate that the grade nine to ten attrition rate for minority students is roughly *triple* that for white students.

To present results by race for just one state, Figure 6.2 shows patterns of attrition between grades nine and ten in New York for roughly the last ten years, 1993–1994 through 2003–2004. As may be seen, the rate of attrition between grades nine and ten for white students in New York has been in the range of 5 to 7 percent. However, for black and Hispanic students, rates of attrition have been far, far worse—on the order of 15 to 25 percent. Attrition of minority students in New York worsened substantially in the late 1990s, but appears to have lessened slightly in recent years. Still, as of 2003–2004, the attrition rate between grades nine and ten for black and Hispanic students in New York (about 18 percent) was triple the rate of attrition for white students (6.1 percent).

These results illustrate dramatic racial inequalities in rates of student progress through the K–12 educational system. They also make clear that test results based on grade-level samples (as in NAEP and most state testing programs) will mask underlying inequalities in our educational system. While much attention has been focused on the so-called "race gap" in test scores, far more severe and of much more consequence is the race gap in progress through the education pipeline.

Figure 6.2 Attrition of Students Between Grades Nine and Ten by Race, New York, 1993–1994 to 2003–2004

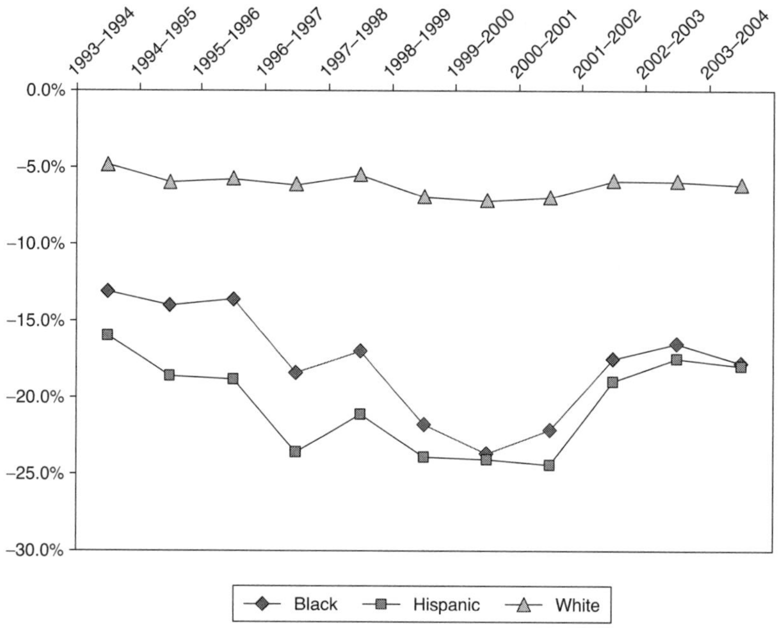

CONCLUSION

High-stakes testing—by which I mean making important decisions based on test results alone—has been increasing in recent decades in the United States. This trend by no means began with the NCLB Act of 2001, but it certainly has been fueled by the NCLB legislation. The mania to make test-score averages appear to increase has resulted not just in fraud in Florida, but also in school administrators in at least three jurisdictions (in Texas, New York, and Alabama) actually pushing young people out of school in order to make high school test results look better. (The three cases are documented in our report *The Education Pipeline in the United States, 1970–2000,* Haney et al., 2004).

In addition to focusing attention on test results as measures of school quality, NCLB also mandated measures of high school graduation rates as indicators of school systems' quality. This has helped promote considerable research, and a dose of controversy, on how best to calculate high school graduation rates (Greene, 2002a, 2002b; Green & Forster, 2003; Mishel & Roy, 2006; Swanson, 2003, 2004; Swanson & Chaplin, 2003; Warren, 2003; Young, 2002). I do not try to recap here the debates about how to calculate high school graduation rates save to mention two points. First, the Miao and Haney (2004) article compares a number of high school graduation rate measures that have been promoted by various parties. According to most measures, high school graduation rates in the United States have been declining in recent decades, remain far short of the "national education goal" of a 90 percent graduation rate, and are far worse for black and Hispanic students than for white students. Second, the increase in the grade-nine bulge in recent years presages worse dropout rates in the future since research has shown that students being overage for grade is a prime predictor of them dropping out before completion of high school, with as many of 70 percent of those overage in grade nine not persisting in school to graduation (see Haney, 2000 and Abrams & Haney, 2004).

In conclusion, I note that while graduation rates surely represent a better summary measure of school-system quality than do test-score averages, they have a fundamental weakness. Whether based on three, four, or five years of data, high school graduation rates always represent a limited and "rear view" look at what is happening in school systems. They are limited in that they have little potential to illuminate what happens to young people before they reach high school. And they are "rear view" because whether based on three, four, or five years of data, they tell us what has happened to students in the past, rather than what is happening to them now.

Hence I suggest simply that in the reauthorization of NCLB legislation some very simple reporting requirements be added. States and LEAs should be required to report not just on test scores but also on grade enrollment and grade retentions, both overall and by race. Such data would allow easy examination of grade-progression rates. As I have argued here, rates of student progress through the grades are a more robust measure of educational quality than are test scores. Also, as I have demonstrated, such data are vital in order to interpret grade-level test results. The apparent dramatic improvement in 2005 grade four NAEP scores in Florida are illusory. Not only is Florida not reducing the race gap, but data on grade progression rates for that state reveal that with three to four times as many minority as white students being flunked to repeat grade three, Florida's policies are helping to cement educational inequalities in place for years to come. Messieurs Bush and Bloomberg are simply myopic and misguided. NAEP may provide some useful information on states' educational progress, but as I have shown, if used in isolation as an "official benchmark for evaluating states' standards," NAEP results may mislead more than inform.

PART III

7

Interstate Inequality and the Federal Role in School Finance

Goodwin Liu

For all that has been said about the nationalizing influence of the No Child Left Behind (NCLB) Act on education policy, one fact endures: states remain in the driver's seat on setting academic standards and distributing the resources needed to achieve results. After decades of state litigation and policy reform, some evidence shows that disparities in educational opportunity within states have lessened (Card & Payne, 2002; Murray, Evans, & Schwab, 1998). But a national goal of equal educational opportunity cannot be realized by addressing only inequality within states. The reason is simple: the most significant component of educational inequality nationally is not inequality within states, but inequality *between* states. This fact casts a long shadow over the ideal of equal opportunity.

In this chapter, I describe educational inequality across states in terms of funding, standards, and outcomes. I then show that interstate disparities in education resources have more to do with the capacity of states to

This chapter is adapted from my 2006 article, Interstate Inequality in Educational Opportunity, *New York University Law Review, 81,* 2044–2128.

finance education than with their willingness to do so, highlighting the need for a robust federal role in ameliorating interstate inequality. I go on to demonstrate how Title I reinforces rather than reduces interstate inequality in school funding, and I conclude with proposals for reforming and enlarging the federal role in school finance.

THE CURRENT STATE OF INTERSTATE INEQUALITY

States vary greatly in their education spending. Column A of Table 7.1 shows each state's current per-pupil expenditures in 2003–2004. To facilitate valid comparison across states, column B adjusts the nominal data for geographic cost differences and for interstate differences in student demographics and educational needs. In cost-adjusted terms, average spending per weighted pupil in the top ten states ($7,345) was nearly 60 percent more than it was in the bottom ten states ($4,591).

Both the extent of spending variation and the ranking of states (with a few exceptions) have remained fairly stable in recent decades, with many low-spending states clustered in the South. The most noticeable modern trend has been a relative decline in per-pupil spending among states in the West and Southwest. In part, this reflects the political dynamics of school finance reform in states like California and Washington (Joondeph, 1995; Rubinfeld, 1995). It also reflects dramatic population growth in states like Arizona and Nevada, whose public school enrollments more than doubled from 1970 to 2000. In sum, the current map of educational inequality is one in which the South, Southwest, and West trail the rest of the country.

States also differ significantly in their student demographics and thus in the magnitude of their educational task. Table 7.2 compares student demographics in 2003–2004 in the top half and bottom half of states ranked by adjusted spending per weighted pupil. Whereas the student body in the top half was 72 percent white, 14 percent black, and 9 percent Latino; it was 51 percent white, 19 percent black, and 24 percent Latino in the bottom half. Poor students and English language learners comprised 19 percent and 12 percent of students, respectively, in the bottom half of states, but only 14 percent and 4 percent, respectively, in the top half. In fact, the states in the bottom half of spending, while enrolling 65 percent of all schoolchildren, served 71 percent of the nation's poor students and 83 percent of all ELLs. By contrast, the states in the top half enrolled 35 percent of all schoolchildren, but only 29 percent of the nation's poor students and 17 percent of all ELLs. In short, children with the greatest educational needs live disproportionately in states with low education spending.

Table 7.1   Current Expenditures in Public Elementary and Secondary Schools, 2003–2004

	A Nominal dollars per pupil	B Cost-adjusted dollars per weighted pupil		A Nominal dollars per pupil	B Cost-adjusted dollars per weighted pupil
Vermont	$11,128	$9,149	Maryland	9,212	5,923
Wyoming	9,363	7,941	Illinois	8,656	5,603
New Jersey	12,981	7,692	Oregon	7,619	5,491
Maine	9,534	7,581	Missouri	7,331	5,391
New York	12,930	7,428	Arkansas	6,740	5,307
Alaska	10,114	7,236	Colorado	7,412	5,267
Pennsylvania	9,979	7,027	Louisiana	7,209	5,228
Montana	7,763	6,981	Virginia	8,225	5,216
Connecticut	10,788	6,835	Georgia	7,733	5,191
Delaware	10,228	6,754	South Carolina	7,184	5,188
New Hampshire	8,860	6,674	New Mexico	7,331	5,119
Wisconsin	9,226	6,656	Kentucky	6,888	5,097
Massachusetts	10,693	6,635	Idaho	6,028	5,097
North Dakota	7,727	6,608	Alabama	6,553	4,875
Nebraska	8,032	6,459	Washington	7,243	4,798
Ohio	8,963	6,331	Mississippi	6,237	4,786
West Virginia	8,475	6,330	Florida	6,784	4,777
Michigan	9,072	6,309	Oklahoma	6,176	4,773
Rhode Island	9,903	6,238	Tennessee	6,504	4,693
Iowa	7,631	6,226	North Carolina	6,702	4,638
Indiana	8,280	6,224	Texas	7,104	4,629
South Dakota	6,949	6,149	California	7,748	4,551
Hawaii	8,533	6,076	Arizona	6,036	4,314
Kansas	7,518	6,025	Nevada	6,399	4,279
Minnesota	8,359	5,967	Utah	5,008	3,812

Current expenditures per pupil in column A are from U.S. Census Bureau (2006a). In column B, the data are adjusted for geographic cost differences using 2004 state-level values of the Comparable Wage Index (Taylor & Fowler, 2006; Education Finance Statistics Center, 2006) and for interstate differences in student needs by assigning weights of 1.9 to students with disabilities (Parrish et al., 2004, p. 24), 1.6 to students from poor families (U.S. General Accounting Office, 1998, pp. 34–35), and 1.2 to English language learners (Parrish, 1994, pp. 263, 276).

Table 7.2   Demographics of School-Age Children, 2003–2004

	(percentages)				
	White	Black	Latino	Poor	ELL
United States	58.3	17.0	18.4	17.3	8.9
States in top half of spending	71.6	13.9	8.9	14.4	4.2
States in bottom half of spending	51.1	18.7	23.5	18.9	11.5

Black, Latino, and white enrollment data by state are from National Center for Education Statistics (2006). Numbers of poor children by state are from U.S. Census Bureau (2006b). Numbers of English language learners by state are from National Clearinghouse for English Language Acquisition and Language Instruction Educational Programs (2006).

We can better comprehend the magnitude of interstate spending disparities by comparing them to intrastate disparities. Figures 7.1a, 7.1b, and 7.1c illustrate the magnitude of interstate spending disparities using cost-adjusted expenditures per weighted pupil in unified districts at the 10th (low), 50th (median), and 90th (high) percentile of spending in each state in 2003–2004 (Common Core of Data, 2006). In Figure 7.1a, each bar represents the range of expenditures among districts from the 10th percentile to the median in a given state. Figure 7.1a shows that the *10th percentile* districts in eighteen states (Wyoming to Maryland) spent more than the *median* districts in nineteen states (Louisiana to California). In other words, even if the nineteen low-spending states were to raise spending in the bottom half of their districts up to the state median, those districts would still trail 90 percent of districts in the eighteen high-spending states.

Figure 7.1a Per-Pupil Expenditures of Unified Districts at the 10th to 50th Percentile by State, 2003–2004

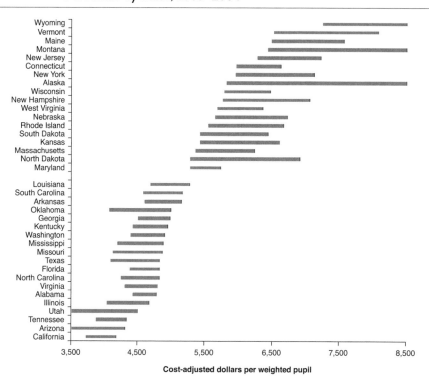

Cost-adjusted dollars per weighted pupil

Figure 7.1b Per-Pupil Expenditures of Unified Districts at the 50th to 90th
Percentile by State, 2003–2004

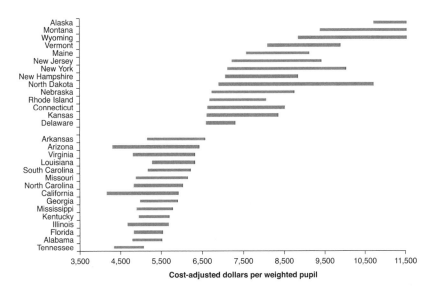

Figure 7.1c Per-Pupil Expenditures of Unified Districts at the 10th to 90th
Percentile by State, 2003–2004

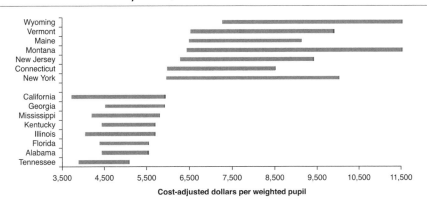

Similarly, Figure 7.1b shows that the *median* districts in fourteen high-spending states (Alaska to Delaware) spent more than the *90th percentile* districts in fifteen low-spending states (Arkansas to Tennessee). Figure 7.1c depicts the starkest interstate inequalities. The *10th percentile* districts in seven high-spending states (Wyoming to New York) outspent the *90th percentile* districts in eight low-spending states (California to Tennessee). Consistent with these data, other research has found that interstate disparities account for well over half of the total extent of interdistrict inequality throughout the nation (Evans, Murray, & Schwab, 1999).

Substantial interstate disparities exist not only in resources, but also in learning standards and outcomes. Figures 7.2a and 7.2b compare the percentage of fourth graders in each state achieving "proficiency" in math and reading on the 2005 National Assessment of Educational Progress (NAEP) with the percentage of fourth graders achieving "proficiency" on 2005 state tests. In each graph, the solid sloping line shows where states would line up if their proficiency standards matched NAEP's. The dotted sloping line is the best-fit line indicating the relationship between NAEP and state tests in an "average" state. The vertical line marks the national percentage of students who scored proficient on NAEP. From these graphs, we learn three things.

Figure 7.2a Fourth-Grade Math Performance, 2005

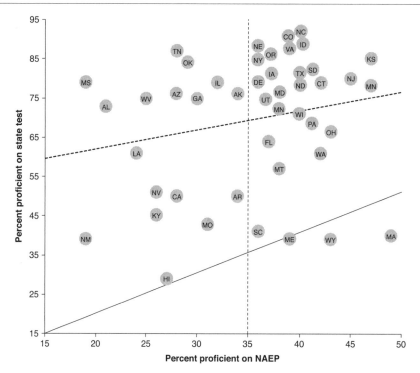

First, state standards are literally all over the map and are mostly less rigorous than NAEP's. In Tennessee, for example, 87 percent of fourth graders achieved a proficient score on the state math test, but only 28 percent scored proficient on NAEP. By contrast, states like Maine, Massachusetts, South Carolina, and Wyoming have proficiency standards that approximate NAEP's. This wide-ranging patchwork is unsurprising in view of the broad discretion states have to set educational standards.

Second, student performance varies considerably from state to state when measured against a common standard. While 35 percent of fourth graders nationwide achieved proficiency on the NAEP math test, state figures ranged from 49 percent in Massachusetts to 19 percent in Mississippi and New Mexico. NAEP scale scores show that the average fourth grader in Massachusetts, Minnesota, and Vermont scored almost twenty points higher in math and reading than her peers in Alabama, Mississippi, and New Mexico—a difference of roughly two grade levels.

Figure 7.2b Fourth-Grade Reading Performance, 2005

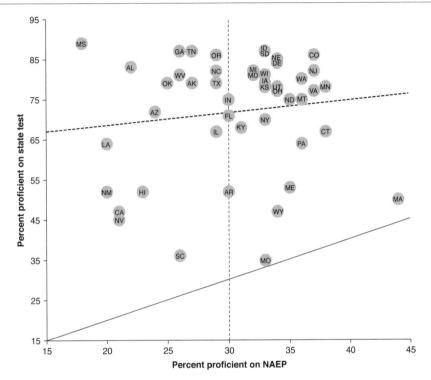

Third, the states with NAEP proficiency rates lower than the national average are almost all low-spending states in the South, Southwest, and West. Among the twenty-one states to the left of the vertical line in either Figure 7.2a or 7.2b, only three (Alaska, Hawaii, and West Virginia) are in the top half of the nation in terms of adjusted spending per weighted pupil. Conversely, while a few low-spending states have above-average rates of proficiency on NAEP (e.g., Idaho, South Dakota, and Washington), the vast majority of high-performing states are high-spending states. Eighth-grade math and reading results produce similar figures.

Although this pattern suggests a relationship between resources and out-comes, it is important to remember that low-spending states have a dispropor-tionate share of poor, minority, and ELL children. Student demographics and family background, as well as differences in state education policies, compli-cate the relationship between resources and results.

However, a leading study of NAEP scores from 1990 to 1996 has shown that, even when parental education, income, race, family size, single-parent status, and other socioeconomic status indicators are taken into account, state NAEP scores varied by as much as one-third of a standard deviation on a national scale (Grissmer, Flanagan, Kawata, & Williamson, 2000). In other words, students in the highest scoring states were roughly one and one-third grade levels ahead of similar students in the lowest scoring states. Some low-spending states (e.g., Texas, Missouri) performed better than average, and some high-spending states (e.g., Rhode Island, Vermont) performed worse. But overall, spending was positively correlated with performance when similar students were compared.

The study further showed that resource-dependent interventions, such as lowering pupil-teacher ratios and increasing access to pre-K programs, are most effective when targeted to low-SES states and, within states, to low-SES districts and schools. These results cohere with three other lines of research. First, randomized experiments on class size reduction have found gains by all students, but gains by minority students, low-income students, and low-achieving students were significantly larger (Finn & Achilles, 1999; Krueger, 1999). Second, some econometric studies have found that greater resources are associated with greater gains by low-achieving students and by students in low-spending districts (Ferguson & Ladd, 1996; Guryan, 2003). Third, from the late 1960s to early 1990s, increased education spending—largely in the form of compensatory programs—coincided with robust achievement gains by black, Latino, and low-scoring white students, with the greatest gains in the South, even as the broad majority of whites made little or no improvement (Grissmer, Flanagan, & Williamson, 1998; Hedges & Nowell, 1998).

Of course, more money does not guarantee better outcomes, and the general relationship has been much debated (Hanushek, 1996; Greenwald, Hedges, & Laine, 1996). But the evidence suggests that additional resources are likely to produce educational benefits—indeed, the *greatest* benefits—for disadvantaged children concentrated in the lowest spending states. It should not be surprising that the relationship between resources and outcomes appears stronger where current spending is low and weaker, or unpredictable where spending is already high. After all, it is what the principle of marginal utility would predict: additional resources make the greatest difference to those who have the least.

STATE FISCAL CAPACITY AND EFFORT

Do interstate disparities reflect differences in state *effort* in support of public schools or differences in state *fiscal capacity*? If the problem is effort, then the emphasis of law and policy should be on encouraging low-spending states to devote more of their own resources to education. If the problem is capacity, then it is important to consider the federal role in expanding resources available to low-spending states.

To address this question, Table 7.3 lists states in rank order by cost-adjusted revenue per weighted pupil from nonfederal sources in 2003–2004

(Column A). Each state's nonfederal revenue is a function of its fiscal capacity (i.e., its resources available to finance education) and its educational effort (i.e., its willingness to leverage its resources). Using a fiscal capacity measure called Total Taxable Resources (TTR; U.S. Department of the Treasury, 2002), we can compare fiscal capacity across states by computing each state's cost-adjusted TTR per weighted pupil. These data appear in column B of Table 7.3. Most states in the Northeast and upper Midwest have above-average fiscal capacity, while most states in the South and Southwest are below average. The fiscal capacity of the ten wealthiest states ($206,000 per weighted pupil) is over 50 percent greater than the fiscal capacity of the ten poorest states ($136,000 per weighted pupil).

Each state's educational effort may be defined as the hypothetical tax rate that, when levied against the state's fiscal capacity, produces the observed level of nonfederal education revenue in that state. So defined, each state's effort can be derived as the ratio of nonfederal revenue per weighted pupil (column A) to state fiscal capacity per weighted pupil (column B). The results appear in column C.

Table 7.3   State Fiscal Capacity and Educational Effort, 2003–2004

	A Nonfederal revenue		B Total taxable resources		C Educational effort (%)	
			(percentage of national average in *italics*)			
Vermont	$8,984	*155*	$194,185	*118*	4.63	*131*
Wyoming	8,500	*147*	243,488	*148*	3.49	*99*
New Jersey	8,499	*147*	195,698	*119*	4.34	*123*
Maine	7,657	*132*	179,170	*109*	4.27	*121*
New York	7,537	*130*	184,955	*112*	4.08	*116*
Connecticut	7,452	*129*	216,652	*131*	3.44	*98*
Hawaii	7,375	*127*	192,807	*117*	3.82	*109*
New Hampshire	7,244	*125*	213,455	*130*	3.39	*96*
Pennsylvania	7,131	*123*	190,262	*115*	3.75	*106*
Indiana	7,082	*122*	178,690	*108*	3.96	*112*
Massachusetts	7,017	*121*	206,918	*126*	3.39	*96*
Wisconsin	6,980	*120*	178,357	*108*	3.91	*111*
Kansas	6,877	*119*	181,367	*110*	3.79	*108*
Nebraska	6,844	*118*	200,110	*121*	3.42	*97*
Minnesota	6,711	*116*	193,076	*117*	3.48	*99*
Rhode Island	6,701	*116*	184,875	*112*	3.62	*103*
Delaware	6,670	*115*	297,756	*181*	2.24	*64*
Ohio	6,612	*114*	168,562	*102*	3.92	*111*
Iowa	6,575	*113*	193,247	*117*	3.40	*97*
Michigan	6,535	*113*	154,300	*94*	4.24	*120*
Montana	6,492	*112*	177,803	*108*	3.65	*104*
Alaska	6,354	*110*	173,654	*105*	3.66	*104*
Maryland	6,313	*109*	196,032	*119*	3.22	*91*
North Dakota	6,266	*108*	199,170	*121*	3.15	*89*
West Virginia	6,075	*105*	142,408	*86*	4.27	*121*
Oregon	5,993	*103*	174,502	*106*	3.43	*97*
South Dakota	5,976	*103*	219,957	*133*	2.72	*77*
Missouri	5,850	*101*	177,310	*108*	3.30	*94*

(continued)

Table 7.3   State Fiscal Capacity and Educational Effort, 2003–2004 (continued)

	A Nonfederal revenue		B Total taxable resources		C Educational effort (%)	
			(percentage of national average in *italics*)			
Illinois	5,770	*100*	172,156	*104*	3.35	*95*
Georgia	5,700	*98*	149,887	*91*	3.80	*108*
Colorado	5,671	*98*	191,557	*116*	2.96	*84*
South Carolina	5,512	*95*	144,761	*88*	3.81	*108*
Virginia	5,428	*94*	183,687	*111*	2.95	*84*
Florida	5,291	*91*	178,732	*108*	2.96	*84*
Idaho	5,216	*90*	146,250	*89*	3.57	*101*
Washington	5,200	*90*	169,214	*103*	3.07	*87*
Arkansas	5,110	*88*	144,634	*88*	3.53	*100*
New Mexico	5,108	*88*	134,753	*82*	3.79	*108*
Kentucky	5,045	*87*	153,903	*93*	3.28	*93*
Oklahoma	4,970	*86*	141,855	*86*	3.50	*99*
Nevada	4,934	*85*	175,499	*107*	2.81	*80*
Louisiana	4,908	*85*	152,120	*92*	3.23	*92*
North Carolina	4,858	*84*	167,637	*102*	2.90	*82*
Texas	4,835	*83*	131,308	*80*	3.68	*104*
Alabama	4,811	*83*	147,205	*89*	3.27	*93*
California	4,731	*82*	138,423	*84*	3.42	*97*
Mississippi	4,603	*79*	126,999	*77*	3.62	*103*
Arizona	4,414	*76*	141,472	*86*	3.12	*89*
Tennessee	4,335	*75*	165,964	*101*	2.61	*74*
Utah	4,134	*71*	124,795	*76*	3.31	*94*

Columns A and B show cost-adjusted dollars per weighted pupil. Estimates of Total Taxable Resources by state are from U.S. Department of the Treasury (2006). Nonfederal education revenue data by state are from U.S. Census Bureau (2006a). The values in column A divided by the values in column B yield the values in column C.

Table 7.3 provides some insights into the nature of school funding disparities across states. States with high revenue tend to have high capacity and high effort. But some states, like Delaware and Maryland, achieve high revenue by exerting low effort against high fiscal capacities, while other states, like Michigan and West Virginia, achieve high revenue by exerting high effort against low fiscal capacities. At the other end, states with low revenue tend to have low capacity and low effort. But some states, like New Mexico and South Carolina, have low revenue despite high effort, and other states, like Florida and Nevada, have low revenue largely because of low effort. In short, both effort and capacity play a role in explaining interstate disparities in educational resources.

We can assess the relative importance of the two factors by comparing the relationship between capacity and revenue with the relationship between effort and revenue. Table 7.4 shows these correlations in nominal and cost-adjusted terms, using TTR and state personal income as alternate measures of fiscal capacity. Although revenue is positively associated with both capacity and effort, the relationship between revenue and capacity is consistently stronger. In other words, variation in fiscal capacity plays a larger role in explaining interstate disparities in education revenue than variation in effort. Indeed, among the twenty-five states with the highest per-pupil revenue in Table 7.4, only two (Michigan and West Virginia) had below-average fiscal capacity in 2003–2004, while most states in the bottom half of revenue had below-average capacity.

Table 7.4   Correlation of State Fiscal Capacity and Educational Effort to Nonfederal Revenue Per Pupil, 2003–2004

	Measure of fiscal capacity	
	Total taxable resources	State personal income
Nominal		
Capacity	0.73	0.83
Effort	0.45	0.58
Cost-adjusted		
Capacity	0.65	0.76
Effort	0.53	0.64

The top panel shows correlations using nominal data on state TTR and nonfederal revenue per pupil. The bottom panel shows correlations using cost-adjusted data on state TTR and nonfederal revenue per weighted pupil. Estimates of state personal income are from U.S. Department of Commerce (2006).

In sum, fiscal capacity and effort are both determinants of interstate disparities in educational resources, but capacity plays the larger role. This reality highlights the need for a robust federal role in ameliorating interstate inequality.

THE FEDERAL ROLE IN INTERSTATE INEQUALITY

Yet the federal government has done little to narrow educational inequality across states. The federal role in education, while greatly expanded by NCLB, does not set common content or performance standards for schools in every state. Nor does it seriously address interstate inequality in school funding. Although federal aid disproportionately benefits poorer states, the equalizing effect is modest primarily because federal spending on K–12 education is small (only 8.9 percent of total education revenue in 2003–2004). Cost-adjusted nonfederal revenue per weighted pupil in 2003–2004 was 60 percent greater in the ten highest revenue states than in the ten lowest revenue states. When federal aid is taken into account, cost-adjusted revenue per weighted pupil remained 54 percent greater in the top ten versus bottom ten states. In short, the federal government cannot buy much equality with nine cents of every education dollar.

The limited leverage of the federal share is attributable not only to its small size but also to the way it is allocated. Remarkably, the single largest federal investment in K–12 education, Title I, does not reduce but instead *reinforces* interstate inequality. This is because each state's Title I allocation is largely a product of two factors. The first factor, poverty, tends to benefit low-spending states because they have disproportionate numbers of poor children. However, the second factor, the average per-pupil expenditure in the state, causes the existing pattern of interstate disparities in education spending to be reproduced in the allocation of Title I funds.

These disparities are evident in Table 7.5. Column A lists each state's 2006 Title I allocation in cost-adjusted dollars, and column B lists the number and percentage of the nation's poor children in each state in 2003. (Title I allocations in 2006 were based on 2003 poverty data.) As these data show, high- and low-spending states do not receive Title I money in proportion to their shares of the nation's poor children. Michigan, for example, had roughly the same number of poor children as North Carolina but received 43 percent more Title I aid. Pennsylvania had 6 percent fewer poor children than Georgia but received 23 percent more Title I aid, and New Jersey had 10 percent fewer poor children than Tennessee but received 6 percent more Title I aid.

Column C shows each state's Title I aid per poor child in rank order. Some of the highest amounts in column C reflect statutory minimum allocations for small states. Leaving those states aside, the amounts per poor child at the top are as much as 50 percent greater than the amounts at the bottom, with the variation essentially mirroring interstate variation in per-pupil spending. As I have shown elsewhere (Liu, 2006), the state expenditure factor neutralizes whatever interstate equalization is achieved by allocating Title I aid based on poverty. The net effect of Title I is to reinforce not reduce interstate inequality. Thus, the small, equalizing effect that the totality of federal education aid has across states occurs not because of but *in spite of* Title I.

The state expenditure factor has no convincing policy rationale (Riddle & Apling, 2000). It does not serve as a valid geographic cost factor. Nor does it provide an incentive for higher state effort, since allocating federal aid based on state per-pupil spending does not reward effort so much as it rewards fiscal capacity. Further, Title I aid is too small to motivate additional state or local spending; states typically do not spend an additional dollar to capture a few extra pennies. Nor does the state expenditure factor reflect a sensible policy of deference to diversity in state educational approaches. To be sure, there is no single optimal level of state per-pupil spending given the many nonresource variables essential to an effective state education policy. But, as Table 7.5 shows, interstate disparities in Title I aid are substantial. However important the value of federalism may be in public education, it would be perverse to characterize this scheme as a national "experiment" to test whether low-spending states can educate poor children as well as high-spending states with 20 percent or 30 percent fewer resources.

Table 7.5   Title I Allocations and Children in Poverty, 2006

	A Title I allocation (percentage of national average in *italics*)		B Poor children		C Title I per poor child
Wyoming	$29,168,800	*0.3*	9,796	*0.1*	$2,978
Vermont	27,327,371	*0.3*	9,667	*0.1*	2,827
North Dakota	30,578,989	*0.3*	11,245	*0.1*	2,719
New Hampshire	27,213,157	*0.3*	13,140	*0.2*	2,071
South Dakota	38,838,332	*0.4*	19,125	*0.2*	2,031
Alaska	28,536,347	*0.3*	14,330	*0.2*	1,991
Maine	44,336,471	*0.4*	25,025	*0.3*	1,772
Montana	44,978,747	*0.4*	25,827	*0.3*	1,742
Delaware	27,133,164	*0.3*	16,038	*0.2*	1,692
Nebraska	49,017,467	*0.5*	32,413	*0.4*	1,512
Pennsylvania	414,421,520	*4.1*	274,088	*3.3*	1,512
West Virginia	94,909,248	*0.9*	63,503	*0.8*	1,495
Hawaii	39,416,551	*0.4*	26,720	*0.3*	1,475
Michigan	357,069,276	*3.6*	251,533	*3.0*	1,420
Kansas	77,767,566	*0.8*	55,419	*0.7*	1,403
Rhode Island	38,012,696	*0.4*	27,313	*0.3*	1,392
Massachusetts	155,790,967	*1.6*	112,570	*1.3*	1,384
Wisconsin	132,606,695	*1.3*	96,223	*1.1*	1,378
New York	878,393,739	*8.8*	638,992	*7.6*	1,375
Ohio	348,142,954	*3.5*	258,749	*3.1*	1,345
Connecticut	74,376,666	*0.7*	55,987	*0.7*	1,328
Indiana	168,964,576	*1.7*	129,878	*1.6*	1,301
Maryland	130,657,915	*1.3*	101,153	*1.2*	1,292
Illinois	430,344,982	*4.3*	333,173	*4.0*	1,292
Louisiana	264,496,628	*2.6*	207,871	*2.5*	1,272
Iowa	63,302,771	*0.6*	49,808	*0.6*	1,271
Oregon	116,296,660	*1.2*	93,069	*1.1*	1,250
New Jersey	192,212,945	*1.9*	155,082	*1.9*	1,239
Kentucky	169,116,502	*1.7*	138,101	*1.6*	1,225
New Mexico	103,678,133	*1.0*	85,331	*1.0*	1,215
Mississippi	167,157,931	*1.7*	139,374	*1.7*	1,199
Minnesota	91,604,340	*0.9*	76,892	*0.9*	1,191
Idaho	42,710,588	*0.4*	35,921	*0.4*	1,189
Arkansas	124,202,423	*1.2*	105,100	*1.3*	1,182
Missouri	169,911,156	*1.7*	146,574	*1.7*	1,159
South Carolina	160,279,213	*1.6*	138,465	*1.7*	1,158
Oklahoma	135,437,658	*1.4*	117,122	*1.4*	1,156
Georgia	338,168,707	*3.4*	292,431	*3.5*	1,156
Florida	578,647,631	*5.8*	512,261	*6.1*	1,130
Colorado	108,848,951	*1.1*	96,512	*1.2*	1,128
Alabama	184,331,990	*1.8*	165,578	*2.0*	1,113
Arizona	231,544,197	*2.3*	213,295	*2.5*	1,086
Texas	967,943,732	*9.7*	902,369	*10.8*	1,073
Virginia	158,751,162	*1.6*	149,256	*1.8*	1,064
Nevada	62,428,141	*0.6*	59,296	*0.7*	1,053
Tennessee	180,692,016	*1.8*	171,970	*2.1*	1,051
Washington	138,967,722	*1.4*	138,049	*1.6*	1,007
North Carolina	250,092,284	*2.5*	248,492	*3.0*	1,006
California	1,272,037,008	*12.7*	1,288,493	*15.4*	987
Utah	48,201,580	*0.5*	49,259	*0.6*	979

The amounts in columns A and C are cost-adjusted dollars. Title I allocations by state are from U.S. Department of Education (2006). Numbers of poor children by state are from U.S. Census Bureau (2006b).

REFORMING THE FEDERAL ROLE IN SCHOOL FINANCE

Just as a patchwork of state standards offers little guidance for educating a national citizenry (Finn, Julian, & Petrilli, 2006; Gordon, 2006; Ravitch, 1995), a patchwork of unequal state funding cannot effectively support ambitious national education goals. Narrowing interstate disparities ought to be a central focus of the federal role in school finance. Here I sketch some key principles to guide policy design, followed by a specific proposal to reform Title I and a broader proposal to increase federal education funding.

Principles for Federal Education Aid

Because poor children in concentrated poverty face special challenges, Congress should continue to target aid to the highest poverty districts and schools within each state, and should push states toward more equitable distribution of their own funds. In addition, federal aid should reduce inequality *across* states consistent with the following policy guideposts.

First, because interstate differences in education funding primarily reflect interstate differences in fiscal capacity, the distribution of federal aid should compensate for differences across states in their ability to support education. Narrowing such differences is a school finance role that only the federal government can fulfill.

Second, in aiding states with low education spending, federal policy should distinguish between low capacity and low effort. Where low spending is due to low effort, the primary federal role should be to motivate states toward greater effort. Similarly, the federal government should do more to ensure that states receiving federal aid do not reduce their effort or use federal money to supplant state or local funds. Because states will continue to bear most of the burden for school finance, narrowing interstate disparities will require a progressive distribution of federal aid that is layered on top of a commitment by each state to do its fair share.

Third, because educational purchasing power varies significantly between states and within states, federal aid should accurately account for geographic cost differences.

Finally, federal aid will not do much to reduce interstate disparities if it remains only nine cents of every education dollar. In addition, there is growing evidence that effective standards-based reform demands significantly more resources than what is now being committed (Driscoll & Fleeter, 2003; Imazeki & Reschovsky, 2004; Mathis, 2003). Given NCLB's goals of educating all children to high standards and closing the achievement gap, it is fair to expect increased federal responsibility for the associated costs. Indeed, "some type of nationwide base per-pupil spending level is the logical school finance policy for the implementation of national education goals" (Odden & Kim, 1992, p. 291).

In sum, the federal role in school finance should (a) foster equitable resource distribution within each state, (b) promote interstate equality by compensating for interstate disparities in fiscal capacity, (c) motivate states to exert reasonable effort in support of education, (d) adjust federal aid for geographic cost differences, and (e) provide aid sufficient to enable the poorest states to educate their children to national standards.

Policy Recommendations

With these principles in mind, I offer two proposals for reshaping federal education aid. First, the state expenditure factor in Title I should be eliminated. This reform would bring Title I into line with the aid formulas for special education, English language instruction, and child nutrition, all of which assign equal weight to eligible children regardless of the state where they reside. Title I should simply allocate aid based on poverty and incorporate a valid cost factor to adjust for geographic cost differences.

Although this reform would make Title I more equitable, its impact on interstate inequality would be modest because Title I would continue to provide only a thin layer of federal aid on top of large interstate disparities in nonfederal education revenue. Any serious effort to reduce interstate inequality must directly address the wide variation in state effort and fiscal capacity. This can be done through a national program of foundation aid that complements the systemic reach of NCLB and the plausible evolution of federal policy toward national standards.

There are many ways to design a foundation program that compensates for interstate disparities in fiscal capacity. One approach is a modified form of "power equalizing" whereby the federal government would guarantee each state a minimum amount per weighted pupil for a given level of state effort. For example, the government could assure each state an amount per weighted pupil at least equal to what the state would have raised had it applied its tax effort against the average fiscal capacity among all states. For poor states, whose actual revenue at a given level of effort is less than the guaranteed amount, federal aid would make up the difference. Richer states whose actual revenue exceeds the guaranteed amount would retain their revenue but would receive no aid. Under this scheme, federal aid would boost the fiscal capacity of poorer states while leaving wealthier states to their superior means, thereby narrowing interstate inequality. Moreover, by treating *weighted* pupils as the unit of analysis, the funding scheme integrates the compensatory thrust of categorical aid like Title I.

This approach is a step in the right direction, but three modifications are warranted. First, if an important objective is to establish a national foundation of aid, then the program must specify a minimum level of effort that participating states must meet. The foundation program should not function as insurance against state indifference. Instead, it should serve as a framework for cooperative federalism in which the federal government would guarantee to every state exerting the minimum effort a foundation level of spending per weighted pupil. Although a state could refuse to make the minimum effort, any serious program of national foundation aid would involve large sums of money that states would find difficult to forgo.

Second, although it would be equitable to limit federal aid to poor states, a power-equalizing foundation program is unlikely to succeed politically unless it spreads federal aid widely. Instead of offering no aid to wealthy states that already exceed the federally guaranteed amount at any given effort level, a better approach would be a graduated system that provides some aid to every state. One example of this approach is the variable "federal medical assistance percentage" used by Medicaid. Under Medicaid, the federal government matches state spending on health-related services for low-income people at a different rate for each state depending on the square of the ratio of its per capita income to national per capita income. States with lower per capita income have a higher matching rate, and states with higher per capita income have a lower matching rate, with a minimum match of 50 percent and a maximum of 83 percent.

An analogous "federal educational assistance percentage" could be created to provide foundation aid to public schools. For each state at or above a minimum effort level, the federal government would match its cost-adjusted spending per weighted pupil at a rate that takes into account the state's fiscal capacity relative to the average fiscal capacity among all states. Fiscal capacity would be measured by a state's taxable resources adjusted for geographic cost differences and then divided by its weighted pupil count. For poorer states, the federal matching rate would be higher and, for the poorest states, high enough to ensure an educationally adequate foundation. For wealthier states, the matching rate would be lower and, for the wealthiest states, bounded by a politically acceptable minimum.

Third, the federal aid program will not serve its purpose unless it furthers not only interstate but also intrastate equality. If we wish to ensure a foundation level of resources per weighted pupil, it makes little sense to allow states to channel large portions of federal aid toward the most advantaged districts or the most advantaged students. To participate in the program, each state should be required to use federal aid not only to bring all districts up to the foundation level but also to narrow interdistrict and intradistrict disparities. One approach would be to require each state to use federal aid to reduce its coefficient of interdistrict variation by a minimum percentage, while offering small increases in the federal matching rate to states that reduce interdistrict disparities by more than the minimum percentage. This approach would drive federal aid to the neediest districts and schools within each state, thereby subsuming the objectives of Title I. To enhance continuity with Title I, the program could specify that within-state allocations in accordance with the current district- and school-level allocation formulas of Title I would presumptively satisfy the intrastate equalization requirement.

In the legislative process, the specific parameters of a national foundation program—pupil weights, cost adjustments, minimum state effort, federal matching rate, and the foundation level itself—would be informed by a complex mix of research, expert judgment, and politics. The practical balance of benefits and burdens is as important as any distributive principle in determining the shape of a viable program. Nevertheless, as long as public demand for high standards can be sustained, and as we learn more from cost studies about current shortcomings in financing an adequate education, the case for a robust federal role in narrowing interstate disparities and ensuring a national foundation level of resources will remain strong.

In other work (Liu, 2006), I compared the interstate equalizing effect of federal education aid in 2002–2003 with the effect of a national foundation plan with the following parameters:

1. *Foundation guarantee.* The program assures every state at least $6,500 in cost-adjusted revenue per weighted pupil, an amount that Congress has hypothetically determined, based on the best available evidence, to be a reasonable estimate of the cost of adequate educational opportunity.

2. *Minimum state effort.* As a condition of federal aid, each state with nonfederal per-pupil revenue below $6,500 must devote (a) at least 3.25 percent of its Total Taxable Resources to education or (b) the level of effort necessary to produce the $6,500 foundation level, whichever is less. In other words, a state is ineligible for federal aid if it has not made sufficient effort to bring its per-pupil revenue up to the foundation level.

3. *Federal matching rate.* Federal aid matches each state's nonfederal revenue at a rate inversely proportional to the ratio of the state's fiscal capacity to the national average.

4. *Minimum matching rate.* The minimum federal match is 4 percent, a figure hypothetically judged by Congress to be high enough to win support for the plan from wealthy states.

This plan would disproportionately benefit states with relatively low fiscal capacity that have exerted at least the minimum effort, such as Alabama, California, New Mexico, and Oklahoma. It would be less generous toward states with relatively high fiscal capacity, including states with historically high education spending, such as Connecticut and Massachusetts, as well as states whose low education revenue is largely due to low effort, such as Florida and Nevada. The plan thus ensures a base level of per-pupil funding by directing substantial aid to poorer states where additional money is likely to yield the greatest educational dividends, while encouraging wealthier states to do their fair share. In 2002–2003, the simulated plan would have reduced the coefficient of interstate variation in per-pupil revenue by nearly one-third (32 percent) at a cost of $43.5 billion. By comparison, actual federal education revenue in 2002–2003 totaled $36.8 billion and reduced the coefficient of interstate variation by only 12 percent.

If Congress were to adopt this foundation plan as a major reform and expansion of Title I, it would require approximately $30 billion in new money above the $13 billion currently spent under Title I. Large as this increase may seem, the federal share of the national education budget would still be less than 15 percent. Moreover, a significant component of the increase is attributable to the 4 percent minimum federal matching rate. Without any minimum, the plan would have produced an even greater degree of interstate equalization (a 37 percent reduction in the coefficient of variation) at a lesser cost ($37.2 billion), although only thirty states—perhaps too few for an effective political majority—would have received significant federal aid. Finally, as costly as this proposal may seem, it must be weighed against the immense social and economic costs of current educational inadequacies (Levin, Belfield, Muennig, & Rouse, 2007).

CONCLUSION

To be sure, the shortcomings of American public education are too complex to be remedied by simply "throwing money at the problem." The national foundation plan I propose must bear a reasonable empirical relationship to learning standards that lend coherence and strategic direction to education policy. Funding reforms also must be nested within ongoing efforts to improve the accountability and efficiency of public schools. Moreover, districts and schools need concrete solutions to work-a-day challenges such as how to align teachers' skills with higher standards and how to implement effective instructional practices for the most disadvantaged students. Given this context, the ideas here are not intended to be panaceas. To succeed, they must leverage other reform agendas in the policy environment.

At the same time, it is difficult to believe that our gaping interstate disparities in educational standards and resources have no bearing on unequal opportunity and outcomes. The problem is one that only the federal government can address. The political alignment necessary for a solution is beyond the scope of this chapter. But the approach must bring together southern moderates who see the benefits of federal aid outweighing the threat to states' rights with northern liberals who support a fairer distribution of the nation's wealth. The coalition might also include legislators from the West and Southwest, where high poverty and immigration have produced formidable educational challenges. The viability of any reform will depend on the balance of winners and losers. But without a new and concerted effort, it will continue to be more rhetoric than reality to speak of a national commitment to equal educational opportunity.

8

Massive Responsibilities and Limited Resources

The State Response to NCLB

Gail L. Sunderman and Gary Orfield

Under the No Child Left Behind (NCLB) Act, state education agencies play the crucial role in supporting and monitoring the implementation of the federal mandates. Because the law's requirements are extraordinary—reaching far into the internal operation of schools—and the federal resources are limited, the law tests the capacity of state educational agencies to impose dramatic educational change and administer the law. Using data collected from six states, this chapter examines the state response to meeting the law's requirements. It identifies significant changes in NCLB from previous legislation that alter the state role and examines whether states have the resources, knowledge, and organizational capacity to implement the law and intervene in low-performing schools on the scale demanded by NCLB. From a civil rights perspective these issues are especially important, since NCLB places responsibility on the states for both sanctioning

This chapter was adapted from our 2006 article, Domesticating a revolution: No Child Left Behind and state administrative response. *Harvard Educational Review*, 76, 526–556.

and reforming the schools in which minority students and teachers are concentrated when many states have not historically had a positive relationship with these schools.

NCLB rested on assumptions about the professional capacity of state educational agencies, which vary from extensive professional staffs in the largest states to modest operations in the smallest and poorest, to implement the requirements called for in the law and provide the support and technical assistance necessary to help low-performing schools and districts. Supporters of the law argued that federal policy should provide the leverage to change how states allocate their resources and that an outcome-based reform strategy would create the professional and political incentives for states to marshal the federal and state resources necessary to respond to the accountability incentives. The law itself provided only modest resources and paid little attention to how the state role would need to change if the ambitious educational goals were to be achieved. One of the interesting aspects of this study is the finding that state administrators did their best to obey the law, at least by implementing the data collection and testing requirements and the market-based sanctions. But when confronted with the much more ambitious goals of ensuring large-scale educational changes and providing support to low-performing schools, the states were much less adept and the resources were few.

Two types of capacity are critical to states' abilities to implement NCLB: (1) human and financial resources available to the state and local agencies, including expertise in a broad range of areas; and (2) organizational capacity, including the systems necessary to meet the data management and testing requirements and the formal and informal organizational networks between state and local authorities to provide technical assistance and support to local districts and schools (McDermott, 2004; Sunderman & Orfield, 2006). In particular, we pay attention to the knowledge base and existence of suitable interventions for improving performance in low-performing schools that would allow state administrators to do what the law requires, since the history of state failures on a much smaller scale makes it difficult to understand how the states could meet these challenges and raises concern about the resulting policies and practices for minority schools and districts.

We use a case-study methodology focusing on interviews with state education officials supplemented with data from other sources. We have negotiated access to a sample of states selected on dimensions we consider of fundamental importance for getting a sense of the issues of state capacity. As part of a larger study on NCLB, we are following implementation of NCLB in six states: Arizona, California, Georgia, Illinois, New York, and Virginia. These six states are geographically and politically diverse, with each state located in each geographic region of the United States. Politically, the degree of state control over local education policies varies, and the states differed prior to NCLB in where they were in the reform process as it relates to the NCLB requirements. Finally, each state has a large portion of minority and low-income students, the intended beneficiaries of the NCLB policies.

The data for this study is drawn from a variety of sources. We interviewed Department of Education officials in each state. These interviews took place between January and May 2005 and included interviews with directors of federal programs, budget directors, officials responsible for accountability systems, assessment directors, officials directing school improvement programs, and information and reporting officers. We also collected state policy documents, descriptions of programs designed to meet the NCLB requirements, and budget and staffing information. Some of the policy and program documents were obtained from state education Web sites. We augmented our state interview data and documents with local and national newspaper articles. The variety of qualitative data sources allowed us to verify information from the various sources. In the following section, we begin by tracing the development of the state role in education and how this reinforced the monitoring and regulatory functions of state education agencies and increased the need for people with specialized professional knowledge in particular areas.

STATE CAPACITY IN HISTORICAL PERSPECTIVE

Public education in the United States is largely controlled by state laws. In important respects, we have fifty independent state educational systems with 15,700 local variations at the district level that are loosely regulated by the states (U.S. Census Bureau, 2006, p. 155). This local variety is related to how different regions of the country developed historically, the demographic makeup of the states' populations, local ideas about how to provide for schooling, and the resources available to support public education in each state (Wirt & Kirst, 1982). Since legal authority for education policymaking is vested with the legislature and governor, the system is highly political. Today, state authority over education derives from policies that determine who can teach; what must be included in children's education; and, in most states, what must be learned to graduate and how it will be assessed.

Until recently, state departments of education have remained relatively small and weak, with little control over education decisions made at the local level. By the 1950s, local school boards and superintendents, particularly in large districts, held considerable decision-making authority and operated relatively autonomously from state or federal control. State education departments were small agencies that performed a limited range of functions, administering some federal grant programs, distributing funds, and collecting statistics.

This began to change in the 1960s with the civil rights movement and the enactment of the Elementary and Secondary Education Act (ESEA) in 1965. The civil rights movement focused attention on achieving equity through improvements in the schooling opportunities for low-income and minority students. For the first time, the federal government became a significant player in education, largely through increased federal aid to public schools. With the increased federal role, a larger role for state departments of education developed, both as a way to funnel money to local districts and to enforce and monitor the emerging federal requirements. With the passage of ESEA, federal officials relied on states to provide an organizational structure to administer federal funds, monitor implementation of the law's requirements, and divert attention away from criticisms of federal control.

The reform movements of the latter half of the twentieth century strengthened the state role in funding and regulating education. States responded to the school finance movement of the 1960s and 1970s and the standards movement of the 1980s and 1990s by introducing laws and regulations designed to monitor local compliance with federal and state requirements. By focusing on funding disparities between districts, states moved toward a more comprehensive approach to funding education. Under the reforms of the 1980s and 1990s, when both federal and state legislation embraced standards-based reform, states extended the scope of regulations to include curriculum standards and expanded state testing. These regulations were demanding but left districts with considerable discretion over implementation and instruction. At the federal level, weak enforcement of the Improving America's Schools Act (IASA) of 1994 allowed the federal government to avoid state and local opposition to an expanded federal role in education.

The particular expertise of state agencies, which allowed them to enforce federal requirements, enact state policies, and act as a conduit for the flow of federal and state money to school districts, and the relative weakness of their staffs in the core areas of educational reform meant they focused less on issues concerning the academic content of the curriculum, assessment, school reform, or organization and management—precisely those areas now demanding attention under NCLB (Elmore & Fuhrman, 1995).

NCLB furthers the trend of making states central to implementing school reform efforts and relies on assumptions about the professional capacity of all state departments of education, which vary from extensive professional staffs in the largest states to very modest operations in the smallest and poorest, to achieve unprecedented educational progress and implement sanctions that will require deep interventions in thousands of schools that do not meet the required annual progress standards of the federal law. It reverses the traditional relationship between the federal and state agencies from one of federal aid and incentives in grant programs to one of federal requirements for producing huge educational gains under pressure of serious federal sanctions. A fundamental question is whether state agencies have the resources, knowledge, and organizational capacity to intervene at the scale demanded by NCLB.

STATE RESPONSIBILITIES UNDER NCLB

State responsibilities under NCLB are extensive. States are required to develop and administer an accountability system that assesses students annually and, on the basis of those assessments, determines whether schools and districts are making adequate yearly progress (AYP). States must create and implement curriculum standards and assessments in reading, mathematics, and science in grades three to eight and in at least one grade level in grades ten to twelve. These requirements increased the number of tests in the three subject areas (reading/language arts, mathematics, science) from six that were required under the 1994 ESEA reauthorization to seventeen under NCLB (Government Accountability Office, 2003). In addition to testing all students in core subject areas, states must provide both appropriate assessments and accommodations where necessary for students with disabilities, and assess students learning English for English proficiency. The law established a timeline for when these tests must be in place and determined that all students must score "proficient" on state tests by 2014.

Because NCLB expanded the data collection and reporting requirements, states now need data collection and information systems that can disaggregate student test scores by race, English language ability, and disability status and that can use this disaggregated data to make AYP determinations. States must monitor teacher and paraprofessional qualifications to insure they are all highly qualified by a date specified in the law.

Three other changes to NCLB from previous legislation significantly alter the state role by placing additional demands and responsibilities on state departments of education. First, requirements that all students, including all subgroups, must reach a state's proficiency goal by 2014 raises the expectations and goals of Title I by requiring that states bring all schools and all subgroups to the same level of performance within a relatively short period of time. NCLB requires universal high achievement for all students and attaches sanctions that become increasingly severe the longer a school or district does not meet the state's achievement goals. The law, which relies on outcomes rather than the provision of additional resources to improve student performance, operates on the assumption that state education agencies and boards will reallocate their state resources in ways that will allow all schools to meet this goal and that it is possible to bring all students to 100 percent proficiency. It ignores huge resource differences between districts that are closely related to the socioeconomic status of the students.

Second, states have a role in helping schools and districts improve under NCLB, a requirement that traditionally has not been a major state function. State agencies developed the expertise and capacity to funnel state and federal funds to local districts and to propagate regulations needed to monitor education. Requiring states to intervene and force change in schools and districts requires a very different sort of capacity and expertise than that required for monitoring or funneling funds to local districts. The law requires states to "establish a statewide system of intensive and sustained support and improvement for local educational agencies and schools" that have been identified for improvement (NCLB, 2002. Sec. 1117(a)(1)). The law is very specific about what this must include, yet the resources provided for this are limited at best.

Third, the inclusion of timelines for when states must meet the NCLB requirements mean all states must be at the same place regardless of where they start. Under NCLB, states must adhere to federally determined timelines for establishing an accountability system and having assessments in place, identifying failing schools and improving student achievement, establishing adequate yearly progress goals, and ensuring teacher quality. The 1994 ESEA reauthorization included the possibility of timeline extensions, something not included under NCLB. It also imposes strict timelines for improving the achievement of disadvantaged students and mandates specific sanctions for schools not performing well.

STATE ACTIONS AND LIMITATIONS ON IMPLEMENTING NCLB

NCLB combines extremely demanding educational goals with extremely limited administrative resources. There is the assumption in the act that drastic change can and should be imposed on the educational system but, at the same time, the law reflects the antigovernment, antibureaucratic assumptions of the conservative political movement that created it. So state agencies are expected to make unprecedented changes with few additional resources.

While NCLB provided additional money, much of this increase came during the first year (FY 2002) when Title I funding increased 18.11 percent and total appropriations for elementary and secondary education increased 17.43 percent (see Table 8.1). Since then, increases have been smaller and are negligible when factoring in inflation. The 3 percent increase in Title I grants to local districts in FY 2005 did not keep pace with the 6 percent increase in the number of children in poverty (Center on Education Policy, 2005). Appropriations for Title I actually decreased in FY 2006 and the president's proposed FY 2007 budget held Title I funding constant while reducing overall appropriations for elementary and secondary education by 4.19 percent. These reductions came at the same time that the federal demands were increasing and states were required to raise proficiency levels, have assessments in place, and ensure all teachers were highly qualified.

Table 8.1   Title I Grants to Local Education Agencies (LEAs) and Total Elementary and Secondary Education Appropriations (in thousands of dollars), FY 1998–2007

Fiscal Year	ESEA Title I Grants to LEAs	% Increase From Prior Year	Total Elementary & Secondary Appropriation	% Increase From Prior Year
1998	$ 7,375,232	1.09	$18,164,490	10.28
1999	7,732,397	4.84	20,951,877	15.35
2000	7,941,397	2.70	22,600,399	7.87
2001	8,762,721	10.34	27,316,893	20.87
2002	10,350,000	18.11	32,078,434	17.43
2003	11,688,664	12.93	35,113,253	9.46
2004	12,342,309	5.59	36,942,478	5.21
2005	12,739,571	3.22	37,530,257	1.59
2006	12,713,125	-0.21	37,863,840	0.89
2007*	12,713,125	0.00	36,276,140	-4.19

Source: U.S. Department of Education, Budget History Table: FY 1980–present. Retrieved August 15, 2006, from www.ed.gov/about/overview/budget/history/edhistory.pdf

Note: *2007 President's Proposed Budget.

While the law gave states modest funding for administration, it simultaneously imposed major new requirements.[1] At the same time, program changes and the set-aside requirements offset much of the overall increases in funds states received. For the most demanding part of the law—the requirement that states provide additional support for low-performing schools and districts—the amount of funding appropriated under NCLB was insufficient and did not represent additional money but rather a reallocation of Title I funds, which reduces the funding that is available for other Title I activities.

State Assessments

One area where states did receive significant new resources was for state assessments. These allocations helped offset some of the costs covered by the state, at least in the initial years, but state officials were concerned because there is no mechanism in NCLB for maintaining the testing system over time. Because Title VI of NCLB does not have a supplant clause, states were able to replace state funds for assessments with federal funds. For example, Illinois reduced the amount of state funds devoted to state assessments from $18.3 million in the 2002 fiscal year to $8.4 million in the 2005

[1] States may reserve 1 percent of the amount they receive from Parts A, C, and D of Title I for administration. There is a ceiling on the amount that can be reserved. (NCLB, 2002, Sec. 1004)

fiscal year. However, to achieve these cost savings, the General Assembly amended the state's testing legislation to eliminate all testing that was not required by NCLB, including dropping tests in writing and social studies.

States that did not have a testing system that met the NCLB requirements contributed substantial resources to augment the federal funds. This was the case in Arizona, where the Arizona Board of Education voted in March 2004 to develop and administer a new test that would replace its previous testing system. The costs of developing this system were huge, and required the state to contribute over half of the funding needed for test development and administration. In addition to the costs of developing the testing system, Arizona officials were concerned with meeting the costs of achievement testing when the federal funding ends, since the state has a growing school-age population requiring additional tests in future years.

System of Support

A central component of NCLB requires states to provide additional support for low-performing schools and districts. Even though this represents a major challenge for states—the record on state intervention is poor—the amount of funding appropriated under NCLB was insufficient and did not represent additional money but rather a reallocation of Title I funds. NCLB includes two mechanisms for states to receive funds for school-improvement activities, one of which has never received appropriations. Section 1003(g) of the act authorizes a separate program for school improvement in which states could receive grants that are awarded to districts for school-improvement activities. A portion of these grants (5 percent), if they were available, could be reserved by the state for administration, evaluation, and technical assistance. Since funds have never been appropriated for this program, school-improvement activities have come from the Title I basic grant to states as a set aside.

The set aside requires states to reserve a portion of their Title I funds for school improvement (NCLB, 2002, Sec. 1003(a)). Beginning with the 2005–2006 school year, this reservation rose from 2 percent to 4 percent. Of this allocation, 95 percent must go to local educational agencies to support school-improvement activities for schools identified for improvement (Sec. 1003(b)). Schools may use these funds to implement the required sanctions and to develop and implement a school-improvement plan, or the district may provide direct assistance to schools needing improvement. The remaining 5 percent may be used by the state educational agency "to carry out states responsibilities... including carrying out the State educational agency's statewide system of technical assistance and support for local educational agencies" (Sec. 1003 (a)). Since this reservation is tied to the overall Title I appropriations, the amount of the set aside is related to overall increases (or decreases) in Title I funding; it does not represent additional funds.

Table 8.2 shows the amount of school-improvement funds available to six states for the 2005 fiscal year. Since the federal legislation sets a ceiling on the amount of funds that can be used for administration, states can convert some of these funds into local assistance in the form of higher grants to districts. This is what the California legislature did, and instead of the $3.5 million that California could set aside under the Title I guidelines, the state set aside $1.78 million and sent the remainder to local districts.

Table 8.2   Amount of Title I Budget Allocated for School-Improvement Activities, FY 2005

State	4% for School Improvement	95% of 4% for Districts	5% of the 4% for State
Arizona	$ 9,957,899	$ 9,460,004	$ 497,895
California	71,061,718	67,508,632	3,553,086
Georgia	16,263,283	15,450,119	813,164
Illinois	21,532,907	20,456,261	1,076,645
New York	49,067,048	46,613,696	2,453,352
Virginia	8,660,702	8,227,667	433,035

Source: U.S. Department of Education. Retrieved February 24, 2006, from http://www.ed.gov/about/overview/budget/statetables/index.html. Calculations are based on the ESEA Title I Grants to Local Education Agencies for FY 2005.

To put the set aside for state administration of school improvement in perspective, we compared the allocation to the number of schools and districts identified for improvement (Table 8.3). If each school that was identified for improvement were to receive an equal portion of the school-improvement grants—an unlikely event since the grants go to the district, which will likely use some for their own administrative costs—the allocation per school ranged from $93,041 in New York to $26,713 in Virginia. Dividing the amount that the state can retain by the number of districts in need of improvement gave states $4,431 per district in Illinois to $67,764 per district in Georgia. These are not large amounts when you consider they barely, if at all, cover the costs of adding just one staff person for every school or district needing improvement.

Data Reporting

To meet the NCLB data collection and reporting mandates, states had to develop a new student-information system that allowed state officials to track students over time as well as collect the student demographic data essential for disaggregating test scores by subgroups. Among the six states, only California had an existing system that included student-level information. Still, California added several data fields to their system in order to collect the data they needed for NCLB.

Table 8.3   Allocations for School Improvement Grants to Schools and Districts Per Number of Schools or Districts Identified for Improvement, 2004–2005

State	Allocation for School Improvement Grants FY2005	Schools Identified for Improvement 2004-2005	Allocation Per School	State Allocation for School Improvement	Districts Identified for Improvement 2004-2005	Allocation Per District
Arizona	$ 9,460,004	151	62,649	$ 497,895	78	6,383
California	67,508,632	1600	42,193	3,553,086	150	23,687
Georgia	15,450,119	354	43,644	813,164	12	67,764
Illinois	20,456,261	661	30,947	1,076,645	243	4,431
New York	46,613,696	501	93,041	2,453,352	58	42,299
Virginia	8,227,667	308	26,713	433,035	79	5,481

In addition to developing the state systems, state officials cited data integrity as a major challenge in meeting the NCLB reporting requirement. Since data was self-reported, the quality of data varied considerably between districts. Many districts simply lacked the infrastructure necessary to collect the required data or their systems were not compatible with the state system. To fully implement a student-information system often required providing resources to districts that did not have the local resources, technology, or staff to develop and implement such a system. For example, Illinois officials estimated that about 25 percent of the districts in Illinois did not have an electronic way of tracking enrollment, attendance, or demographic information. Georgia spent an estimated $26 million to develop the district-level infrastructure necessary to establish a student-information system.

Although the law focused on outcomes, the limited resources were often absorbed with collecting data on inputs and tests, leaving little time for using data to facilitate educational reform. Consequently, staff devoted their time to collecting, correcting, and analyzing the data for NCLB reporting purposes but did not have the time or resources to analyze data for program effectiveness. For example, to meet the data-reporting requirements of NCLB, the policy and evaluation division of the California Department of Education reallocated staff time to complete NCLB tasks and gave up doing research studies using the data they collected, no longer responding to outside studies using California data or providing analyses to the superintendent, legislature, or news media. Because of the increased amount of data required under NCLB, insuring the integrity of the data and responding to school and district challenges to improvement status consumed staff time according to a California state official.

> We end up crunching 4 or 5 million student records and creating massive reports and with 20 percent of the schools, the data is wrong. So they go back, correct it. . .and then send it back and we re-crunch it again, and on and on and on. . .And it's gotten even

worse with the high stakes of NCLB. Districts and schools are going back more and more to make sure all the data are correct. . .This whole concept of getting good data into the department is loosely coupled and that's that biggest point of breakdown, which keeps us busy constantly (personal communication, California Department of Education, February 16, 2005).

Since the data states collected was used to comply with NCLB, not the separate and preexisting state reforms, the new statistical data was often not very useful to state officials or district educators. In Illinois, districts questioned the usefulness of the data since it did not tell them which programs worked or how it would help their schools. For example, the state collects data on the number of students taking advantage of the transfer option, but does not provide information on "what it means in the long run in terms of policy. The data tells us which [supplemental educational services] vendors are chosen more frequently than others, but it doesn't really speak to the issue of which programs are more effective than others" (personal communication, Illinois State Board of Education, January 26, 2005).

Federal grants to support the development of longitudinal data systems have done little to address the capacity differences between states. To qualify, states had to demonstrate that considerable capacity already existed, including the capacity to support research on student academic growth, to exchange data across institutions within the state and, to provide reports and analysis to stakeholders and the staff and technical and monetary resources to sustain the system over time (U.S. Department of Education, 2005).

Human Resources

The state experts who are required to mount massive new assessment and data systems and do whatever is needed to achieve huge educational gains are on the one hand given tremendous responsibilities and, on the other, spoken of as if they were a waste of money. The act sets aside a much larger share of the Title I budget for two market-driven reforms that are assumed to have powerful impacts on school reform—supplemental educational services and the transfer option—than it does to support state intervention activities. Neither district administrators, school principals, nor state administrators were dealt with in a coherent way in the act, although studies of systemic school reform show that strong and consistent leadership is crucial to successful school reform.

Opposition to bureaucracy is also evident at the state level. In some states the antibureaucratic assumptions in state politics led to slashes in state professional staff even as the responsibilities for complex educational intervention soared. Since teacher organizations are always one of the dominant forces in state educational policy while state bureaucrats have little political constituency, it is often popular to cut the "bureaucracy" to fund teacher salaries.

It was not unusual for state education agencies to experience a decline in the number of staff in the period prior to the passage of NCLB that continued during the first years of implementation. To illustrate, Figure 8.1 shows historical staffing data from three states—Illinois, New York, and Georgia. The number of staff in the Illinois State Board of Education declined from 787 in FY 2000 to 492 in FY 2005, a 37.5 percent decrease during the time the state was implementing NCLB. The decline in the number of staff in the New York Office of Elementary, Middle, Secondary, and Continuing Education began in FY 1995. Over a ten-year period, the staff declined 36.4 percent in this office, compared to a 9.4 percent decline over the same time period in the umbrella agency, the New York State Education Department (New York State Education Department Office of Human Resources Management, 2004). A significant drop in staff in Georgia occurred in FY 1997, when there was a 26.7 percent decline in one year. These staff reductions were tied to budget reductions and resulting hiring freezes; agency reorganizations where divisions were eliminated, consolidated, or moved to other agencies; staff turnover and retirements; and political factors. Since states could not substantially increase staff, to meet the NCLB requirements they added additional responsibilities onto existing staff.

Figure 8.1   Staffing Count, Illinois State Board of Education, New York Office of Elementary, Middle, Secondary, and Continuing Education, and Georgia Department of Education, FY 1995 to FY 2005

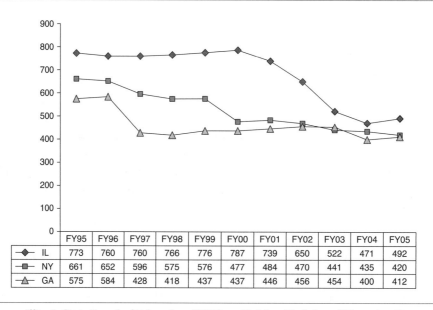

	FY95	FY96	FY97	FY98	FY99	FY00	FY01	FY02	FY03	FY04	FY05
IL	773	760	760	766	776	787	739	650	522	471	492
NY	661	652	596	575	576	477	484	470	441	435	420
GA	575	584	428	418	437	437	446	456	454	400	412

Source: Illinois State Board of Education (2005), p. 11; New York State Education Department of Human Resources Management (2004); Georgia Department of Education personal communication (September 2005).

STATE CAPACITY TO INTERVENE IN SCHOOLS AND DISTRICTS

NCLB incorporates not only requirements for achievement gains and for assessments, but also directives about what to do when districts and schools fail—a litany of state-driven reforms that appear in the law as if they were well-documented methods of improving schools, and as if the states have the resources and knowledge and leadership to effectively implement them. These range from state takeovers, state advisors, state decisions to convert failing schools to charter schools, mandates to develop a new school-level reform plan, and, of course, implementation of supplemental educational services and transfer options for families in the many schools not making "adequate yearly progress" for all subgroups of students. The basic idea was to provide an array of strong tools states could use to force change in failing schools and districts and to demand that state and local officials do something to produce changes.

The idea of drastic action by states was not new in NCLB. As is true in NCLB, there is the assumption that reform is often blocked by recalcitrant local forces and that it can be imposed more successfully in some cases by a distant force less entangled in local pressures, antiquated institutions, and politics. In fact, twenty-nine states have the authority to take control of a district and simply override local authorities under specified circumstances, and about a third of the states also have the authority to cease local control of individual schools and impose changes (Education Commission of the States, 2006). The actual record of state interventions is surprisingly long and extensive but also disappointing.

The idea of state takeovers blossomed in the reform era in the late 1980s and became widespread in the following decade. It often began in cases of financial collapse where the state was forced to step in; in court orders; in cases of massive corruption; or, as the standards-based reform movement became more intense, in cases of persistent academic disaster. New Jersey was the first state to take over a district for poor academic performance, but there were major efforts in a number of states, including California, Illinois, Ohio, Maryland, New York, Connecticut, and others. A study by the Education Commission of the States, a compact of state education agencies hardly hostile to or critical of the idea of a vigorous state role in education policy, concluded in a 2004 report that takeovers were "yielding more gains in central office activities than in classroom instructional practices" by helping to straighten out accounts and business practices and upgrading facilities. Little progress was noted on academic gains, certainly nothing like the gains required by NCLB: "Student achievement still oftentimes falls short of expectations . . . In most cases, academic results are usually mixed at best, with increases in student performances in some areas . . . and decreases in student performance in other areas" (Education Commission of the States, 2004).

In the many cases where states displaced the local school authorities and appointed outsiders to implement reform, there is just very little evidence that any state is capable of achieving the vast transformations and rapid progress for all subgroups required by NCLB (Hunter, 1997; Mathews, 2000; Strauss & Loeb, 1998; Weizel, 1997; Wyatt, 2000). With NCLB, Congress was requiring changes no state had been able to accomplish with its own takeovers, even though they involved far fewer schools and districts than those facing sanctions under NCLB. The assumption that there were practical remedies in the reach of state agencies had very little empirical grounding.

Not surprisingly, when it came to developing a system of support for school improvement, state efforts were limited at best. Prior to NCLB, most efforts apart from federal school improvement monies for comprehensive school-reform models stemmed from state accountability requirements and were not very effective (Mintrop & Trujillo, 2005; O'Day & Bitter, 2003). These programs were typically characterized by voluntary participation of a limited number of schools. While some included onsite personnel or intervention teams, they were more likely to rely on a school-based improvement planning process and school-improvement plans, comprehensive school-reform models, or external audits of school performance. For example, a California program that was designed as part of the state accountability system to help a limited number of schools that failed to demonstrate significant growth allowed for voluntary participation. In Georgia, districts could request a School Effectiveness Review for a school, but any recommendations coming from this review were left up to the school or district to implement. In Illinois, state officials assigned an Educator in Residence to a poorly performing school, but did not define his or her responsibilities and later abandoned this program. Arizona did not provide school intervention services prior to NCLB.

The low level of federal investment in state school improvement under NCLB limited what states could do to compliance and monitoring activities and forced states to prioritize which schools or districts would receive support. They could serve only schools already identified for improvement and could do little for schools that were at risk of being identified for improvement. Because of limited federal and state resources, states put the burden for school improvement on districts, relied on regional centers to provide assistance to schools and districts, and made schools central to their own improvement through the school-improvement planning process. Officials cited a lack of available strategies to improve the achievement of English language learners and special education students, the two categories that most often caused a school or district to be identified for improvement, and insufficient time for schools to make improvements under the NCLB timelines as constraints on their ability to help schools.

Most often, state officials filled a management function. According to a California official: "I don't think the state can do it alone. . . I think we can help them identify areas that are of need and make them better consumers of the product that is likely to be the next step. . .and then maybe be a broker using our county office partners and other partners" (personal communication, California Department of Education, February 16, 2005). Since the Illinois State Board of Education (ISBE) did not have the staff to go out and work directly with schools or districts, Regional Educational Service Providers (RESPROS), already under contract with the state, were given primary responsibilities to work with schools and districts. Developing school- and district-improvement plans was a central component to the improvement process, and staff time at the state level was devoted to reading these plans. Georgia developed a regional support team to bring the Regional Education Service Agencies and other entities together to coordinate and collaborate on school-improvement efforts. The state played a management role in coordinating the services a school might receive from different entities in order to avoid duplication or conflict between different types of services. State officials recognized that as districts moved into the corrective action phase of the NCLB sanctions they might have to become more involved, but since they were not there yet, they had not addressed that issue. The very dramatic sanctions in the Act were not yet being used, and a law that was highly regulatory was, so far, being administered largely as data collection and technical assistance functions much more compatible with normal state-local relations.

CONCLUSIONS AND POLICY RECOMMENDATIONS

With a modest and temporary infusion of additional federal aid funds, the most conservative government in generations adopted policies that required levels and kinds of educational gains for every group of students within every school that had never been achieved anywhere. The requirements were set down as nonnegotiable, and major progress was required under deadlines that did not fit what research had shown to be the preconditions and time required for successful reform. The fact that the law attached very strong sanctions and embarrassing publicity about educational failure for not reaching goals deepened the conflict over the law.

Most educational professionals were good soldiers, trying to implement the policies, treating them as possible goals, at least in the early stages, and thinking positively about complying with as many provisions as possible. Most state officials, though they were being asked to play a role that was new and very difficult, perhaps objectively impossible, collected data and released findings of widespread "failure" as defined by NCLB. Some saw the law as a lever to increase their own reach and power in pursuing goals that were congruent with those of NCLB.

This study shows striking good faith at the administrative level but also a striking lack of resources and knowledge to accomplish the extraordinary goals. States focused on the data collection and procedural parts of the law because they were things administrators could actually do, spheres of action that they could actually control. For the most ambitious goals of large-scale drastic educational interventions that produced fast and consistent gains, the law provided few resources and often absurdly small amounts of money and staffing, and the previous experience of the states in dealing with much smaller numbers of schools and districts was usually deeply disappointing. It is not surprising that the administrators put off facing these problems in favor of those they could actually solve.

For states to develop the capacity to implement anything like the NCLB requirements will take more than a massive infusion of resources. It will also require a restructuring of how the state education agencies function and the development of new expertise in areas where state agencies have not operated before, such as the provision of school-improvement support, and which have typically been left to other levels of the education system. But it is far from clear that such a restructuring is appropriate or feasible. In fact, we found that many state officials did not see school intervention as an appropriate role. Since state agencies traditionally rely on regulatory mechanisms to control education, they lack the expertise to effectively intervene in schools and districts and the organizational networks that would facilitate a cooperative relationship between state and local authorities. Rather than require states to take on new responsibilities, it may be better to build on their current roles and develop the infrastructure to improve current functions. Indeed, that is the approach states took when they continued to use conventional approaches to implementing Title I instead of using the new powers they have under the law.

Congress can begin to address the state capacity challenge by providing much-needed oversight to determine if the deadlines, performance targets, and data requirements mandated by NCLB are helping and, if not, to determine what low-performing schools need to improve. At the same time, a serious independent, federally funded analysis of what it takes in administrative and financial resources for states to have a reasonable chance of turning around low-performing schools is needed. This should include considering the role states should play in this effort, the level of resources that are necessary given the number of low-performing schools, the record in states with a history of such interventions, the probability of failure, and the length of time needed for schools to improve and sustain improvement in those cases that have succeeded.

If state intervention in schools is to have any chance of succeeding, additional resources for school improvement are needed. One way to meet this is to give local officials control of the 20 percent set aside targeted for supplemental educational services and transfers, two interventions with little or no research documenting their effectiveness and with obvious implementation problems. Finally, Congress should request a study reflecting the judgment of state and local educators and researchers about an appropriate mix of assessments, sanctions, and rewards and an appropriate time frame that would produce greater gains by schools with weak results.

9

Low-Performing Schools' Programs and State Capacity Requirements

Meeting the NCLB Educational Goals

Heinrich Mintrop

The federal No Child Left Behind (NCLB) Act is an unprecedented national response to the persistent achievement gap between children from poor and ethnic minority backgrounds and white, middle-class children in U.S. public schools. The policy instruments for influencing school performance that the law compels state governments to use, however, are not entirely new. A number of "first-generation" states began experimenting with outcome-based accountability systems some ten years prior to the passage of the federal act. While the federal act imposes some uniformity on the states regarding formal assessment procedures and sanctions, it leaves the definition of educational goals and the actual business of school improvement to the states. Just as they did prior to NCLB, states have opted for different levels of rigor and support for school improvement under the law. Thus, the first-generation accountability systems, with their extended performance history and wide variation, provide a useful "laboratory" from which we can infer important lessons about NCLB implementation (Council of Chief State School Officers [CCSSO], 2003; Education Commission of the States, 2002; Rudo, 2001). For this chapter, data and reports from three smaller states (Kentucky, Maryland, and North Carolina) and two larger ones (California and Texas) are used, in addition to three urban districts (New York, Chicago, and Philadelphia) to understand the scope of low-performing schools' programs and the level of state capacity needed to reach the ambitious NCLB goals (Mintrop & Papazian, 2003; Mintrop & Trujillo, 2006).

In this chapter, I argue the following points:

- Worthwhile goals are the foundation of a good accountability system (Porter & Chester, 2002). The need for capacity building in struggling schools is determined by the system's educational "goal horizon."
- School improvement within an accountability environment remains an enterprise of muddling through, despite new diagnostics and sanctions, and contrary to the idea of "proven" strategies.
- To reach educational goals of at least medium rigor, low-performing schools programs must be sophisticated and intensive.
- Even the most elaborate state programs for low-performing schools to date are not up to the task of successfully reaching NCLB goals. The challenges for state capacity are enormous.

GOAL HORIZONS AND THE NEED FOR SUPPORT

Worthwhile performance demands within outcome-based accountability systems flow from definitions of the good school, and in the context of NCLB, from visions of educating poor children and children of color. There is broad agreement that all children need to learn basic skills (i.e., literacy, numeracy), and for the large number of nonnative speakers, ability to communicate in English. And there is a solid body of research on effective schools and effective instruction (Scheerens & Bosker, 1997; Teddlie & Reynolds, 2000) that has yielded characteristics of schools and instructional programs from which reformers can usefully draw when they design improvement strategies. The problem is that this body of literature has very little to say about more complex goals and schooling processes; and research about the latter is not nearly as unanimous (Creemers, 1994).

While in earlier historical periods, educational values and moral zeal may have been the driving forces of school change, as in the school wars of the sixties (Ravitch, 1974), in the current phase of high-stakes accountability, ideas about *what works* putatively drive educational aims and notions of quality. Many proponents of outcome-based accountability systems, the early designs of the Maryland and Kentucky systems being a case in point, assume that complex educational goals can be reached within this model. And there is a priori no reason why they may not, given proper design. But it seems that, in light of the evidence discussed in this chapter, the specific architecture of NCLB may set us up for a rather limited horizon. One could imagine an accountability system that hones in on the most basic of skills, poses within-easy-reach proficiency targets, puts high pressure on reaching these targets, and measures them with repeatedly used test forms. In all likelihood, we may have designed something that works, probably requiring little investment in capacity building, but do we value it, given the propensity in such a system for test training rather than substantive learning? And so, when we reflect on designs for low-performing schools programs (and states' reform capacities to implement them), we need to persistently ask ourselves, not only if the programs work, but also if we value what they deliver.

Michael Fullan (2003) drew the following lesson from his extensive evaluation of national systemic reform efforts in English schools. He found that in the first years, schools in the system improved remarkably, but noted that this improvement came with a price: on the side of the teachers, serious morale problems, a high degree of program prescriptiveness, and teacher dependency; on the student side, a stagnation of performance once organizational tightening up and improvements on basic skills had been accomplished. In Fullan's language, this is Horizon 1, distinguished from Horizon 2, characterized by reasoning and problem solving. The idea of goal horizons emphasizes that for many schools, Horizon 1, achieving basic proficiency for most students, is a great challenge and a worthy goal to achieve in the future, and it avoids playing one set of goals—basic skills—against another—higher-order thinking.

It is troublesome, however, if a state system as a whole gets stuck on this level. Low-performing schools programs need to encourage schools to move toward Horizon 2, while not losing sight of teaching the basic skills. If we just look at what works within Horizon 1, we have a model that may be workable within the present architecture of NCLB, *given current efforts at school capacity building*: fairly low test rigor, goals pegged to presently available state and teacher capacity, pressure on districts and schools, and consequently fairly light—that is, affordable and manageable—capacity building needs (Peterson & Hess, 2006). The problem with such systems is not that they concentrate schools on Horizon 1 challenges, but that they tend to squelch teacher activities in Horizon 2, particularly when these systems *work well*. And once a system has operated within the confines of Horizon 1 for a while, and educators have internalized the intellectual habits rewarded in such a system, school improvement dynamics cannot simply be switched over into Horizon 2. Thus, the system gets stuck.

By contrast, we have systems that are more ambitious in their performance demands while at the same time producing an intervention burden that seems to make the system *unworkable*. Table 9.1 shows how testing rigor, using the National Assessment of Educational Progress (NAEP) as a common yardstick across state systems, fundamentally structures a state's burden of intervening in low-performing schools.

Table 9.1   Percentage Point Differences Between Students Scoring Proficient on NAEP and State Tests in Relationship to Numbers of Schools in Need of Improvement (2003–2004)

	Reading 4th grade	*Reading 8th grade*	*Math 4th grade*	*Math 8th grade*	*Number of schools*	*Percent of total*
CA	18	8	20	8	1626	~20%
KY	31	23	16	7	130	~12%
TX	58	62	54	47	199	~6%

Figures calculated based on statistics supplied by Education Week, Jan. 6, 2005, pp. 77–78, 80.

States with high testing rigor, such as California, indicated here by a small difference between NAEP and state definitions of proficiency, produce an enormous intervention burden, in combination with challenging demographic conditions. While states with less rigorous tests and more lenient definitions of proficiency in NAEP terms, such as Texas, face a relatively modest challenge. Kentucky is a state with medium testing rigor and, correspondingly, with a medium intervention burden. Thus, if states were to adopt definitions of proficiency close to NAEP, as California did, the result would be a high number of schools in need of improvement.

SCHOOL IMPROVEMENT IN OUTCOME-BASED ACCOUNTABILITY SYSTEMS

School improvement is an intricate business. Whether a school succeeds in improving depends on a host of internal and external factors that come into play. The motivation of the workforce; the strength of interactions among staff; the school's programs for students' cognitive, emotional, and social development; and the implementation of specific improvement strategies are, to a large degree, under the control of schools. The supply of material and human resources; the design of sound policies, regulations, and incentives; the adoption of effective programs; and the provision of technical assistance are to a larger degree externally generated, primarily by districts and states, but also by nongovernmental third-party providers. As these multiple factors interact, embedded in the context of the school's socioeconomic environment, they produce idiosyncratic constellations that make success in school improvement efforts an uncertain and contingent outcome for individual schools.

Outcome-based accountability systems are designed to introduce a greater degree of rationality into school improvement. Most notably, they reduce the number of goals to a few easily measurable achievement targets and set up a streamlined incentive system by adding pressure to reach these targets. Given higher goal clarity and more performance information, they encourage the development and adoption of purportedly robust programs and school restructuring efforts that work. Clear goals, focused pressures, and ready-made programs and interventions seem to simplify the task of school improvement. The record from first-generation accountability systems, however, cautions us not to overestimate these rationality claims.

Sanctions

Pressure and the threat of more severe sanctions were conspicuous features of low-performing schools programs when high-stakes accountability systems first came into existence in the 1990s, and they are a prominent feature in NCLB. Practically all of the sanctions suggested by NCLB had been on the books or had been tried by the first-generation systems examined here (see Mintrop & Trujillo, 2006, for more detailed description and documentation). But these sanctions were very rarely imposed, and their centrality faded over time. Kentucky is a good example. The original language of schools "in decline" and "in crisis" was replaced by schools "in need of assistance" (David, Coe, & Kannapel, 2003). The state-appointed "Distinguished Educators," whose role initially was a combination of technical assistance and probation management, were renamed "Highly Skilled Educators," and they shed their evaluative function (David et al., 2003). Actual imposition of final sanctions has been a negligible feature in Kentucky. In Texas and Maryland, very similar patterns played out (see Mintrop & Trujillo, 2006, for more detailed description and documentation). Reflecting this turn from pressure to support, the California accountability system, designed in 1999, already began with voluntary participation of qualifying schools. Schools selected into the program accepted increased scrutiny and accountability from the state in return for funds usable for capacity building at the site (Mintrop, 2002; O'Day & Bitter, 2003; Posnick-Goodwin, 2003).

Why this turn from pressure to support? Some have suggested that states shrink from the responsibility and political costs that the heavy hand of sanctions entails (Brady, 2003). This is one plausible explanation, but other research suggests that, political costs notwithstanding, the pressure strategy is not as promising a motivation strategy as perhaps originally perceived (Consortium for Policy Research in Education [CPRE], 2001; Elmore, 2006; Malen, Croninger, Muncey, & Jones, 2002; Mintrop, 2003, 2004). This is so for a number of reasons. Increasing pressure on schools that do not have the baseline capacity to meet performance goals is not motivating; rather, it further fragments already precarious organizations.

Sanctions turn off high-performing teachers that are present in most low-performing schools. And lastly sanctions, widely seen as unfair for schools that educate poor children, violate the professional norms, values, and expectations of many teachers.

Thus, in their majority, first generation states have either rarely used, or turned away from, high pressure as a main lever to motivate teachers. Instead, they came to emphasize mild pressure. By contrast, under NCLB, pressure as an improvement strategy is a central feature, and schools may face severe sanctions in a rather short time. If experiences of the first-generation accountability systems are any indication, system designers are advised not to rely too much on the power of pressures and sanctions to bring about needed improvements.

Proven Strategies

School improvement would indeed be rather simple if it merely was about matching an identified performance problem with a proven strategy implemented by willing educators. The record from first-generation systems speaks otherwise. A number of strategies, envisaged by the law, have been tried for corrective action and school redesign within first-generation accountability systems. They seemed to have worked in some contexts, but not in others (Brady, 2003), confirming the contingent nature of school improvement even within the context of stringent accountability systems. I will briefly summarize findings on the most commonly used strategies (see Mintrop & Trujillo, 2006, for more detail).

Reconstitution. In Maryland, some local reconstitutions actually exacerbated schools' capacity problems, reduced schools' social stability, and did not lead to the hoped for improvements, although a number of schools also benefited from the fresh start (Malen et al., 2002). Results from reconstitutions in Chicago (Hess, 2003) and in New York's "Schools Under Registration Review" (SURR) program, were inconclusive as well (Brady, 2003; New York Education State Department [NYSED], 2003).

Educational management organizations. School take-over by educational management organizations (EMOs) has worked in some cases, but not in others, as examples from Baltimore and Philadelphia suggest. In Philadelphia, a high number of schools have been taken over. Preliminary data, at the time of this research, suggest that management company takeovers have helped in some cases, but the results are not universally positive (Blanc, 2003; Bracey, 2002; Molnar, 2005; Travers, 2003; Useem, 2005).

External partners. This feature, where each school on probation was assigned an external partner, was widely used in Chicago (Hess, 2003). Originally, external partners developed their own models of intervention, but disparities in the quality of services concerned the district. (O'Day & Finnigan, 2003). An inherent problem in external partner—as well as diverse provider—models is the lack of focus on state or district goals and the uneven quality of consultant services (Blanc, 2003; Murphy & Datnow, 2002).

Charters. While the research base on charter schools is expanding, little is known about charter school conversion as a means of corrective action and school redesign (Bulkley & Wohlstetter, 2003). Available data seem to suggest that converting district-administered schools into charter schools has had uneven results (Brown Center, 2003). Charter schools also tend to show up on states' lists of failing schools in larger proportions than regular public schools. Anecdotal evidence collected through interviews from Philadelphia suggests that charter school conversion without the benefit of an external provider model may be the least successful conversion of the ones tried there.

District takeovers. State takeovers of entire districts have also produced uneven outcomes. Financial management is often cited as the most promising area for potential success by states (Garland, 2003). However, equally dramatic *academic* success has been much harder to achieve (Ziebarth, 2002). Academic gains have been mixed at best, most often occurring only after multiple years of intervention (Garland, 2003).

Intervention teams. These teams enter schools as authoritative interveners. They are charged to evaluate schools, prescribe remedies, and help with implementation. In North Carolina, these teams were said to be rather successful; in California, they worked with mixed success, encountering much resistance at the school level (Ladd & Zelli, 2001; see also Mintrop & Trujillo, 2006, for more details).

In summary, a variety of corrective action strategies have been tried by the examined systems, but none stick out as universally effective or robust enough to overcome the power of local context. Competence of provider personnel, intervention designs, political power of actors in the system, and district and site organizational capacity to absorb the strategies all strongly influence how a particular strategy will turn out. Thus, first-generation accountability systems demonstrate, firstly, that creating motivation through pressure is not as powerful an option on the ground as it might appear in the language of the law, and secondly, that robust and universally effective interventions are hard to come by. School improvement, even under conditions of stringent accountability, is (and remains) far more complex than matching an identified performance problem with a proven strategy implemented by willing educators. As a consequence, states are advised to design low-performing schools programs that are professionally sophisticated enough to address the complexity and contingent nature of the task.

THE NEED FOR CAPACITY BUILDING

By looking at variations among first-generation systems across states, we gain a better understanding of the requirements for capacity building. In two of the four states examined here, Maryland and Texas, capacity building was not a prominent feature of the low-performing schools programs; in two others, California and Kentucky, it was.

Maryland. The Maryland system in the 1990s, a system that operated, using Fullan's (2003) terminology, in Horizon 2, created the toughest challenge. The system targeted extremely hard cases in decline, demanded that schools adjust to highly complex assessments (which fewer than half the state's student population managed to pass with satisfaction), and set the exit criteria for its low-performing schools program very high. The state did not develop an elaborate capacity building structure. State monitors were the eyes and ears of the state, but their role in internal school improvement efforts was minimal. Very few low-performing schools managed to exit the program; and indeed, schools statewide stagnated until the system was abandoned. In the Maryland case, state performance demands, pegged to goal Horizon 2, were decoupled from existing capacities; and with a lack of compensatory capacity building, pressures became ineffective or counterproductive (Mintrop, 2004).

Texas. Texas took an approach that contrasted with that of Maryland in testing rigor, but exhibited similarities regarding capacity building. Operating within Horizon 1, the state pegged performance demands at levels that challenged schools in the bottom 20 to 40 percent of the performance distribution with cognitively simple tests. The state has a decentralized form of governing schools and did not take a strong leadership role in providing support to ailing schools, relative to more intensive efforts in other states (Ferguson, 2000). Apart from peer review teams that received very limited training, the state organized educational support centers that offered their services to low-performing schools and districts, but not exclusively so. The state, however, had strong mechanisms built into its accountability system that directly identified low-performing districts and threatened them with further sanctions. Given that performance demands were more closely pegged to existing teacher capacities, the state could bank on a pressure strategy that succeeded by motivating schools to raise test scores while keeping the need for state support relatively limited. Scores on the state tests rose, and low-performing schools exited the program in large numbers.

California. As we saw earlier, California's rigorous performance demands, relative to NAEP definitions, coupled with challenging student demographics, led to a burgeoning number of schools identified as low-performing that experienced mild accountability pressures. For capacity building, the state banked on a massive disbursement of grants attached to a very loosely constructed oversight structure (Mintrop, 2002). Not all schools that could have received these grants did so. The state selected schools according to priority and by chance.

Identified schools had to contract with an external evaluator who was chosen from a state-approved list. Educational reform projects, consultants, county offices of education, and later, even district offices themselves could apply to this list. Training in evaluation was not provided. The state, however, did require vendors to reapply to the list showing evidence of success. To receive grant money, schools were to write a school improvement plan that was, however, kept on file locally. Thus, in the California case, the state department kept a low profile. It relied primarily on grant making at a magnitude far greater than most other states we examined, on the capacity of local vendors, the willingness of local districts, and the wisdom of schools to spend the money wisely. A management structure that could ensure quality of the support system was only weakly developed. Reports showed that schools' responses to the program varied widely and depended on the varying quality of external evaluators (California Department of Education [CDE], 2001; Goe, 2001). A systematic evaluation of the program (O'Day & Bitter, 2003) did not show significant program effects. Qualitative data suggest that the schools lacked sustained quality support. The number of low-performing schools in the program remained high.

Kentucky. Of the state programs we surveyed, Kentucky used a fairly elaborate system that provided oversight and support to schools under direct supervision from the state department. Services were sustained over one school year or longer, and were specifically targeted to low-performing schools achieving state goals. As part of the state's support for its schools "in need of assistance," Kentucky provided modest additional school improvement funds. A school inspection was conducted by state-sponsored Scholastic Audit Teams (Kentucky Department of Education [KDE], 2000a, 2000b). The audit teams were trained for their task and they visited each school for about a week. Once the scholastic audit was conducted, schools used the results to write their school improvement plans.

Highly skilled educators (HSEs) were assigned to assist low-performing schools. HSEs had to demonstrate prior ability to bring about high levels of student performance and went through a rigorous hiring and training process. Each HSE received two weeks of training and follow-up training at quarterly meetings. Mentors from the state department provided HSEs with assistance in problem solving and support. HSEs were expected to serve on-site at least 80 percent of their work time. Their activities included, but were not limited to, staff development, classroom observations of instruction, demonstration lessons, grants writing, tutoring, and creation of model lessons (David et al., 2003; Holdzkom, 2001). In addition, a team of HSEs that specialized in organizational management was formed and could be assigned to more than one school at a time, given the needs of particular schools. In the 2002–2003 school year, fifty-two HSEs worked with thirty very low-performing schools and provided support to others on a voluntary basis. The program succeeded in exiting most of the schools. Significant challenges for the program were sustaining the change once HSEs had left school grounds, creating an appropriate match between the HSE and the school, and maintaining a strong pool of HSEs (David et al., 2003; Kannapel & Coe, 2000).

We can infer from the comparison across states that the need for strong state support grows in proportion to performance demands. Programs can be successful without intensive capacity building for struggling schools as long as they operate within a low goal horizon. But as soon as goals move beyond the most basic of skills, the lack of capacity building seems to bode ill for success. California's program disbursed generous grants for capacity building, and its decentralized structure made it adaptable to local conditions, but it lacked a management structure at the state level that was strong enough to assure quality of services and focus. Its effect dissipated. Programs such as the one in Kentucky (see also North Carolina in Mintrop & Trujillo, 2006), which coupled rigor with focused, intense, and comprehensive support, were fairly successful (as indicated by schools exiting the program). Kentucky's program stresses support over sanctions, supervises this support centrally, and manages recruitment and training of personnel and quality control of services. Services are geared toward the comprehensive reform of schools with a focus on the state's programmatic mandates and performance goals. But at the same time, on-site support providers are sophisticated enough to flexibly adapt their intervention to individual school needs, though curriculum and instructional alignment are key points of intervention.

The necessity for comprehensive support is underscored by New York's Chancellors District, now defunct. This effort, emulated by other inner-city districts, consisted of the following elements (Phenix, Siegel, Zaltsman, & Fruchter, 2005; Snipes, Doolittle, & Herlihy, 2002):

- Reduced class size.
- Extended school day, school year, and afterschool program.
- Prescribed instructional program, schedule, and curriculum; supervisory and instructional support; more intense monitoring and mentoring.
- Professional development: a minimum of four on-site staff developers and a teacher specialist assigned to each school.
- Restaffing and replacement of most principals and many ineffective teachers; incentives for recruiting qualified teachers (e.g., signing bonuses).

However, even with this intense intervention, data suggest that Chancellor's District schools achieved only modest improvement in student performance; only half of the enrolled schools were removed from the state list of low-performing schools; and one-fifth had to be closed (Phenix et al., 2005). This sobering result highlights the pervasive need for capacity building in the most challenging educational environments.

NCLB GOALS AND PROGRAM SCALE

The goals of NCLB are ambitious and commendable: all students should reach rigorous proficiency levels within a fairly short time frame. Rigorous definitions of proficiency—for example, by using NAEP criteria—would push states' performance demands well into goal Horizon 2 and would in all likelihood create a huge intervention burden. The California system with a proficiency definition fairly close to NAEP and an intervention burden of one-fifth to one-quarter of all schools would be a likely scenario for the country as a whole (or at least for states with similarly large numbers of poor and immigrant students). That this scenario has not become reality is due to the fact that many states eschew these high standards and the specter of unmanageable loads of troubled schools in need of support and, at some point, requiring sanctions.

Echoing this concern, first-generation accountability systems typically kept their programs on a manageable scale or downscaled them over time. In Maryland, a state with a relatively large program, the state department limited the burden by capping the number of schools at around one hundred (about 7 percent of all schools), although many more schools could have qualified according to the state's criteria. Texas kept the intervention burden even smaller. In 1995 the system identified 267 low-performing schools. The numbers dropped to 59 in 1998, and rose again, continuously, to 150 in 2002 (Texas Education Agency [TEA], 2002). The thresholds for entrance and exit had risen in the meantime, but the state department saw to it that state capacity was not overwhelmed. With these numbers, the program fluctuated in the 2 to 4 percent range of the total number of schools in the state. The Kentucky program started out with 250 schools, or about 20 percent of all schools. But these numbers were swiftly curtailed (Cibulka & Lindle, 2001). In the 2002 accountability cycle, the state identified merely 90 schools as low-performing, or about 7.5 percent of the total (KDE, 2000b). Only one-third of those were required to accept state intervention, which, in Kentucky's case, as we saw, was intensive.

If the record of first-generation systems is any indication, it seems that over time, state intervention burdens leveled off at around to 2 to 4 percent of the total number of schools. Even in California, with large numbers of identified schools, the state severely curtailed the number of schools that received grant money from the state. Moreover, with educational goals of

at least medium rigor, even a small intervention burden requires a sophisticated, intensive, and comprehensive capacity building effort. But even
comprehensive approaches, as we saw in the case of the special district in
New York City, are sometimes hard-pressed to overcome performance
barriers that exist in the highest need and lowest capacity schools and
districts.

One can infer from the records of the most developed first-generation
accountability efforts that a strategy of realistically meeting the ambitious
NCLB goals—that is, closing the achievement gap based on rigorous educational goals in a fairly short time period—would require states to adopt
programs for low-performing schools on an unprecedented scale and with
an intensity, focus, and comprehensiveness of capacity building that has
heretofore only been tried for relatively small numbers of schools. The alternative would be either a capping of the number of identified schools tai-
lored to available state capacity—a strategy that a number of states
pursued, but is no longer an option under NCLB—or a downscaling of performance demands while increasing pressure, with the danger of confining
schools to a low goal horizon.

IMPLICATIONS FOR NCLB REDESIGN

Growth Goals and Design Competition

The purpose of this chapter is to gauge the scope of low-performing
schools programs and the level of state capacity needed to reach ambitious
NCLB goals. I draw my conclusions from the literature on low-performing
schools and especially from the successes and shortfalls of first-generation
accountability systems that preceded NCLB by up to a decade. I was
guided by the conviction that we need to design systems that work, but at
the same time, that deliver on educational goals we value. An accountability system that emphasizes basic skills, poses within-easy-reach performance targets (i.e., within the margins of available educator capacity), and
uses high pressure to reach these targets may "work" without expanding
investments in school and state capacity. But if such systems constrain the
education of poor children within what Fullan (2003) has called goal Horizon 1, do we value these systems enough to advocate for them? On the
other hand, we have looked at systems that have more ambitious goals, but
that suffer from straining intervention burdens and serious overload. Unrealistically ambitious goals relative to schools' available performance capacity and states' support for further capacity building make an
accountability system dysfunctional. In the long run, such a system becomes illegitimate and demotivating.

The current NCLB architecture, with its fixed proficiency targets, fixed
time lines, and automatic sanctions for schools and districts not meeting

these targets, rewards Horizon 1 accountability systems and punishes Horizon 2 systems with strain, delegitimation, and the need for unprecedented investments in school capacity that overextend the fiscal resources of even the wealthiest states. We need systems with ambitious performance goals that consistently encourage educators to venture into goal Horizon 2 while meeting expectations in goal Horizon 1 for all students. Setting a fixed proficiency target for all to be reached within a fixed time period is deceivingly simple, but will not get us there. Instead, it will encourage the design of systems that cage schools within Horizon 1. We need an NCLB design, instead, that establishes continuous growth in absolute performance and in closing the achievement gap with ever-increasing rigor based on the real improvement capacities of state systems. The strains experienced in the more ambitious systems (e.g., California, Maryland in the 1990s) show that most states could not get to NAEP-like rigor overnight and would need to take intermediate steps.

Toward this end, growth goals for each state ought to be pegged to real growth achieved by a sizable number of demographically similar, high-performing, Title I schools in a given state. As a consequence, lower-performing schools have realistic goals to aim for and models to emulate, and system overload is avoided. Rather than wrestling with states on compliance issues, the federal government should set up system design competitions among states that encourage states to continuously upgrade their performance expectations as new capacities are opening up. These design competitions should be facilitated by an independent and authoritative nonpartisan commission or nongovernmental agency that monitors state progress based on multiple indicators: differential growth on state tests and NAEP for various levels of cognitive complexity, completion rates, years-to-completion, and so forth. The agency's effort ought to be supported by independent researchers who are recognized in their field as specialists. Monitoring of multiple data should result in yearly ratings of states' progress. Exceptionally strong designs are then publicly and authoritatively recognized. Thus, states have a strong incentive to learn from powerful designs, and schools operate within accountability systems that are ambitious, but at the same time, are realistic and functioning.

Treatment Flexibility

As soon as we move into the realm of at least medium-rigor systems, such as the one in Kentucky, severe sanctions do not work as a fallback solution, and fresh-start measures heighten the need for sophisticated support that is sensitive to contextual conditions and flexible enough to respond to idiosyncratic constellations of internal and external factors, mentioned earlier, that make school improvement such an uncertain process. Overreliance on sanctions leads to undesirable distortions, such as restrictive goals within Horizon 1, a narrowing of taught curriculum to measured indicators, and a focus on students with the greatest statistical weights. In many instances, unduly high pressure leads to hasty quick fixes, to the implementation of context-insensitive "solutions," and to organizational fragmentation rather than organizational health. Inflexible staging and limited intervention menus lead to unproductive turbulence, rather than a fresh start and sustainable renewal. In order to avoid this situation, the law should stipulate that districts develop, based on state growth goals, a growth plan for each identified low-performing school. In this plan, schools and districts commit to realistic and complex goals and multiyear programmatic improvement.

Districts hold schools accountable to this plan through regular lines of authority. States give advice on, approve, and monitor individual school plans or districtwide improvement plans. The latter applies if high numbers of schools in a given district are identified as low performing. In a first round, schools are *identified* as low performing if they fail to meet state growth goals. In a second round, multiple performance and process indicators are taken into consideration when states *classify* schools as low performing. State audits that can assess a school's organizational health with sophisticated professional judgment intervene between identification and classification. Such audits help the accountability system to become better anchored in educators' sense of system fairness and validity. For the district, reaching state performance goals is high-stakes, involving increasing state oversight and loss of governance autonomy. Districts, in cooperation with state agencies, decide what mixture of pressure, sanctions, corrective action, or support they want to exert on their low-performing schools, depending on local conditions and available alternative resources.

Support Structures

Some of the most vigorous and stringent pre-NCLB accountability systems restricted their intervention load to about 5 percent of the total number of schools after an initial "high-flying" phase. And even this relatively reduced scale required focused, intensive, and comprehensive support for struggling schools, the scope of which grew with increasing educational rigor of the system. Reaching performance goals of at least medium rigor in all schools hinges on sizable state support for low-performing schools and districts. Given the enormous variation in states' size, political culture, administrative structure, degree of centralization, and educational reform history, it does not make sense to mandate a specific program design for all states. States used various designs to meet schools' needs. Small states organized a more centralized effort of support provision, while larger states relied either on regional centers or on third-party providers. But independent of size, performance demands of at least medium rigor require elaborate capacity building structures. Whether support and oversight is provided directly by the state or through third-party consultants, low-performing schools programs need a management structure that allows for careful recruitment and quality control of service providers. This entails the expansion of states' administrative capacity.

What I have tried to show is that what is needed in terms of programs for low-performing schools all depends on the goals, or goal horizon, a system strives for. As to systems with more ambitious goals (California, Maryland, and Kentucky), we saw that California's approach of loosely granting money and leaving assistance largely to a market of providers is not very promising, nor is the (old) Maryland approach of foregoing a capacity building strategy. Judging from the systems I have surveyed in this chapter, the approach advanced in Kentucky holds more promise. But since we do not have a common metric across these states that would enable direct connections between design features and outcomes, we have to hedge our judgment.

First-generation attempts have shown that the task of continuous school improvement requires states and districts to "move on all fronts" and go beyond incentives and sanctions. Even generous additional grants for capacity building are not sufficient. The enormity of the task requires the federal government, states, districts, and schools to search for powerful, high-quality, and comprehensive methods of reform and institution rebuilding. Alternatively, states could reduce testing rigor or keep rigor down; and we could be faced with the undesirable trade-off between the ends of achieving basic literacy and numeracy by means of severely curtailing the spectrum of educational goals. In Lauren Resnick's words in a presentation at the American Educational Research Association in 2006, we would have succeeded in creating a twenty-first-century accountability system that delivers on a nineteenth-century model of learning.

PART IV

10

Improving High Schools and the Role of NCLB

Linda Darling-Hammond

Civil rights advocates hailed the 2001 reauthorization of the Elementary and Secondary Education Act (ESEA), optimistically entitled No Child Left Behind (NCLB), as a step forward in the long battle to improve education for those children traditionally left behind in American schools—in particular, students of color and those living in poverty, new English learners, and students with disabilities. The broad goal of NCLB is to raise the achievement levels of all students and to close the achievement gap that parallels race and class. The act intends to do this by focusing schools' attention on improving test scores for all groups of students, providing more educational choices, and ensuring better qualified teachers. This chapter looks at how NCLB supports or undermines the current national movement to reform high schools—a movement that advances similar goals but approaches them from a different perspective. The chapter also proposes specific amendments to the act that could help to achieve the goals of high-quality, equitable education for all youth.

This chapter is adapted from my 2006 article, No Child Left Behind and high school reform. *Harvard Educational Review*, 76, 642–667.

THE NEED FOR HIGH-SCHOOL REFORM

Of all the ways in which urban schoolchildren are being left behind, their experiences in large, factory-model high schools are, arguably, the most egregious. In fact, in many such schools, young people are not only left behind but also actively thrown overboard. In urban areas, dropout rates from large comprehensive high schools are typically 50 percent or more. These schools are structured as huge warehouses, often housing three thousand or more students in an organization focused more on the control of behavior than the development of community. With a locker as their only stable point of contact, a schedule that cycles them through a series of seven or more overloaded teachers, and a counselor struggling to serve the "personal" needs of several hundred students, teenagers struggling to find connections have little to connect to. Heavily stratified within, and substantially dehumanized throughout, most students experience such high schools as uncaring or even adversarial environments—where "getting over" becomes important when "getting known" is impossible. For adults, the capacity to be accountable for the learning of 150 to 200 students daily—students whom they do not share with other teachers—is substantially constrained by the factory-model structure that gives them little control over or connection to most of what happens to the students they see only briefly.

For more than forty years, large urban high schools have been critiqued for their impersonal structures, their fragmented curricula, their segregated and unequal program options, and their inabilities to respond effectively to student needs (Barker & Gump, 1964; Goodlad, 1984; Lee, Bryk, & Smith, 1993). A number of recent studies have found that, other things being equal, smaller schools appear to produce higher achievement, lower dropout rates, lower rates of violence and vandalism, more positive feelings about self and school, and more participation in school activities (Darling-Hammond, Ross, & Milliken, in press). These outcomes are more pronounced for students who are traditionally lower achieving (Lee & Smith, 1993, 1995).

A number of small urban schools serving high-need students have experienced striking success, graduating more than 90 percent of their students and sending equal shares to college (Darling-Hammond, et al., in press). School size is not the only thing that makes a difference, however. A number of studies have found that, all else equal, schools have higher graduation rates and stronger achievement when they create small, personalized units in which students see a smaller number of teachers over a longer period of time (Gottfredson & Daiger, 1979; Lee, et al., 1993). Researchers suggest that in such "communitarian" schools, students are better known, and faculty develop a collective perspective about their work.

In response to these kinds of findings, major reforms of comprehensive high schools are underway in many cities, in part with the assistance of the federal government through the Small Schools Act and charter-school development funds and with the help of a number of philanthropists. NCLB has a complex relationship with these reforms, both helping and hindering the efforts that are underway to remake the most dysfunctional element of the American schooling system.

ELEMENTS OF HIGH-PERFORMING URBAN HIGH SCHOOLS

Not all small schools are equally successful. Those that have implemented fewer personalizing features and less intensive instructional changes have produced fewer benefits (Darling-Hammond, et al., in press). More effective schools have instituted important changes in organization and instruction. In addition to smaller learning communities where students are well known, research suggests that at least the following elements are critical:

1. *Personalization* achieved through teams of teachers working with shared groups of students—usually numbering no more than eighty and sometimes over multiple years—and through "advisories" in which each teacher takes responsibility for about fifteen students for whom he or she serves as advocate, counselor, and primary family contact. These smaller pupil loads are achieved, in part, through offering longer block classes, some of them interdisciplinary (e.g., humanities courses that combine English and social studies), which allow teachers to teach fewer students for longer blocks of time.

2. *Well-qualified teachers* supported by ongoing peer collaboration and professional development. Successful schools have teachers who have solid academic backgrounds and are well prepared for teaching, who have skills for teaching students with special needs, English language learners (ELLs), and the wide range of other students they encounter (Darling-Hammond, 2000). Furthermore, these teachers create strong, coherent curriculum by having time in their schedules to plan together around subject matter and students and to pursue ongoing professional development.

3. *A common core curriculum organized around performance-based assessment*, which engages students with intellectually challenging work that resembles what they will do outside of school. Most highly effective urban schools require students to complete portfolios and performance tasks in which they conduct research; design science experiments; amass and analyze evidence; apply math skills to real-world problems in engineering, physics, or topography; and demonstrate competence in writing and the arts. Students revise their work in response to feedback guided by standards, and they

defend their work before committees of teachers and external judges, much like a dissertation.

4. *Supports for struggling students.* Students are not tracked in these schools, but are supported in a variety of ways to meet the demands of an intellectually engaging and challenging curriculum. Teachers use a wide repertoire of instructional strategies to adapt to students' needs. Schools offer afterschool and Saturday tutoring for all students who need additional help, integrating supplementary supports into the core curriculum, rather than offering disconnected services that fragment, rather than concentrate, effort. They also use special education models that "push-in" expert teachers to assist in the core classroom and provide resource room supports to help students complete the same challenging work that other students are assigned, rather than "pull-out" classrooms where students are kept busy with workbooks and lower level tasks.

These practices are not only found in case studies tracking small groups of schools, but also in large-scale studies finding higher and more equal achievement in restructured schools that create smaller units, form teaching teams with common planning time, keep students together with teachers over multiple years, involve staff and parents in decisions, and foster cooperative learning (Lee & Smith, 1995). Higher achievement on both traditional tests and complex performance tasks is also found in schools and classrooms where students experience "authentic instruction" calling for higher order thinking, consideration of alternatives, extended writing, and performance assessments that provide an audience for student work (Newmann, Marks, & Gamoran, 1996; Lee, Smith, & Croninger, 1995).

HIGH-SCHOOL REFORM AND NO CHILD LEFT BEHIND

The efforts of NCLB to support more equitable education have leveraged attention to the relative success of students of color and low-income students who have traditionally been poorly served by comprehensive high schools. This spotlight has been useful to focus attention on inequalities not only in the cities, but also in suburban and rural communities where deeply entrenched tracking systems relegate most "minority" students who attend "integrated" schools to the lower tracks where they often receive less challenging and lower-quality instruction from less well-qualified teachers.

At the same time, the complicated rules that have accompanied NCLB have unintentionally made it more difficult for many heroic schools in low-income neighborhoods to do their work well and to keep the neediest students in school and moving toward productive futures. Some key elements of redesigned high schools that are associated with greater success for high-need students are not reinforced by the law, in part because NCLB was not conceptualized with new model schools in mind. Many of its provisions implicitly assume high schools will continue to operate as they have in the past—for example, with departmental structures, which contribute to a fragmented experience for students and a large pupil load for teachers, and with standardized tests that are easily scored but do not represent the kinds of thinking and performance skills students actually need to succeed at work and in higher education. These assumptions have led to incentives in the law that undermine the ability of successful, redesigned schools to offer more personalized, interdisciplinary instruction and to organize teaching and learning around intellectually ambitious performance assessments.

In addition, although the law's rhetoric about highly qualified teachers and adequate yearly progress (AYP) in student achievement sets important goals, the legislation lacks resources and incentives for developing and recruiting high-quality teachers for urban schools, and it lacks incentives for keeping struggling students in high school. Indeed, it punishes schools that enroll the neediest students and keep them in school, while rewarding schools that select them out. Addressing these unintended negative consequences as well as the disjunctures between the law and useful high-school reforms requires particular attention to two major areas of NCLB:

- the definition and development of "highly qualified teachers," and
- the design of testing and accountability regulations.

Each of these areas is described now, followed by recommendations for amendments that will enable more high schools to leave fewer children behind.

ENSURING HIGHLY QUALIFIED TEACHERS

One of the most important aspects of NCLB is that it requires all schools to provide highly qualified teachers who are fully certified and show competence in the subject areas they teach to all students. This requirement is intended to correct the longstanding problem that schools serving our neediest students typically have the least experienced and least qualified teachers, even though such students need our most skilled teachers. And it is a problem that can be solved. What often looks like a teacher shortage is actually mostly a problem of getting teachers from where they are trained to where they are needed and keeping teachers in the profession, especially in central cities and poor rural areas. About one-third of beginners leave teaching within five years, and those with the least preparation and the least access to mentoring leave soonest (Darling-Hammond & Sykes, 2003).

In low-income schools suffering from even higher turnover rates, producing more teachers—especially through fast-track routes that tend to have high attrition—is like filling a leaky bucket rather than fixing it. Yet, NCLB also encourages the creation of alternative certification pathways—some of which skirt key elements of teacher learning—and allows teachers to be deemed "highly qualified" as soon as they enter such programs, rather than when they complete them and demonstrate they are competent. Perversely, on the other hand, many well-prepared teachers are deemed *not* highly qualified because they teach in multiple subject areas and have not completed a major or passed a test in each. The interdisciplinary teaching that is central to many successfully redesigned high schools is jeopardized by the current administration of the law.

NCLB's emphasis on highly qualified teachers has been generally productive—and many states are investing in the preparation and recruitment incentives needed to produce better-prepared teachers and distribute them where they are needed. Initiatives have included precollege recruitment programs, subsidies for preparation, and even pay incentives for teaching in high-need schools. However, these efforts have not always solved shortages in the most hard-to-staff urban and rural schools, particularly high schools. Such solutions will require more aggressive measures to improve working conditions in these schools and more systemic reforms of inadequate school-funding systems that will, in turn, enable more competitive and equitable salaries across districts. Meanwhile, some states have unfortunately spent more energy seeking to avoid the law's intentions—for example, by defining even teachers on emergency permits as highly qualified—than actively pursuing the Act's goals. Consequently, poor and minority students are still disproportionately taught by under-qualified teachers (Darling-Hammond & Sykes, 2003).

Although NCLB specifies that states report what they are doing and the progress they are making toward ensuring that poor and minority students are not taught by unqualified, inexperienced, or "out of field" teachers at higher rates, the requirement for equitable access to well prepared teachers has not been a focus of federal enforcement. Thus, the first area for attention is teacher quality. The law should provide the subsidies and incentives needed to attract well qualified teachers to urban schools, while not defining teacher quality so narrowly as to impede restructuring of the curriculum that supports engaging and personalized instruction.

1. The federal government should enforce the equity provisions of NCLB to reduce disparities in access to qualified teachers for students of color and low-income students. One of the great ironies of federal education programs designed to support the education of students with greater needs is that poor schools have often served these students with unqualified teachers and untrained aides, rather than the highly skilled teachers envisioned by federal laws. An additional irony of NCLB's administration is that federal attention to student test scores has not been matched by attention to the equitable provision of qualified teachers. The Department of Education should require states to report on their progress in closing the teaching gap as well as the achievement gap among schools serving different groups of students, and to develop plans that will increase the provision of truly qualified teachers to students in high-poverty schools. States and districts should publish a teacher quality index alongside their accountability reports, evaluating progress toward providing qualified teachers to students in different kinds of schools.

2. The law should allow states to develop appropriate standards for teachers who teach multiple subjects or interdisciplinary courses. These kinds of courses are a necessity in many small schools and districts and an advantage in reforming secondary schools. The act currently requires a major, or passage of a subject-matter test, in each subject taught, in addition to full certification. While this seems straightforward, it turns out to be highly problematic in small schools in remote rural areas (where a single teacher may teach every grade level and subject area) and in redesigned middle and high schools (where interdisciplinary teaching allows both curriculum integration and smaller pupil loads for teachers, so that they can individualize instruction). Small schools that use block schedules with interdisciplinary configurations—such as humanities courses combining literature with history—can cut pupil load from 150 or more students per teacher to as few as 40 or 50 students per teacher, without additional funding, thus allowing much greater attention to pupil learning (Darling-Hammond, Ancess, & Ort, 2002).

Many states have developed sensible certification laws for handling these kinds of real-world situations in ways that evaluate subject-matter knowledge and teaching skills appropriately, and some have developed certification rules that specifically take into account interdisciplinary or multidisciplinary teaching. Current steps to increase flexibility in this regard have postponed but not resolved these concerns for rural schools, and have not addressed the issue for small urban high schools that have been redesigned to personalize and integrate instruction. The federal government should delegate to states the ascertainment of subject-matter competence for teachers who teach multiple subjects through their certification systems, rather than trying to specify from Washington the only means for teachers to meet the intent of the law.

3. The act should ensure that teachers are not labeled "highly qualified" until they have completed preparation and mastered essential teaching skills. While the NCLB is overly prescriptive regarding how subject-matter knowledge is to be demonstrated, it has simultaneously promoted alternative certification programs that allow individuals to be deemed "highly qualified" the moment they *enter* a program rather than when they have finished training and demonstrated their competence. While some excellent alternative certification programs have been constructed, the range of program quality is extremely wide. Many programs do not provide student teaching or coursework in essential areas like student learning and development, subject-matter-teaching methods, or the teaching of special needs students, all of which are associated with greater teacher effectiveness (Darling-Hammond & Bransford, 2005). Furthermore, many programs place candidates in classrooms as teachers of record after a few weeks of summer training and long before they have encountered much of the coursework the program offers. Promised mentoring does not always appear. This happens almost exclusively in high-need schools serving the most disadvantaged students.

For these reasons, candidates in many alternative routes are less effective in their initial years of teaching than those who enter having completed their preparation, and they have higher attrition rates (Boyd, Grossman, Lankford, Loeb, & Wyckoff, 2006; Darling-Hammond, Holtzman, Gatlin, & Heilig, 2005). Candidates who do not receive student teaching or critical coursework are twice as likely to leave teaching after the first year, adding to the instability that plagues high-need schools. Typically, this attrition is greatest in low-income secondary schools.

When prospective teachers experience programs that do not prepare them to succeed, they flounder and feel inadequate, often leaving in despair rather than continuing in the profession. Although NCLB regulations require alternative routes to meet specific standards, few states enforce the standards. This disadvantages all schools that hire such teachers, and the students they serve. If states can fool the public into believing that they are using highly qualified teachers when they are not, this also reduces pressures for them to put in place the necessary incentives to recruit truly prepared teachers, thus leaving schools with insufficient supports to solve their staffing problems.

NCLB should recognize teachers as "highly qualified" only when they have *completed* preparation, and should require that alternative programs, like others, meet standards of quality. In addition, as described below, greater incentives are needed to develop high-quality preparation programs that prepare teachers in high-need communities and to subsidize candidates so that they can afford to take the time they need to be well prepared.

4. Greater federal supports and incentives are needed to recruit and prepare highly qualified teachers and to distribute them to the schools where they are most needed. Schools in the United States should not have to experience teacher shortages, as there are actually many more credentialed teachers than there are jobs, and many states and districts have surpluses (Darling-Hammond & Sykes, 2003). Not surprisingly, though, teachers are less likely to enter or stay in schools with poor salaries and working conditions. They are also more likely to leave if they have not had preparation, and if they do not receive mentoring in their early years on the job. These problems can be solved. States and districts that have increased and equalized salaries, created strong preparation programs so that teachers are effective with their students, and provided mentors have shown how we can fill classrooms with well-prepared teachers (Darling-Hammond & Sykes, 2003).

But solving this problem everywhere requires a national agenda. The distributional inequities that lead to the hiring of unqualified teachers are caused by disparities in pay and working conditions, inadequate recruitment incentives to distribute teachers appropriately, and fiscal conditions that produce incentives for hiring the least expensive rather than the most qualified teachers. At the same time, some specific teaching fields experience real shortages. These include teachers for children with disabilities and those with limited English proficiency (LEP) as well as teachers of science and mathematics. Boosting supply in the fields where there are real shortfalls requires targeted recruitment and investment in the capacity of preparation institutions to expand their programs to meet national needs.

While NCLB sets an expectation for hiring qualified teachers, it does not yet include the policy support to make this possible. In other high-achieving nations, teachers receive a much more extensive preparation (usually one to three years of graduate-level teacher education) entirely at government expense (Darling-Hammond, 2005). Schools that hire beginners are given extra veteran teachers to support intensive mentoring in the first year (Darling-Hammond, 2005). The United States has adopted none of these policies on a wide scale.

The federal government should play a leadership role in providing an adequate supply of well-qualified teachers just as it has in providing an adequate supply of well-qualified physicians for the nation through the Medical Manpower Act and the Health Professions Education Assistance Act. These have supported medical training, teaching hospitals, scholarships and loans to medical students, and incentives for physicians to train in shortage specialties and to locate in underserved areas. Similar federal initiatives in education were effective during the 1960s and 1970s but were eliminated in the 1980s. Federal involvement is essential both because the problems and potential solutions are national in scope and because the federal mission in education—to equalize the educational playing field—requires, more than anything else, systemic solutions to the problems of teacher supply, demand, and quality. We need a federal teacher policy that will:

- *recruit substantial numbers of new teachers* who will teach in high-need fields and locations, through service scholarships that underwrite their preparation;
- *reduce barriers to interstate mobility* by supporting the development of license portability based on a performance assessment of teaching skills, so that teachers can more easily move from places with surpluses to areas with shortages;

- *strengthen teachers' preparation* through incentive grants to improve preparation for teaching diverse students and to create professional development schools, like teaching hospitals, to train prospective teachers in urban areas;
- *improve teacher retention and effectiveness* by ensuring they have mentoring support during the beginning teaching stage when 30 percent of them drop out (Darling-Hammond & Sykes, 2003; National Academy of Education [NAE], 2005).

Of all the problems facing the nation's schools, the problem of teacher supply and quality is one of the most solvable if a purposeful set of initiatives is developed. For the equivalent of one week's combat costs in Iraq, the nation could eliminate teacher shortages and produce a more competent teaching force, providing top-quality preparation for enough new teachers annually to fill all of the vacancies currently filled by underprepared teachers—and mentor all of the new teachers who are hired over the next five years (Darling-Hammond & Sykes, 2003). To ensure that schools can employ highly qualified teachers, this kind of focused initiative is needed.

Fixing Testing and Accountability Provisions

The goals of NCLB are to improve achievement for all students, to enhance equity, and to ensure more qualified teachers. However, its complex regulations for showing AYP toward test score targets aimed at "100 percent proficiency" have created a bizarre situation in which most of the nation's public schools will be deemed failing in the next few years—even many that score high and are steadily improving from year to year. Ironically, states that have set higher standards for themselves will experience greater failures than those with low standards, and many have abandoned assessments that measure critical thinking and performance, just as the labor market increasingly demands these skills.

The accountability provisions of NCLB have been the subject of much analysis and considerable protest. In particular, the AYP metrics were set without an understanding of what they would really mean. Studies suggest that at least 80 percent of schools in most states will have failed to achieve AYP by 2014 (Wiley, Mathis, & Garcia, 2005); and in diverse states like California, 99 percent of schools are expected to "fail" by this date (Packer, 2004).

One fundamental problem is that the act's goals are unrealistic. Using a definition of proficiency benchmarked to the National Assessment of Educational Progress (NAEP), one leading measurement expert has calculated that it would take schools more than 160 years to reach such a target in high school mathematics if they continued the fairly brisk rate of progress they were making during the 1990s (Linn, 2003). There are several especially problematic aspects of NCLB for diverse urban schools, especially high schools, which undermine high-quality instruction and efforts to keep the most vulnerable students in school. These include:

- disincentives for using intellectually ambitious performance assessments;
- a "diversity penalty" experienced by schools serving many groups of high-need students, especially for assessing the progress of ELLs;
- incentives for pushing students out of school in order to boost test scores.

The necessary changes to address these problems are now described.

5. The law and regulations should encourage states and schools to use performance assessments that motivate ambitious intellectual work. Performance assessments that require students to evaluate and solve complex problems, conduct research, write extensively, and demonstrate their learning in projects, papers, and exhibitions have proven key to motivating students and attaining high levels of learning in redesigned high schools. These kinds of assessments are the norm in European and many Asian high schools, whose examination systems rely mostly on essays and oral examinations, as well as student work products, rather than multiple-choice tests. Although NCLB explicitly calls for the use of multiple measures to evaluate student and school progress, its administration has discouraged states from using robust assessment systems that go beyond multiple-choice tests or from evaluating schools based on multiple measures of learning.

One of the first perverse consequences of NCLB was that many states which created forward-looking assessment systems during the 1990s began to shrink or abandon them, since they are more costly than machine-scored tests, and do not fit the federal mandate for annual testing that allows students and schools to be compared. NCLB's requirements caused Maryland to drop its sophisticated performance-assessment system and Maine to eliminate performance assessments in some fields, as well as a teacher-scoring process that provided strong professional development. Oregon had to fight to get the U.S. Department of Education to allow it to use its sophisticated computer-based adaptive testing system for the diagnostic purposes it was designed to serve. States like Nebraska that previously used only local performance assessments to evaluate student learning were forced to adopt norm-referenced standardized tests to meet the law's requirements (Erpenpach, Forte-Fast, & Potts, 2003). States that built systems relying on multiple measures, including performance assessments at the school level, had difficulty getting their state plans approved. Federal officials discouraged several New England states from using performance-based assessments, and suggested that Connecticut drop its sophisticated open-ended assessments and use multiple-choice tests when the state asked for a waiver, on fiscal grounds, from adding more grades to its testing programs. Connecticut sued the federal government for the funding needed to maintain its system of performance assessments.

Relatively few states now encourage high schools to engage in performance assessments or acknowledge such assessments in state accountability systems, thus reducing the incentives for schools to focus on higher order skills and proficiencies. The administration of NCLB has pushed states back to the lowest common denominator in testing, undoing progress that had been made to improve the quality of assessments and delaying the move from antiquated norm-referenced, multiple-choice tests to more thoughtful systems that measure real performance.

Analysts have raised concerns about how the law's requirements are leading to a narrower curriculum, to test-based instruction that ignores critical real-world skills, especially for lower income and lower-performing students, and to less useful and engaging education (Erpenpach et al., 2003; Sunderman, Kim, & Orfield, 2005; Wood, 2004). Constraints on testing not only reduce the chances that schools will focus on helping students acquire critical thinking, research, writing, and production abilities; they also reduce the opportunities that students who learn in different ways and have different talents will have to show what they have learned.

Amendments to the law and regulations should encourage rather than discourage the use of diagnostic assessments and high-quality state or local performance assessments as a key part of state accountability systems aimed at improving curriculum and teaching. Unless more federal funds are available to support high-quality annual testing that includes performance components, the requirement for annual testing should be relaxed so that states can afford to maintain such high-quality assessments. And evidence about school progress should be expanded to include information from multiple measures, including performance assessments and information about student learning opportunities and progression through school.

6. The law should be amended to accurately assess student progress—including the progress of ELLs and students with disabilities—without penalizing schools serving the most diverse student bodies. NCLB requires that schools be declared "failing" if they fail to meet test-score targets for each subgroup of designated students annually. It requires the largest gains from lower-performing schools, although these schools serve needier students and generally have fewer resources than those serving wealthier students.

Two separate teams of researchers have found that schools serving poor, minority, and ELL students experience what researchers have called a "diversity penalty" (Novak & Fuller, 2003; Kim & Sunderman, 2005) even when they show test-score gains. This occurs because schools must meet test-participation rates and test-score gains for each subgroup on each test to "make AYP," with each racial/ethnic and income group, plus ELLs and students with disabilities, counted separately. Thus, a diverse school might need to meet each of thirty separate targets, while a homogenous school serving few low-income students or ELLs might need to show progress in only five or six categories.

Of two schools with identical overall gains, one may easily make adequate yearly progress while the other, more diverse school, does not. Even if students in every single subgroup make gains, the gains made by one group may be smaller than required, or a single subgroup may have 94 percent of students take one test in one grade rather than the required 95 percent. In some small schools, the absences of just a couple of students, or requested waivers from tests by a couple of parents, can cause participation rates to dip below 95 percent. In one small school with a large immigrant population in California, for example, the month long absence of three migrant students who returned to Mexico with their parents was enough to cause the school to fail to make AYP, despite showing large test gains. (In a subgroup of fifty, having three students absent puts the participation rate just below 95 percent.) Small schools with many subgroups serving transient populations are especially vulnerable to this problem. Many schools with strong, consistent gains for all groups nonetheless are falsely labeled "failing" because of this system.

Perverse outcomes are frequently reported. For example, one account documented two schools that were penalized for closing the achievement gap: their literacy reforms produced steep gains for African American and Latino students while the gains made by high-scoring white students who were already near the test ceiling were small, and thus did not make AYP (Darling-Hammond, 2004). In schools that serve special education students, allowing more than a few of them to be tested in accordance with their individualized education plans also causes the school to fail to make AYP, even if all groups have improved, including special needs learners.

Schools that serve large numbers of new ELLs—what the law calls limited English proficient (LEP) students—and students with disabilities are subject to the most nonsensical rules, which guarantee that they cannot ultimately meet the law's standards. Since students are assigned to these subgroups *because* they cannot meet the proficiency standard, and they are typically removed from the subgroup when they do meet the standard, these schools will not ever be able to meet the 100 percent proficiency benchmark the law has set.

For example, Section 9101(25)(d) of NCLB defines a LEP student as one "whose difficulties in speaking, reading, writing, or understanding the English language may be sufficient to deny the individual *the ability to meet the State's proficient level of achievement* on State assessments." It seems not to have occurred to policymakers that ordering schools to show 100 percent proficiency for students in a subgroup that by definition scores below that level creates an impossible goal. Furthermore, as students gain proficiency in English, they are transferred out of this subgroup within two years; thus, it is impossible for 100 percent of this subgroup ever to reach proficiency. Thus, schools and districts that serve substantial numbers of LEP students will never be able to show the required gains because of how this subgroup is defined under law. Some advocates have suggested that students who are classified as LEP count in the AYP calculations for this subgroup as long as they stay in a school (even after they become proficient in English and achieve proficiency on the state content tests). However, the U.S. Department of Education has not approved this definition (Erpenpach et al., 2003).

The same issues pertain to the testing of students with disabilities and to the schools that serve them. Many such students who cannot demonstrate their learning on grade-level tests have individualized education plans that prescribe different assessments for charting their progress, including "instructional level" tests. The U.S. Department of Education has ruled that using such tests is permissible only if the results are counted as "non-proficient" or if they apply to fewer than 2 percent of all test-takers. In addition to the fact that this appears to violate special education laws, schools that serve large numbers of special education students will always be penalized in their AYP rankings. Furthermore, because disabilities are correlated with poverty (which is linked to poor prenatal and childhood health care, low birth weight, poor nutrition, lead poisoning, maternal substance abuse, and many other conditions that predict learning problems), this rule punishes schools that serve large numbers of low-income students.

The law should credit gains for subgroups without applying mechanistic rules for targets, allow the appropriate IEP testing of special needs learners in all cases, require appropriate modes of testing for all ELLs—in line with published professional testing standards—and abandon the impossible 100 percent proficient rule for this subgroup or modify it to pertain only to ELLs who have had a reasonable amount of time to learn English (e.g., at least three years), keeping all of these ELLs in the subgroup throughout their school careers for the purpose of calculating progress. In addition, the goal of tracking subgroup progress should be accomplished without the complex system of rigid targets for both scores and participation rates that sets thirty or more categories on each test, any one of which can cause a school to fail AYP.

7. The flawed system of measurement should be changed to eliminate current incentives to push out students in order to raise scores. Perhaps the most adverse, unintended consequence of NCLB's accountability strategy is that it undermines safety nets for struggling students rather than expanding them, and it creates incentives for such students to be kept out or pushed out of school. As low-scoring students disappear, test scores go up. This is because targets are measured in terms of average achievement for noncomparable groups, rather than in terms of actual student growth. In combination with the "diversity penalty" already described, this creates a "double hit" in the NCLB accountability system for schools serving many high-need students—especially if they succeed in keeping struggling students in school (Kim & Sunderman, 2005). The problems with this approach are especially dangerous in high schools: because the law does not require tracking student progression and graduation rates, and because it requires inappropriate testing of ELL and special needs students, the most expedient thing for schools to do to get their scores up is to allow or even encourage such students to leave.

Table 10.1 shows how this operates. At "King High School," a hypothetical school representing the nature of the problem, average scores increased from the 70th to the 72nd percentile between the 2003–2004 and 2004–2005 school year, and the proportion of students who met the standard (a score of 65) increased from 66 percent to 80 percent—the kind of performance that test-based accountability systems celebrate and reward. Looking at subgroup performance, the proportion of Latino students meeting the standard increased from 33 percent to 50 percent. However, *not a single student* at King improved his or her score between 2003–2004 and 2004–2005. In fact, the scores of every single student in the school went *down* over the course of the year. How could these steep improvements in the school's average scores have occurred? A close look at Table 10.1 shows that the major change between the two years was that the lowest-scoring student, Raul, disappeared. As has occurred in many states with high-stakes testing programs, students who do poorly on the tests—special needs students, new ELLs, and those with poor attendance, health, or family problems—are increasingly likely to be excluded by being counseled out, transferred, expelled, or by dropping out.

Table 10.1 King High School: Rewards or Sanctions? The Relationship Between Test Score Trends and Student Populations

	2003–2004	*2004–2005*
Laura	100	90
James	90	80
Felipe	80	70
Kisha	70	65
Jose	60	55
Raul	20	
	Average Score = 70	Average Score = 72
	% Meeting Standard = 66%	% Meeting Standard = 80%

If this school had been judged using a "value-added" index that looked at the changes in individual students' scores from one year to the next, it would have been clear that the students' scores decreased by 8 percentile points on average rather than registering an apparent, but illusory, gain caused by changes in the student population. Recent studies have found that systems that reward or sanction schools based on average student scores create incentives for pushing low-scorers into special education so that their scores won't count in school reports, retaining students in grade so that their grade-level scores will look better, excluding low-scoring students from admissions, and encouraging such students to leave schools or drop out (for a review, see Darling-Hammond & Rustique-Forrester, 2005). Studies have linked dropout rates in many states and cities to the effects of grade retention, student discouragement, and school exclusion policies stimulated by high-stakes tests (Advocates for Children, 2002; Haney, 2002; Jacob, 2001; Lilliard & DeCicca, 2001; Orfield & Ashkinaze, 1991; Roderick, Bryk, Jacob, Easton, & Allensworth, 1999; Wheelock, 2003).

Meanwhile, steep increases in test scores have often occurred in schools with high rates of grade retention and dropout. For example, Wheelock (2003) found that Massachusetts high schools receiving awards for gains in tenth-grade pass rates on the state tests showed substantial increases in prior year ninth-grade retention rates and in the percentage of "missing" tenth graders. A Texas study found a similar relationship between ninth-grade retention, dropouts, and school rankings (Heilig, 2005). Paradoxically, schools that work to keep struggling students in school are disadvantaged by such accountability systems, and NCLB's requirement for disaggregating data increases the incentives for eliminating those at the bottom of each subgroup, especially where schools have little capacity to improve the quality of services such students receive.

The consequences for individual students who are caught in this no-win situation can be tragic, as most cannot go on to further education or even military service if they fail these tests, drop out, or are pushed out to help their schools' scores look better. The consequences for society are also tragic, as such policies lead to more students leaving school earlier—some with only a seventh- or eighth-grade education—without the skills to join the economy. These students join what is increasingly known as a "school-to-prison pipeline" (Wald & Losen, 2003) carrying an increasing number of undereducated youth almost directly into the criminal justice system. Indeed, prison enrollments have tripled since the 1980s, and the costs of the criminal justice system have increased by more than 600 percent (while public education spending grew by only 25 percent in real dollars). More than half of inmates are functionally illiterate, and 40 percent of adjudicated juveniles have learning disabilities that were not addressed in school (Darling-Hammond, 2004).

The annual costs of incarceration are three to five times the cost of educating the same individuals in schools years earlier, and the annual costs of dropouts are extremely high. Increasingly, this growing strain on the economy deflects resources away from the services that could make people productive. If test scores are increased by pushing students out of school, the result is not higher levels of education in the society.

Addressing this problem will require measuring of individual student progress rather than using cross-sectional averages that compare one year's average scores to the next. It will also require placing a value on keeping students in school as part of the accountability system; greater investments in improving the capacity of schools to teach, not just to test, struggling students; and appropriate means for assessing students with special needs.

While these are troubling aspects of the law's implementation, one could also argue, quite legitimately, that at least some of the schools identified as "needing improvement" (a designation that changes to "failing" if targets are not met after three years) indeed are dismal places where little learning occurs, or are complacent schools that have not attended to the needs of all of their students—schools that need to be jolted into action to change. And it is fair to suggest that underserved students in such schools deserve other choices if the schools cannot change. These arguments are part of the law's theory of action: that low-quality schools will be motivated to change if they are identified and shamed and that their students will be better served if given other educational options. Unfortunately, access to more successful schools has proved to be a mirage in most high-need communities. Meanwhile, the law creates incentives that can reduce the quality of education schools serving the neediest students can provide.

How might the goal of improving schools actually, paradoxically, undermine them? In North Carolina, analysts found that labeling schools as failing made it more difficult for the neediest schools to attract or retain high-quality teachers (Clotfelter, Ladd, Vigdor, & Diaz, 2003). Florida's use of average test scores, unadjusted for student characteristics, in allocating school rewards and sanctions led to reports that teachers were leaving the schools rated "D" or "F" in droves, to be replaced by teachers without experience or training (DeVise, 1999). As one principal asked, "Is anybody going to want to dedicate their lives to a school that has already been labeled a failure?" NCLB's approach of labeling schools and threatening staff dismissals is a disincentive for qualified staff to stay in high-need schools when they have options to teach in better resourced and better regarded schools with more affluent students (Tracey, 2005).

FIXING NCLB

If we are to achieve the noble goals of NCLB, the law must be amended so states are encouraged to use thoughtful performance assessments and so that tests are used diagnostically for informing curriculum improvements rather than for punishing students or schools. Learning progress should be evaluated on multiple measures—including such factors as attendance, school progress and continuation, course passage, and classroom performance on tasks beyond multiple-choice tests. Furthermore, within a multiple-measures system, gains should be evaluated with "value-added" measures showing how individual students improve over time, rather than solely by school averages that are influenced by changes in who is assessed.

Rather than using unrealistic targets to evaluate schools, schools should be evaluated in terms of their ongoing contribution to learning progress for students. The system should ensure appropriate assessment for special education students and ELLs, and credit for the gains these students make over time. While progress for subgroups of students should be reported, these reports should include evidence about continuation and success in school as well as academic achievement for members of each group. Determinations of school progress should be constructed to reflect a better-grounded analysis of schools' actual performance and progress rather than a statistical gauntlet that penalizes schools serving the most diverse populations. These reporting changes should be designed to ensure that schools that are identified as failing are indeed those that are offering poor education, not those merely caught in a mathematical mousetrap. And progress should be gauged against sensible benchmarks for success. As policy analyst Bruce Fuller (2004) notes of the law's current 100 percent proficiency standard:

> Would government ever require automakers to produce emissions-free cars in the space of a decade, then shut down companies that failed to meet a pie-in-the-sky goal? Of course not! Better to set demanding yet pragmatic standards and require clear signs of progress. Schools should be rewarded for elevating achievement levels by some degree, rather than penalized for not meeting an absolute, unrealistic standard. The ideal level of proficiency for all— just like emissions-free cars—could then be approached over time.

Most importantly, schools that are struggling should receive intensive help to strengthen their staffs and redesign their work. Teachers should be fully prepared and have demonstrated competence before they are recognized as "highly qualified." At the same time, such definitions should not create straitjackets that prevent interdisciplinary teaching that creates more engaging and coherent learning and that enables small schools to personalize instruction. Full funding of NCLB should include supports and incentives for preparing well-qualified teachers and getting them to the schools where they are needed, including a major federal initiative to underwrite strong preparation and recruitment incentives for well-qualified teachers who will teach in high-need schools. With this in place, states should be held accountable for providing highly qualified teachers to all students— the key element of genuine accountability.

In addition to incentives for recruiting and retaining high-quality teachers in the places where they are most needed, fixing NCLB will require a new approach to measuring and supporting school success. This approach should:

- replace the counterproductive AYP formula with more instructionally useful state accountability systems designed to assess student progress through multiple measures, including performance assessments and student continuation in school;

- evaluate gains using approaches that assess the progress of individual students, not changes in average scores that encourage schools to push out low-scoring students;
- appropriately assess the progress of ELLs and students with disabilities based on professional testing standards and "count" the gains of these students throughout their entire school careers.

These changes will reward the efforts of those high schools that have redesigned themselves to better serve the students who are routinely left by the wayside in their adolescent years, rather than penalizing or obstructing their efforts to keep students in school and enable them to learn in rigorous and relevant ways. Really leaving no child behind requires a law that creates "two-way accountability"—accountability to parents and children for the quality of education they receive as a means for greater learning for all.

11

NCLB and Continuous School Improvement

Willis D. Hawley

The theory of reform embedded in the federal government's primary instrument for improving schools, the No Child Left Behind (NCLB) Act, is that holding schools accountable for increased student performance will result in continuous improvement because educators will reallocate human and financial resources in order to narrow the gap between student performance and high goals for all students. There is evidence that NCLB is pushing states and districts to make use of student performance data to promote improvement, better align standards and instruction, and focus more attention on the performance of lowest achieving students (Center on Education Policy [CEP], 2006a). However, there are also numerous problems with the provisions of NCLB, including the measurement of school improvement, the adequacy of funding, ways of assessing and ensuring that all students have quality teachers, and the timing, fairness, and effectiveness of sanctions when school and districts fail to meet improvement targets.

This chapter examines whether the provisions of NCLB maximize its potential to develop in schools and districts the capacity to foster continuous and meaningful improvement. The first section provides an overview of the organizational conditions that continuous improvement requires, describes why such processes are essential to ensuring that all students learn at high levels, and examines how NCLB affects the conditions needed for continuous school improvement. The second section recommends changes in NCLB that might strengthen the law's effects on long-term improvements in student learning.

PROVISIONS OF NCLB THAT AFFECT THE POTENTIAL FOR CONTINUOUS IMPROVEMENT

Developing a capacity for continuous improvement is important for all purposeful organizations, but it is particularly critical for schools because goals for student learning change constantly as a result of political, economic, and social change; knowledge about effective schools evolves and is conditional; the efficacy of specific practices depends on the unpredictable dispositions and needs students bring with them to school; and extraordinary changes in student demography and teacher mobility that characterize many schools.

There appears to be considerable agreement about the conditions and processes that enhance the capacity of schools to learn how to improve and to act on that learning (Fullan, 2001; Hawley & Sykes, 2007; Leithwood & Louis, 1998). The most important of these are the following:

- Clear and ambitious goals for students' learning
- Data on student learning that provide an accurate picture of student progress over time
- The opportunity, motivation, and capability of personnel to engage in collaborative, evidence-based problem solving and related professional practice
- Human and financial resources to identify and implement promising practices
- Sufficient time and support to implement promising initiatives, assess their effects, and modify initial improvement efforts

Clear and Ambitious Goals for Student's Learning

Like no other federal (or state) policy, NCLB has driven schools to focus on achieving specific predetermined goals for student performance, not just for students as a whole, but for students of color, English language learners, socioeconomically disadvantaged students, and students with disabilities. On the other hand, most states and districts have set goals that do not reflect the breadth and depth of what students need to know and be able to do, not only in students' own interests, but also in the interests of their communities and nation. For example, Popham (2005) observed that few content standards include the development of students' capacity to analyze, access, manage, integrate, evaluate, and create information in a variety of formats and media. Given the political risk and the uncertainty of state and local policymakers and educators that they have the know-how and the resources to achieve ambitious goals, most states are unlikely to enhance their goals even as schools improve. In effect, contrary to the intent of NCLB, the sanctions required by the act appear to encourage relatively low achievement standards and cap state goals for student performance (Carey, 2006; Koretz, this volume).

Virtually every study of the effects of NCLB finds that it has narrowed the taught curriculum—and therefore, the goals of education—by causing educators to deemphasize subjects for which schools are not held accountable under NCLB (CEP, 2006a; Sunderman, Tracey, Kim, & Orfield, 2004). Moreover, even in the subjects used to measure school progress, the content of lessons is often dumbed down. This is because teachers are teaching to tests that tend to focus on skills that are easily measured (Toch, 2006) and that are aligned with the less demanding content standards (Popham, 2005). It is not surprising that the curriculum is becoming narrower and less ambitious. In organizations that seek accountability by attaching high stakes to desired outcomes, everyone involved seeks to define goals and their attainment in terms that can be more or less easily measured and attained.

As our expectations for student learning become more ambitious, measuring outcomes in ways that are technically valid and reliable becomes increasingly problematic. Consider the challenge of assessing traits that most employers and college admission officers expect schools to develop, such as work habits, oral and written communication proficiency, collaborative dispositions and skills, analytical thinking, and the ability to solve complex authentic problems (cf. New Commission on the Skills of the American Workforce, 2007). For example, while it is not difficult to determine whether a student can spell words or correctly apply rules of grammar and punctuation, it is not easy to assess—especially for purposes of external accountability—how well students understand a complex work of literature or write a persuasive essay.

Data on Student Learning That Provide an Accurate Picture of Student Progress Over Time, Including Subgroups of Students

Positive Effects of NCLB

Public and private organizations capable of reliable improvement over time build and use powerful databases consisting of multiple measures to assess outcomes and to analyze what contributed to those outcomes (Stringfield, 1998). NCLB has almost certainly accelerated the movement toward data-based decision making in schools (CEP, 2006a). By requiring that measures of student learning be disaggregated to draw attention to the performance of all students, NCLB has pushed schools and districts to allocate resources to students who are underperforming for a number of reasons. This disaggregation is essential to securing NCLB's goals and ensuring that continuous improvement serves the needs of all students.

How NCLB Impedes the Effective Use of Data to Improve Schools

NCLB impedes the development of understandings about how and when schools improve and introduces incentives that undermine the data-based pursuit of continuous and ambitious school improvement in at least two important ways: promoting inaccurate measures of school improvement and negatively affecting instruction.

Promoting Inaccurate Measures of School Improvement

Although NCLB has motivated schools to pursue continuous improvement, it appears to be impeding the pursuit of sophisticated approaches to evidence-based (not just data-based) improvement strategies. This is because it largely ties sanctions to a single measure of student learning to determine "adequate yearly progress" (AYP). While AYP does include more than one achievement indicator, the law puts almost all of the emphasis on standardized test results. A widely accepted maxim among assessment experts is that even when there are alternative measures, the one with the highest stakes attached will push out other measures.

Current policy related to the measurement of AYP is one of the most controversial aspects of NCLB. The concern of this chapter is whether AYP requirements help schools engage in continuous improvement. If schools do not have accurate data on student progress that is linked directly to those students' experiences in school, it is very difficult to know what schools need to do to enhance student achievement. And, of course, if schools are actually improving student achievement, but are being defined as unsuccessful—and there are many ways this can happen under NCLB—this will demoralize educators and lead to inappropriate sanctions that undermine school improvement.

Most experts who assess complex phenomena urge the use of multiple measures. For example, economists use multiple indicators to establish the health of the economy, and they apply these indicators frequently and vary the weight assigned to them depending on their interrelationships. Measuring complex learning goals with single measures once a year—as is the case with most assessments of learning used to hold schools accountable—results not only in narrowing the goals pursued, it introduces instability and other sources of error in the measurement of whether schools achieve desired goals (Koretz, this volume; Linn, 2005).

High-stakes tests focus the people to be held responsible on the assessment itself rather than on the standards it purports to measure (Stecher & Kirby, 2004). Standards describing what students should know and be able to do are usually more ambitious and broad than the content being measured in the standardized tests used in meeting the requirements of NCLB. Indeed, standardized tests typically cover only about 50 percent of state standards (Toch, 2006, p. 14). Both the politics of high-stakes accountability and the cost of test development and administration create incentives for states and test contractors to design tests that measure relatively low-level skills and move away from more challenging assessments of student knowledge and competency (Toch, 2006, p. 15). Thus, teachers who teach to the test are not teaching to standards.

In addition to problems with using a single state test of student learning, other concerns with AYP need to be addressed if policymakers and educators are to develop accurate school performance data upon which they can build new organizational and professional capabilities. Among these concerns are the following:

- Student mobility and technical problems with cohort analysis mean that an individual student's academic growth cannot be determined; this, in turn, results in weak measures of school improvement (Koretz, this volume).
- Current AYP provisions relating to students with disabilities and English language learners (Kieffer, Lesaux, & Snow, this volume) undermine effective measures of school quality.
- Better measures of the rate of school improvement are needed. Test scores often vary substantially from year to year in the best schools. And, as previously noted, improvement is seldom linear. Moreover, schools serving low-income students start from a lower base in their pursuit of state proficiency goals. This means that "underperforming" schools must make greater progress each year than those serving higher performing students. For this reason and others, schools actually making progress will become subject to NCLB sanctions (CEP, 2006b).
- Because NCLB focuses attention on the percentage of students who get over the "proficient" bar, overall student progress is masked, at both ends of the achievement distribution (Kim & Sunderman, 2005; Koretz, this volume).
- When subgroups make progress in one content domain but not another, schools are not failing to improve. For example, by focusing on literacy, schools may set the stage for students to do better in mathematics—which requires greater literacy capabilities with each grade level—but not meet AYP mathematics requirements.
- Many proposals for improving high schools call for reducing the scale of student learning environments. The smaller the school, the

less reliable the assessments can be, especially if the smaller schools (or schools within schools) are highly diverse.

These concerns about current approaches to assessing the improvements that schools and districts are making do not invalidate the importance of establishing rigorous ways to hold schools accountable for improving the learning opportunities of all students. They do represent an imperative to improve the law if NCLB is to foster continuous school improvement.

In short, when learning is assessed in simplistic ways, people learn simple things. Ironically, this means that students who rely most on schools for their knowledge, skill, and dispositions related to learning are likely to have their cognitive development capped by the very strategy that seeks to assure that the quality of their schools improve. It also means that the ultimate goals of continuous improvement will be less ambitious than both students and our society require.

Negative Effects on Instruction

Measuring school improvement by using standardized state tests not only narrows the goals of instruction (CEP, 2006a; Linn, 2005; Toch, 2006; Sunderman et al., 2004), it also shapes the character of instruction. One of the most important reasons why state tests may undermine school improvement is that they are not very sensitive to variations in instruction (Popham, 2006; Koretz, this volume). This not only means that they are not helpful in giving direction to improvements in teaching, but they do not capture improvements that are made. This, of course, has the consequence of deemphasizing instructional improvement. Once-a-year tests of the sort used to assess AYP are not useful in helping teachers modify instruction to meet the needs of individual students, and they may actually reduce teacher effectiveness. This can happen when teachers focus on getting through the prescribed curriculum rather than pursuing reasons why students do not understand core ideas or complex techniques (Kennedy, 2005). Further, to maximize student performance measured by typical standardized tests in the short run, many teachers spend considerable time on test-taking skills and review and memorization of low-level skills (Koretz, this volume). Spending time on test preparation and teaching for rote learning essentially reduces students' opportunities to learn and almost certainly contributes to student disengagement from school (National Research Council & National Institute of Medicine, 2004, pp. 44–54). Thus, one of the consequences of high-stakes assessment is to diminish the quality of instruction; and this, in turn, particularly disadvantages students who do not enjoy substantial learning opportunities out of school in their families and communities.

Opportunity and Capability of Administrators and Teachers to Engage in Collaborative, Evidence-Based Problem Solving

Schools that are capable of continuous improvement facilitate collaborative effort and are predictable in everyday work while remaining flexible and ever-evolving (Louis, Toole, & Hargreaves, 1999). Such collaborative work not only requires that appropriate evidence be available upon which to identify and address problems, but also that educators have the skills and the time to do such work. Restructuring and reculturing schools in ways that promote coherence, trust, and collaboration and enhance the relevant expertise of educators to foster continuous improvement are difficult tasks that require time and resources. This is particularly true in high schools because of their disciplinary structures, their size, and (sometimes) the diversity of their students (Gunn & King, 2003).

Significant changes require a willingness to take risks. If a primary goal of educators is to avoid NCLB sanctions, they will not risk implementing major changes necessary to support continuous improvement and ever more ambitious goals for student learning.

Human and Financial Resources to Implement Promising Practices

The resources that enable schools to sustain the conditions for continuous school improvement are adequate financial support, quality teaching, students ready to learn, and engaged families.

Moving in new directions and sustaining those initiatives that are successful can require additional funding as well as the reallocation of existing resources in districts with little fiscal slack. If NCLB pushes scarce financial resources at ineffective strategies, its effect on improvement will, of course, be counterproductive. That may be the case with the supplemental educational services (i.e., tutoring) requirement for schools and districts that fail to make AYP. There is little evidence that the types of tutoring programs being implemented under NCLB make a difference. They are most effective when well-trained teachers carry them out and both the content and the pedagogy complement in-class instruction (for example, as tutoring is used in Success for All). But, with some exceptions, the Department of Education has insisted that NCLB tutoring be carried out by providers who have a weak connection to schools and for whom there is no accountability.

The quality of teaching students receive is the most influential determinant of student success (Rice, 2003). Districts and schools serving the students that NCLB most seeks to help usually have substantial difficulty recruiting and retaining competent teachers. It seems likely that hard-to-staff schools that have been or might be sanctioned for poor performance will be seen as even less attractive places to work by teachers and teacher candidates. NCLB fosters the routinizing of teaching with common scripts and standard operating procedures that limit teacher effectiveness. Limiting teacher effectiveness, of course, greatly complicates the development of organizational capacities for continuous improvement (Shepard, 2000).

Student achievement is also influenced by peers, both directly and indirectly (Betts, Zau, & Rice, 2003; Hoxby, 2003). NCLB provides that students may transfer from schools sanctioned for not meeting AYP to other schools, and it gives preference to the lowest-performing students and to students from low-income families. However, since the burden of the transfer decision lies with parents, not surprisingly, the students who have been the first to leave low-performing schools are those students who are the highest achievers (Smrekar & Goldring, 1999). Thus, NCLB effectively reduces the overall quality of the educational resources available to those students left behind.

The movement of higher achieving students from a given school community is, of course, accompanied by the "transfer" of their parents (or guardians) to the new school as well. This has the unhappy consequence of schools losing those advocates for children who are most likely to seek and contribute to school improvement. In almost all organizations, when those who insist most on quality move to new products or services, the quality of the old products and services often declines (Hirschman, 1970). When there are profits to be made and capital to invest, new providers *may* enter the market to provide quality options, but that incentive is a doubtful motivator in public education (Belfield & d'Entremont, 2005; Levin, 2005). Once quality consumers have moved on, they are difficult to wean away from the product or service to which they switched, even if it is not everything they expected. The flight of higher achieving students and their parents from schools that are labeled as underperforming almost certainly complicates the problem of staffing those schools. All of these effects combined mean that the transfer provision of NCLB, whatever its value to the students who transfer, makes it more difficult for the *schools left behind* to improve.

Sufficient Time and Support to Implement Promising Practices, to Assess Their Effects, and to Modify Initial Improvement Efforts

Time

Research on effective schools shows that meaningful change usually (a) takes at least three to five years and (b) tends to vary in pace from year to year. This poses significant challenges for creating effective accountability processes. As Elmore (2003) observed, "Developmental processes—both individual and organizational—are not linear, but rather nonlinear, proceeding in stages. Performance-based accountability systems—especially NCLB—treat improvement as a linear process....[S]chools increase their internal coherence and capacity around instruction in several discernible stages. These stages often involve significant gains in externally measured performance, followed by periods in which improvement in quality and capacity continue but improvement in performance slows or goes flat" (p. 9).

Not only is the pace of *progress* in school improvement uncertain and difficult to predict, but the implementation of ambitious new approaches to facilitating student learning can result in a short-run decline in student achievement as teachers learn new skills, and as curriculum, assessment, and instruction are brought into alignment (Fullan, 2001). Changes in school structures, cultures, and professional capacity necessary to enable continuous improvement often require considerable time to develop and institutionalize.

It is difficult enough to change a given school meaningfully, but the process of scaling up and sustaining successful practices across a district requires extensive organizational capacity. The development of this capacity, which few states or districts now have, takes time and resources, in addition to changes in organizational cultures (Glennan, Bodilly, Galeher, & Kerr, 2004).

There are, of course, examples of schools that bring about significant improvement in student test scores in a year or two. Among the most likely explanations for these exceptional achievements may be the following:

- Extraordinary leadership from principals and teachers
- Order beats chaos every time. Schools in disarray can improve substantially by aligning curriculum with assessment, routinizing (e.g., scripting) teaching practices, and reducing social disorder
- Unusual parent-school relationships (such as those involving parental contracts) that result in motivated student populations
- Significant increases of time on task for the subjects tested, usually at the expense of other subjects
- A focus on test preparation
- Extensive and expensive external support

In most cases, dramatic short-run improvements in student outcomes occur around what Cuban (2001) and others have called "first order" change—the kinds of changes that involve "dealing with the mess," aligning curriculum, trying to minimize teacher error, scheduling smartly, and controlling disorder. While these are important things to do, first order change does not lead, in itself, to more substantial, "second order" changes needed for significant and continuous improvement (Waters, Marzano, & McNulty, 2004). For example, steps taken to deal with disorder may not set the stage for developing a school culture of shared values and responsibility related to appropriate and socially responsible behavior. Scripting teacher behavior may improve teaching among weaker teachers, but it also limits teacher effects on student learning. "Strong" top-down leadership that works in a crisis may impede the development of a culture that fosters collaborative problem solving and shared responsibility. In short, some strategies for bringing about short-run improvements do not lead to—and may even constrain—long-run gains, especially if we have ambitious goals for students' intellectual development.

Significant increases in learning opportunities for all students will require that schools in need of improvement engage in second order change. Such changes involve changes in values and expectations; restructuring roles, time, and resources to foster collaborative problem solving and shared responsibility for student learning; developing caring and trustful relationships among teachers and administrators and among students, families, and educators; and significantly enhancing the professional expertise of teachers and school administrators. Second order change, of course, requires time and substantial support (Spillane, 2005; Vernez, Karam, Mariano, & Demartini, 2006).

Schools serving low-income students and students with exceptional needs, which are the most likely schools to be affected by the provisions of NCLB (CEP, 2006a: Sunderman, Kim, & Orfield, 2005), must account for a greater share of the educational progress their students make than do most schools. And dealing with the exceptional challenges they face means that creating the conditions for continuous improvement takes more time and support than needed changes in other schools (Spillane, 2005).

Support for Continuous Improvement

Most educators enter and persist in their profession because they want to improve the lives of the students they serve. They do not choose to be less effective than they believe they need to be. When people who care about their work are told they are ineffective and see little chance of dealing constructively with the challenge to their competence, they are likely to find ways to discount the validity of the challenge, find explanations for their alleged inadequacy in the indifference or incompetence of others, find ways to "beat the system" (such as manipulating the assessment process; Booher-Jennings, 2005; Nichols & Berliner, 2005), or find new jobs. Thus, identifying the need for improvement should be accompanied by sufficient support to make those improvements. This includes money for new facilities, equipment, and learning resources, in some cases.

One of the most common observations in the literature on continuous improvement is that meaningful change is difficult to initiate and even more difficult to sustain (Downs, 1966; Fullan, 2001, 2005; Hargreaves & Fink, 2004; Hawley, 1976; Levin, 2005). Among the reasons for this are the following:

- The problems that are easiest to solve and are within the current capability of personnel are addressed first and, as more difficult challenges are undertaken, human and financial resources may prove to be insufficient.

- As the more difficult challenges are confronted, success is more elusive, and people become discouraged and return to what they did prior to initiation of the improvement effort.
- Those who opposed the changes, but did not have the influence to stop the initiative, renew their opposition after implementation and undermine others' confidence in the effort.
- Once initial progress is made, those who were leading the charge often move on to new challenges believing, wrongly, that their job is finished.
- Adopting new initiatives and the fanfare that often goes with such efforts can lead advocates, especially those outside the organization, to think that they have succeeded. They then move on to other concerns.
- New resources important to instigating and implementing the continuous school improvement initiative at the outset, such as consultants and extra financial support, are redirected to other needs.
- People become fatigued from the extra effort often associated with improvement initiatives, and resources for renewal are inadequate.

These propositions apply to all types of organizations, but schools—public and private—often face additional difficulties in sustaining continuous improvement. High productivity in schools often increases consumer expectations, but does not yield greater resources, as is the case in business. In schools facing the greatest challenges, teacher and staff turnover often is high (see the studies cited in Loeb, Darling-Hammond, & Luczak, 2005). When staff turnover is extensive in organizations that depend on effectiveness of professional expertise, as do schools, the stabilization of new initiatives is difficult, and the costs of professional development are high. As noted earlier, policies that stigmatize schools as ineffective, as does NCLB, are likely to increase the difficulty of recruiting and retaining teachers and principals in schools serving students most in need of expert teaching.

The difficulties of putting in place the structural, cultural, and procedural conditions necessary for continuous improvement is nicely illustrated by the experience of Edison Schools. Edison is the largest and apparently the most effective private company in the business of running public schools (American Institutes for Research, 2006). A recent evaluation of Edison Schools by the Rand Corporation found that students in Edison Schools showed somewhat greater gains in achievement than students in comparison schools, but only after *five years and only in those schools where the model was faithfully implemented* (Gill et al., 2005). Consider, too, that Boston, which has consistently been identified as among the most successful urban school systems and has been led by an outstanding superintendent and a supportive and active mayor, took ten years to reach relatively high levels of student performance. And, despite this success, students fall well short of the goals set by NCLB.

Recent studies hold little hope that NCLB's goal of having all students proficient by 2013–2014 will be reached without significant and seemingly unattainable increases in the rate of improvement (Lee, 2006; Linn, this volume; Stullich, Eisner, McCrary, & Roney, 2006; Wiley, Mathis, & Garcia, 2005). For schools and districts serving many struggling students, the rate of improvement is likely to decline rather than accelerate. This is because students closest to meeting proficiency will be the first to respond to initial improvements. Indeed, schools wanting to make AYP focus on these students. But the students who are performing at the lowest level will then have to be served, and the rate of progress in their collective achievement will have to be even greater than that of their higher achieving peers. Moreover, what worked with easier-to-reach students may not work with students with the greatest needs.

Organizations that need to improve usually need expert help to negotiate the change process, and they need help to enhance staff competence. The ever-increasing number of companies, groups, and individual consultants entering the school improvement business testify to these needs. Many of these advice providers do good work, but they do not usually build the capacity within school districts and schools that is needed for continuous improvement. Further, in too many cases, the help provided is inadequate to the task, having been selected because of personal contacts or unrealistic promises of success. NCLB envisioned states providing help to districts and schools. But it is clear that most states lack this capacity (CEP, 2006a; Goertz, 2005; McClure, 2005; Mintrop, this volume; Sunderman & Orfield, this volume).

ENHANCING THE EFFECTIVENESS OF NCLB IN FOSTERING CONTINUOUS SCHOOL IMPROVEMENT

NCLB has accelerated concern for the academic achievement of all students and has created incentives for schools to engage in evidence-based decision making driven by systematic analysis of student performance. However, as identified above, NCLB may impede the building of a capacity for and commitment to continuous improvement. The following proposals suggest ways NCLB could be changed to increase its contributions to continuous school improvement.

Develop Incentives for States to Strengthen Goals for Student Learning

State definitions of student proficiency vary dramatically. Some states have set student achievement goals too low to encourage significant improvements in student performance, and states have little reason to push their schools to achieve new and higher standards. Kevin Carey (2006) recently studied how states set goals for student achievement and concludes that NCLB creates "a system of perverse incentives that rewards state education officials who misrepresent reality. Their performance looks better in the eyes of the public and they're able to avoid conflict with organized political interests. By contrast, officials who keep expectations high and report honest data have hard choices to make and are penalized because their states look worse by comparison" (p. 3).

As demands for higher and different knowledge and skill develop in response to changes in the economy or in social values, states are not likely to adapt their goals accordingly. States could be encouraged to pursue ever more ambitious content standards and performance goals by providing states with high goals and additional funding to support schools in need of improvement. More uniform and rigorous goals for student learning across states would result if the federal government supported the development of national standards against which state standards can be readily compared. While Congressional endorsement of national standards is problematic, at least the federal government could promote "suggestive accountability" by making differences among schools and states more visible and understandable (Manna, 2006). And, though complicated, the law's application of sanctions for lack of school progress might take into account the level of achievement called for by state goals in ways that benefited districts and schools in more ambitious states.

Changes in NCLB that measure school improvement more effectively and give schools and districts more time and support to improve before sanctions are applied, as proposed below, would likely encourage states to specify and honestly pursue higher goals. At the same time, research on motivation tells us that people pursue ambitious goals only when they perceive that goals are realistically attainable (Lawler, 1994). This means that the pace of change expected of particular schools needs to be adapted to their extant capabilities and the support they have to improve.

Judge School Improvement by Multiple and Realistic Measures Over Time

Resting the determination of school improvement on a single and simple measure of student performance and the use of the current AYP method of determining school quality are likely to narrow curriculum, diminish the importance of higher order learning, discourage implementation of fundamental improvements (so-called "second order changes," previously discussed), and lead to unfair assessment of the actual contributions schools make to the academic achievement of individual students. There are a host of problems here, but there is no shortage of potential alternatives to the current approach to assessing school improvement (Hoxby, 2005; Linn, 2005; Lissitz, 2005).

Stecher and Kirby (2004) studied accountability strategies in other sectors and concluded that using multiple measures of organizational performance is common and desirable. On the basis of this evidence, they join many other students of accountability in proposing that multiple measures of students' academic performance should be used to foster school improvement (Kornhaber, this volume). In addition to standardized tests (which themselves should be enriched), measures of school effectiveness could include assessments of students' ability to solve complex problems, portfolios of student work, and evidence of ability to communicate effectively for diverse purposes. The assessments of high school improvement might include the increased weighting of graduation rates, and success in the workplace or in college. Trends on standardized tests might trigger expert qualitative reviews that could serve both as measures of current progress and as sources of technical assistance for improvement. Reville (2005) suggested, for example, that review teams could be charged with "making qualitative judgments about such important topics as school climate and expectations; the quality of teaching and learning; the degree of rigor of the curriculum; the availability of Advanced Placement and college-level courses; the availability of support services; dropout prevention and retrieval; occupational preparation; and success in the development of nonacademic skills in problem solving, interpersonal relations, and collaboration" (p. 4).

A major obstacle in addressing the limited usefulness of current standardized tests for fostering continuous improvement that ensures all students achieve high standards is the cost of productive, multidimensional assessment *systems*. More robust systems of assessment serve not only accountability purpose but should also be seen as a form of technical assistance and, as such, an investment in school improvement. The Congress should provide adequate funding for the development of more appropriate assessments of student learning *and for the administration of these tests*. Such assessments should include tests of higher order learning, accommodations, and alternative evaluation tools for students with disabilities and students who are English language learners. And, as Toch (2006) suggested, Congress could provide incentives for states to collaboratively develop student assessments.

Promote Collaborative Evidence-Based Problem Solving

Collaborative problem solving that is essential to continuous improvement requires time for professional interaction, communication skills, trust, and common understandings about instruction and how students learn. Changing the requirements for the pace and characteristics of school improvement to take into account the difficulties of bringing about significant change could reduce levels of dysfunctional stress that educators report (CEP, 2006a) and open up opportunities for the development of the capabilities for improvements that are ambitious and likely to persist over time.

While there seems no feasible or desirable way to mandate the use of certain practices, Congress should step up efforts to establish an authoritative knowledge base to enhance the likelihood that schools will adopt effective practices in the context of NCLB. This means increased but focused funding of educational research and the development of expert consensus about the meaning of the extant body of research.

Enhance Resources for Implementing Promising Practices

Congress should recognize that NCLB's supplemental educational services and student transfer provisions often remove valuable financial and human resources from schools that need these resources more than ever if they are to improve. This reality embodies more than one dilemma. Why continue to invest in a sinking ship? And, why shouldn't students be allowed to attend better schools, even if only some of them do? The supplemental educational services provision of the law seems to have little to recommend it. The efficacy of investing in schools that do not meet standards for improvement before invoking the transfer provision—much less the school takeover option—depends on whether there is sufficient expertise available to turn the school around. This, in turn, might be a focus of federal policy that would support the building of such capacity in various ways. Clearly, the most promising strategy for enhancing the prospects for schools serving students with the greatest needs is to strengthen the teaching corps in these schools. This would involve resources to improve working conditions, incentive pay attached to demonstrated expertise, and significantly greater investments in professional development focused specifically on the challenges individual schools face.

Sufficient Time and Support to Implement, Assess, and Modify Promising Practices

Schools need time and support to improve. Of course, the assertion that "these things take time" may well be used to justify intransigence or mask incompetence. Policymakers are typically and understandably impatient with promises of results in three to five years, especially when they are trying to address a perceived crisis. Giving struggling schools more time and resources is risky, but the risk needs to be compared to the alternative of not doing all we can to develop viable public school *systems* (i.e., districts or well-organized constellations of schools) that serve all students well. The prospect of thousands of schools more or less unrelated to one another seeking to serve a highly mobile and increasingly diverse student population in ways that meet rigorous standards is mind-boggling. How would these schools be held accountable? How would the strategic movement of personnel and resources to address the weaknesses of these schools be accomplished? How would more or less independent charter or private schools serve students who change schools often and thus need a common curriculum? How, in the absence of school *systems*, would the needs of students who are highly mobile or who need services not effectively provided by individual schools be met? How, in the absence of strong public school *systems*, would cooperation with other service providers, such as health and social services, be accomplished?

Even if significant numbers of "alternative providers" of educational services were motivated to introduce innovative reforms to the nation's schools, the outcomes would be uncertain and unlikely to produce the changes needed to substantially enhance student learning in the near future (Levin, 2005). As R. Maranto and A. G. Maranto (2005) asserted, "policymakers and philanthropies deciding which market-based alternative to back face a paradox: the models that can expand most rapidly offer more incremental prospects for educational success, while those most assured of educational breakthroughs can expand only gradually, meaning that for the foreseeable future they will leave most children behind and have limited influence on traditional public schools. ...we should expect most gains to come over decades rather than years" (pp. 1–2).

NCLB recognizes the importance of providing schools in need of improvement with substantial assistance and identifies various types of support. However, the funds available for such support may not come close to meeting the need. As noted earlier, the capabilities of states to support school improvement are generally inadequate. Thus far, districts bear the largest burden of support, and many districts lack capacity (CEP, 2006a). Schools identified as in need of improvement are unlikely to receive resource-intensive assistance, such as school support teams, full-time staff assigned to support teachers, and mentoring for the principal (Goertz, 2005). It appears that most technical assistance is focused on first order changes, such as how to better plan, use data, construct and follow curriculum guides to align instruction with priorities, and hire instructional coaches (CEP, 2006b). This is important help, but it is not sufficient to bring about new capacity for continuous improvement.

The need for support in creating and sustaining the capabilities for continuous school improvement throughout the country is unlikely to be met by a fragmented array of consultants and profit-making organizations. Federal technical assistance and research and development programs could be better designed, focused, and coordinated to help states and districts support their schools' efforts to improve.

Given the difficulty and importance of bringing about a capacity for continuous improvement in schools serving the neediest of the nation's students, and the limited expertise and financial resources to achieve such change, it seems likely that the more schools in which resources for change are invested, the less likely it is that the schools serving students who most need quality schools will become successful. This suggests that focusing support for improvement on the schools most in need of assistance may be the most productive way to enhance the quality of education for those who need good schools most.

CONCLUDING OBSERVATIONS

NCLB is grounded on the belief that far too many educators and state and local policymakers lack the motivation and capability to adopt and successfully implement effective practices and a conviction that schools can serve the needs of all students well, no matter what the level of resources and family and community support for student learning there might be.

Policies based on distrust and disapproval of those involved in service delivery inevitably seek to limit the discretion of service providers, define performance in narrow ways that can be easily measured, and punish rather than remedy what the policy defines as poor performance. The consequence of policies like this is that they often are replete with unintended effects, not the least of which are to "work around" or narrowly focus on how to meet (or defeat) the specific provisions of the policy rather than finding effective ways to achieve the goals of the policy about which there is wide agreement. In high-threat environments, the first impulse is to avoid the risk, the second is to hunker down and do only what is necessary to get by, and the third is to undermine the policy, both directly and indirectly.

If policymakers believe that the problem involves intransigence or fundamental ineptitude, there is little motivation to be flexible in the administration of the policy or to build system capacity. But, in the long run, the welfare of the nation's students, and thus the nation, depends not on an educational system driven by concerns about avoiding sanctions for poor performance. It depends on developing of the capability of educators, improving the school conditions that facilitate teaching and learning, and eliminating the social conditions that place so many students at risk of failure to maximize their potential.

12

NCLB and Reforming the Nation's Lowest-Performing High Schools

Help, Hindrance, or Unrealized Potential?

Robert Balfanz and Nettie Legters

Nationwide, over one million students drop out of high school each year. That amounts to 7,000 students each day and nearly 12 million students over the next decade (Alliance for Excellent Education, 2006). Current analyses indicate that out of an entering high school freshman class, only about seven in ten students will graduate, four or five will go on to college, and only two or three will achieve a bachelor's or associate's degree (Green & Winters, 2006). The numbers are worse for students of color, with only about half of African American and Hispanic youth receiving

Some analyses presented in this chapter are drawn from Balfanz, R., Legters N., West, T. C., & Weber, L. M. (2007). Are NCLB's Measures, Incentives, and Improvement Strategies the Right Ones for the Nation's Low-Performing High Schools? *American Education Research Journal, 44(3),* 559-593, Copyright AERA 2007.

high school diplomas. In an economy where low-skill, living-wage jobs have all but disappeared and where 80 percent of new jobs require post-secondary training and credentials, our current system is squandering the potential and limiting the life chances of far too many young people (Hecker, 2005).

The individual and societal costs of sending this many students into adult life without high school diplomas and/or unprepared for success in college and career are enormous. High school dropouts in today's economy are far more likely to be unemployed, to suffer from health problems, to be dependent on social services, or to be in prison than their peers who graduate (Levin, Belfield, Muennig, & Rouse, 2007). In 2000, in thirteen states in our union, the number of young African American men incarcerated exceeded the number enrolled in institutions of higher education (Ziedenberg & Schiraldi, 2002).

A recent study finds that our nation can recoup forty-five billion dollars in lost tax revenues, health care expenditures, and social service outlays if we cut the number of high school dropouts in half (Levin et al., 2007). These funds could be put toward reducing the national deficit and reinvested in ways that secure, strengthen, and extend our economy and civil society. Better educating our nation's young people is also simply the right thing to do. It is what we must do to raise the quality of life and elicit the best from our youth, from ourselves, and from our nation as a whole.

Our own research finds that half of the nation's dropouts are concentrated in less than a fifth, or about 2,000, of our regular and vocational high schools (Balfanz & Legters, 2004). We also find that No Child Left Behind (NCLB), the centerpiece federal initiative for stimulating improvements in low-performing schools, is not providing the information, support, or incentives necessary to improve these schools significantly. In the remainder of this chapter, we review these findings and discuss ways in which NCLB must be strengthened to reduce the number of students dropping out of high school and help ensure that all graduates are prepared for success in college, career, and civic life.

LOCATING THE DROPOUT CRISIS

One of the most poignant aspects of the nation's dropout problem is that students who drop out actually show up in high school, at least for a time. Though many are overage for their grade and have poor literacy and math skills, recent surveys indicate that they aspire to graduate and go on to college (High School Survey of Student Engagement, 2005). As places where students show up with a sense of possibility, high schools are critical sites of intervention to stem the dropout tide.

With this understanding, we set out to "locate" the dropout crisis by identifying the high schools that appear to produce the most dropouts in order to provide a guide for targeting resources and interventions. To identify low-performing high schools, we used a measure of schools' promoting power.[1] As the ratio of twelfth graders to ninth graders three years prior, promoting power estimates the success with which a high school achieves on-time promotion of a cohort of students from their freshmen to their senior year. Based on widely available enrollment data found in the national Common Core of Data (CCD), promoting power provides a good estimate of a school's dropout rate and a school's capacity to keep students on track to graduation.[2] We identified schools as "low performing" if they displayed chronically weak promoting power, that is, if they promote 60 percent or fewer freshmen to senior status on time averaged across three successive cohorts of students.[3]

We found that just more than 2,000, or about 18 percent, of regular and vocational high schools in the United States produce nearly half of the nation's dropouts. In these high schools, a freshman cohort shrinks 40 percent or more by senior year and a majority of students fails to graduate in the standard number of years, if at all. Predominately poor and minority students attend these schools. More than 600 of these high schools educate only minority students. Nearly half of the nation's African American and 40 percent of Latino students attend one of these high schools where graduation is little more than a fifty-fifty proposition. These schools are concentrated in urban areas across the northeast and Midwest, in the three large megadistricts (i.e., New York City, Chicago, and Los Angeles), and throughout the southern states (Balfanz & Legters, 2004).

The NCLB Act of 2001 is designed to identify such schools—schools that are consistently failing to serve poor and minority students—and to instigate school-based and systemic remedies so that all students are provided with access to a high-quality, standards-based education. At the high school level, the intent of NCLB is to identify schools in which students are not achieving proficient levels of academic skills and/or graduating with a regular high school diploma in the standard number of years. If schools fail to make adequate yearly progress toward proficiency and graduation goals within the framework established by their states, NCLB

---

[1] We could not use extant graduation or dropout rates given the high degree of variability within and between states in measuring these outcomes and the large amount of missing data related to these outcomes in national data.

[2] The CCD is a dataset compiled annually by the U.S. Department of Education's National Center for Education Statistics. It is the department's census, providing basic demographic, administrative, and financial data for every school in the United States.

[3] We use the term *promoting power* intentionally to emphasize the schools' role in promoting or failing to promote students successfully to graduation. Research on high school dropouts suggests that demographic, family, school, and community factors all play important roles in students' success in school. Our promoting power indicator focuses attention on the school-related factors that can be directly influenced with resources dedicated to educational interventions and school reform efforts.

requires schools and districts to take action to improve the schools and provide students with access to enhanced or alternative educational options.

Has NCLB fulfilled its intent of identifying, measuring progress, and stimulating improvement in low-performing high schools? We explore this question in the following section.

NCLB AND LOW-PERFORMING HIGH SCHOOLS

To examine the impact of NCLB on the nation's lowest-performing high schools, we drew a 10 percent random sample of the 2,030 high schools in 2003 whose three-year average (classes of 2000–2001, 2001–2002, and 2002–2003) for promoting power was 60 percent or less. This enabled us to identify a set of schools that were clearly low performing at the outset of NCLB and to examine to what extent they have been identified and improved by the NCLB accountability framework. The 202 high schools in the sample reflect the main characteristics of the nation's 2,030 high schools with weak promoting power.[4]

We examined state and district report cards from 2003–2004 and 2004–2005 for these 202 high schools to learn about states' adequate yearly progress (AYP) requirements and about schools' academic performances, graduation rates, AYP statuses, subgroup breakdowns for AYP, and NCLB improvement statuses and about whether AYP was met directly or through Safe Harbor provisions (e.g., In Improvement, Corrective Action, Restructured/ing).[5] We also drew from the Education Watch 2004 State Summary Reports published by the Education Trust to assess the rigor of state AYP exams through a comparison of states' performance on the state exams to their performance on the National Assessment of Education Progress (NAEP) exams.

NCLB is designed to focus schools' attention and efforts on students' academic achievement. Hence the state accountability systems mandated

---

[4] That is, the 202 high schools are predominately located in the cities of the Northeast, industrial Midwest, and West, as well as throughout the South and Southwest. Included are high schools from the nation's largest urban school districts, as well as rural, single high school districts. The sample includes high schools from thirty-four different states and slightly more than half the high schools are located in eleven southern states (110 of 202). Texas has the most high schools in the sample (twenty-two), followed by Florida (nineteen), Georgia (fifteen), New York (fourteen), and California (fourteen). Eleven high schools are located in New York City, the district with the most high schools in the sample.

[5] Adequate yearly progress, or AYP, toward academic and graduation goals is the central measure of success or failure for high schools under NCLB. AYP formulas vary widely by state, but typically require schools to demonstrate that a certain proportion of their students (overall and in every eligible subgroup) are performing at proficient levels on state assessments and are graduating in the standard number of years (or are showing expected gains in graduation rates). Schools may achieve AYP through a Safe Harbor provision by reducing the percentage of students who are not academically proficient by 10 percentage points.

under NCLB treat academic assessments as the primary indicator of performance. The law also requires that AYP include a secondary academic indicator (e.g., attendance, dropout rates, and graduation rates) to balance the assessment mandates with other areas in which schools may demonstrate improvement. At the high school level, legislation requires that this secondary indicator be the graduation rate to discourage schools from raising their achievement levels by pushing out lower-achieving students. So, for high schools, AYP is based on demonstrated progress in academic performance and graduation rates for the entire school and for eligible subgroups.

States, however, have considerable latitude in developing the achievement and graduation measures used to gauge progress and in establishing the levels and rate of growth required to achieve AYP in a given year. This is especially the case for graduation rates. While NCLB sets a goal of 100 percent proficiency in math and reading for all students by 2013–2014, there is no comparable NCLB requirement for graduation rates. Our analysis uncovered major shortcomings in NCLB to effectively identify and measure improvement in low-performing high schools due to wide variation in how the law has been put into practice in state accountability systems.

Does NCLB Identify and Measure Improvement in Low-Performing High Schools?

In our subsample of low-performing high schools, we found that 41 percent actually made AYP. The vast majority of those that made AYP met state standards for achievement and graduation, with about 8 percent making AYP through a Safe Harbor provision. We also found that those that made AYP tended to be better resourced, smaller, southern, and less urban than those that did not make AYP (Table 12.1).[6]

At first glance, one might conclude that school-level factors such as large size, fewer resources, and urbanicity contribute to lower high school performance. Recall, however, that *all* 202 high schools promote 60 percent or fewer of their ninth graders to twelfth grade on time, regardless of whether they made AYP. More fine-grained analyses revealed that state differences in how NCLB is being implemented at the high school level appear to drive whether a particular school makes AYP over and beyond other factors.

---

[6] Though only just over half of all sample schools were in the South, two-thirds of the high schools that made AYP were located in southern states (Virginia, West Virginia, Kentucky, Tennessee, Mississippi, Alabama, North Carolina, South Carolina, Georgia, Florida, Arkansas, Louisiana, Texas, and New Mexico). Nearly 47 percent of sample high schools in these states make AYP compared with 33 percent in other states, and 41 percent across the whole sample.

Table 12.1 Poverty Levels, Resources, Enrollment, and Locale of
Low-Performing High Schools that Did and Did Not
Make Adequate Yearly Progress (n = 202)

	Made AYP	*Did Not Make AYP*
# of schools (n)	82	120
% Free Lunch	53%	57%
School Title I	47%	47%
Pupil-Teacher Ratio	15.85 to 1	17.18 to 1
Total Enrollment	901	1426
City	30%	52%
Rural	43%	21%

Low-Performing High Schools That Made AYP Have Less Subgroup Accountability

One state-determined factor is the number of subgroups that must make AYP. Here school characteristics and state policy choices in implementing NCLB intersect. One of the central features of NCLB and AYP is that schools not only have to show continual overall progress toward proficiency for all students, but that they need to show progress for ethnic/racial and economic subgroups as well (e.g., African American, Latino, Special Education, economically disadvantaged students, etc.). States have some latitude, however, in establishing how many students in a school need to belong to a subgroup in order for a school to be responsible for improving the achievement and graduation rates of the subgroup. In our sample, states required anywhere from thirty to fifty students to be in a subgroup for that subgroup to be counted in a school's AYP calculation. These relatively small state differences can have large impacts on schools when they intersect with state and urban/rural differences in the size of schools and the racial/ethnic and economic composition of schools' student populations. Large and diverse schools may have eight or more subgroups that need to make AYP, whereas smaller schools can have half as many or fewer. Thus, the apparent AYP advantage of fewer students in a high school, in part, may reflect the fact that high schools with fewer students may face less subgroup accountability. On average, schools that made AYP had to do so for 25 percent fewer subgroups.

Schools with at least one subgroup that had to meet AYP made AYP only 34 percent of the time. Low-performing high schools without racial/ethnic subgroups made AYP 61 percent of the time. More than half of the low-performing high schools without racial/ethnic subgroup accountability are rural and nearly all are small with less than 500 students. Of the fifteen rural high schools in the South, which did not have to meet AYP for any racial/ethnic minorities, 87 percent made AYP.

Low-Performing High Schools That Did Not Make AYP Faced Higher Levels of NCLB Sanctions and Interventions

NCLB is designed so that each year a school does not meet AYP, there will be higher levels of scrutiny, interventions, and, ultimately, sanctions. This, in part, is based on the theory that the higher the level of intervention and sanction a school faces, the more it will be motivated to do whatever is necessary and possible to meet AYP. Following this reasoning, schools facing greater consequences for not making AYP might be more likely to achieve it than schools where the likelihood for intervention and sanction are small. An alternative view is that schools that have repeatedly failed to make AYP have done so, in part, because they lack the capacity to improve themselves or because the level of improvement required to make AYP is greater than even a school that puts forth effort and implements effective reforms can achieve. This second theory predicts that schools facing high levels of NCLB sanction and intervention might be less likely to achieve AYP.

To test these competing theories, we used each low-performing school's NCLB improvement status in 2004–2005 to classify schools into a three-category scale, indicating minor, moderate, and major levels of NCLB improvement pressure. The minor NCLB improvement pressure category encompasses schools that are not in any sort of NCLB improvement status. The moderate NCLB improvement pressure category includes schools that are at risk or under watch for improvement (meaning they are on alert that they could be placed in Year One Improvement in 2005–2006); schools that are making progress (schools that were in improvement in 2003–2004 but that are improving); and finally, schools that are in Year One Improvement. The major NCLB improvement pressure category includes schools that are in their second through seventh years of improvement status; schools that are under Corrective Action; and schools that are undergoing full restructuring.

In this sample, half of the schools are in the minor improvement category, 18 percent are in the moderate category, and 32 percent are in the major category. Current NCLB improvement status is inversely related to high schools making AYP. Of the low-performing high schools in the minor improvement pressure category, 66 percent made AYP compared to only 5 percent of the high schools facing the highest levels of intervention or sanction. Equally telling is the fact that 80 percent of the schools in the sample that made AYP in 2004–2005 are in the minor improvement pressure category, while slightly more than half of the schools that did not make AYP are in the major improvement category. In sum, low-performing high schools facing the lowest levels of NCLB improvement pressure more often than not made AYP, while only three of the sixty-four schools facing the strongest interventions or sanctions were able to make AYP in 2004–2005.

The NCLB improvement status of a school in our sample in 2004–2005 was not determined only by the school's absolute level of performance. Variation in state policy choices in implementing NCLB also played a significant role. High schools with the same absolute level of performance found themselves in very different improvement statuses. These depended, in part, on whether their state grandfathered in existing state accountability systems (if a school was found to have been low performing under state accountability systems for several years prior to NCLB, it could begin NCLB already in a Needs Improvement Category); how low or high a state set the baseline achievement levels for AYP regardless of any improvement they might have demonstrated (each state sets a baseline achievement level from which incremental progress toward proficiency is measured; if a school does not reach the baseline it does not make AYP, even if it has made improvement towards the baseline, unless the gains are large enough to trigger the Safe Harbor provision); and finally how much improvement the state requires in a given year to reach AYP (states set their own paths to proficiency, with some selecting even incremental gains each year and others expecting smaller gains in the initial years and larger gains in the later years).

As a snapshot of the 2004–2005 school year, our data remain suggestive and cannot establish a direct causal negative relationship between high degrees of pressure to improve under NCLB and schools' failure to make AYP. It is possible, and even likely, that the schools subjected to stronger accountability pressures were the most poorly performing to begin with. What these data do not indicate, however, is any positive relationship between pressure to improve under NCLB and a school's likelihood of making AYP. Many of these schools in the moderate and major improvement pressure categories had been identified as in need of improvement for multiple years (either under NCLB or under previously established state accountability systems). It does not appear from our analyses that this pressure has triggered sufficient improvement to move many of these schools in the direction required to make AYP. For now, our analysis suggests that pressure to improve is an insufficient stimulus for actual improvement. Longitudinal and more fine-grained case study data are required to further explore this relationship and to determine what levels of support are needed for a school under a high degree of pressure to actually turn itself around.

Low-Performing High Schools That Made AYP Are Concentrated in States in Which It Appears Easier to Reach the Required Proficiency Levels

Because states establish their own performance standards, design their own assessments, and establish the pace at which students must improve to reach 100 percent proficiency, the difficulty of reaching NCLB proficiency goals in a given year varies considerably from state to state. The ability of a school to reach NCLB proficiency goals can be influenced by at least three factors.

The first factor is the percentage of students required to demonstrate proficiency in a given year. In 2004–2005, the math proficiency levels required by the thirty-four states in our sample varied greatly, from a low of 17.5 percent in Missouri to a high of 75 percent in Tennessee. However, where states set their proficiency goal in 2004–2005 does not appear to be a determining factor in whether a low-performing high school makes AYP. In fact, low-performing high schools that made AYP faced slightly higher proficiency standards than schools that did not make AYP.

A second factor influencing whether a low-performing high school reaches NCLB proficiency goals in a particular state is the academic skill of its incoming students and the relationship between that average skill level and the state-established percentage of students required to demonstrate proficiency in a given year. In other words, what may be determinative is where the proficiency level needed for high schools to make AYP is set relative to the proficiency of the school's entering ninth graders. It was not possible, however, to measure the entering academic skills of the high school students attending the low-performing high schools in our sample.

We were able to use state-level data, however, to compare the percentage of eighth graders who scored proficient and above on a state's NCLB mathematics exam in 2003–2004, with the percentage of high school students required to obtain proficient levels in mathematics in 2004–2005 for a high school to make AYP. We found that 60 percent of the southern schools that made AYP were in states in which the 2004–2005 high school mathematics proficiency goal was at least 10 percentage points lower than the percentage of eighth graders scoring proficient on the NCLB exam in 2003–2004. By comparison, only 33 percent of the northern and 8 percent of the western low-performing high schools that made AYP were in a state with similar conditions. This indicates that the high rate at which low-performing high schools in the South made AYP, in part, may be related to the fact that proficiency goals were more often below existing proficiency levels.

A third factor that can influence a high school's ability to reach NCLB proficiency levels is the difficulty of the test used to establish proficiency in mathematics and English. We examine this by comparing the percentage of eighth-grade students currently scoring at proficient levels on their state NCLB mathematics exam to the percentage of students scoring at proficient and at basic on the most recent eighth-grade NAEP exam.

When comparing the percent proficient on the NCLB exam to the percent proficient on the NAEP exam in the 196 schools for which we were able to make this comparison, only five of the low-performing high schools in our sample are located in a state (Missouri) where the NCLB tests appear to be more difficult than the NAEP exam. Of the schools, forty-two come from states in which the NCLB and NAEP exams appear to be of similar rigor. However, 149 of the schools are in states in which the NCLB exam appears to be easier than the NAEP exam. In these states, the percentage of students who are proficient on the eighth-grade NCLB math exam is more than 10 percentage points greater than the percentage of students who are proficient on the NAEP eighth-grade math exam.

This analysis also revealed a clear association between NCLB test difficulty in the eighth grade and the likelihood that low-performing high schools will make AYP. The percentage of low-performing high schools making AYP increases as the NCLB eighth-grade mathematics exam gets easier. Missouri, which appears to have the most rigorous exam, seems to be an anomaly in this trend, but it also has the lowest proficiency target in 2004–2005 (17.5 percent).

Overall, there are clear indications that low-performing high schools that made AYP tended to be in states where high school proficiency goals were substantially below existing middle-grade proficiency levels and/or the NCLB proficiency exams themselves were less rigorous.

Are Low-Performing High Schools Improving Under NCLB?

Case studies of the schools in our sample reveal other state differences in NCLB implementation that make it impossible to answer this most basic question. State-to-state differences in the grade in which students are tested, how graduation rates are measured, and where the initial baselines are measured all work to undermine the ability to conclude that a low-performing high school that made AYP is actually performing better or improving faster than a school that did not make AYP. Two practices stand out.

First, in a number of states, high schools can make AYP by improving the performance of only those students who make it to the eleventh or twelfth grade. This is because these states test students in the eleventh and twelfth grades (and not in early grades). Though graduation rates are an additional indicator that states must include when determining AYP, for high schools to counteract the incentive to hold back or push out low-performing students prior to the testing year, graduation rate goals in many states are minimal and often require very little, if any, improvement.

For example, a New York City high school made AYP in 2004–2005 with seemingly impressive proficiency levels of 72 percent in math and 80 percent in English on the twelfth-grade test used in New York State. This, however, is paired with 58 percent cohort graduation rate and an 81 percent attendance rate. This indicates that only 58 percent of the entering freshmen graduated and only 41 percent graduated proficient in mathematics and 46 percent in English. Yet for all practical purposes, because this school made AYP, it is being sent the signal that it is doing fine and that it should keep focusing on making students who survive to the twelfth grade proficient rather than on the nearly 50 percent of students who are dropping out with weak academic skills.

A school in Missouri is an even stronger example of how current implementations of NCLB at the high school level can obscure more than they reveal. This school made AYP with proficiency levels of 21 percent in mathematics and 25 percent in English based on modest gains of 8 percentage points in mathematics and 4 percentage points in English. Its graduation rate, however, *declined* 12 percentage points to 77 percent. The school made AYP, however, because 77 percent is above the minimum required to meet AYP in Missouri in 2004–2005. The signal being sent to this school is that fewer graduates are okay as long as proficiency levels keep rising on the state tests given in the tenth and eleventh grades. This in turn provides a strong incentive to retain students in ninth grade or push them out.

A second practice that plays a large role in making it nearly impossible to use AYP results to determine if the nation's lowest-performing high schools are improving is that each state sets its own baseline from which high schools are supposed to progress until 100 percent of students demonstrate proficiency on state tests. Some states have set initial baseline pass rates on state tests at 20 percent or even lower. In California high schools, for example, in 2002–2003 and 2003–2004 only 11 percent of students had to score proficient in English and 10 percent in math for a school to make AYP. In 2004–2005, the bar was raised to 22 percent in English and 21 percent in math. From 2006–2007 on, the bar will steadily progress toward 100 percent in 2013–2014. Other states, however, set their initial or early baselines at 40 percent or higher. In Pennsylvania, for example, proficiency rates of 45 percent in mathematics and 54 percent in reading were required to make AYP in 2004–2005. In short, more than twice as many students needed to be proficient in Pennsylvania than in California for a high school to make AYP.

One result of this wide divergence in initial and early baselines is that a low-performing high school in California with stagnant proficiency rates in the low twenties could make AYP yearly from 2002–2003 to 2006–2007. By contrast, there is a high school in Pennsylvania that has seen a 15 percentage point increase in its math proficiency, a 20 percentage point increase in its English proficiency, and a 30 percentage point increase in its graduation rate over four years. Yet it is in Corrective Action 2, one year away from possibly being turned into a charter or seeing its faculty replaced because, despite these gains, it has not reached the baseline set by the state.

The same is true for graduation rates. In Georgia, for example, a high school could make AYP in 2004–2005 with a 60 percent graduation rate. In our sample, eight Georgia high schools made AYP in 2004–2005 and seven did not. Four of the high schools that made AYP, however, had graduation rates of around 60 percent, one actually had a rate in the fifties but made AYP through a confidence interval (a statistically allowable range built into the graduation rate measure), and another saw its graduation rate decline from 67 percent to 60 percent. Georgia is far from alone. In a recent publication, the Education Trust reports that no fewer than thirty-four states had set AYP goals for high school graduation that were lower than the states' reported average graduation rates (Hall, 2005).[7] Moreover, in thirty-seven states, any microscopic (0.1 percent) gain, or even no progress, enables a high school to make AYP for graduation rates.

There are, however, at least a dozen states with more ambitious graduation rate baselines and growth targets. California, which has a low test score baseline, has a much higher graduation rate minimum of 83 percent. Thus, a high school with a 61 percent graduation rate could make AYP in Georgia but fall far short in California. In addition, a high school with a very low initial graduation rate of say 40 percent in a state with a high baseline graduation rate could improve its graduation rate by 30 percentage points over four years—more than high schools making AYP in many states—and still find itself facing corrective action.

In sum, the case studies indicate that there is an "Alice in Wonderland" character to current implementations of the NCLB accountability framework: for high schools, up is down, and down is up. Some high schools that are making AYP and by implication being told they are doing fine have extremely low, or even declining, graduation rates. Other high schools are making significant improvements in both achievement proficiency levels and graduation rates and are facing the most extreme NCLB sanctions because their starting points were so far below the baselines established by their state. As a result, it is not possible to use the AYP indicator to determine how many or to what extent the nation's lowest-performing high schools are improving. This is deeply problematic because it means NCLB is not achieving one of its core missions.

Does NCLB Support Improvement in Low-Performing High Schools?

Problems with the implementation of the NCLB accountability framework for high schools are not limited to making it impossible for the public at large to know if low-performing high schools are improving. Even more problematic, the accountability requirements encourage teachers and administrators in low-performing schools to act in ways that are counterproductive to the intent of the law. This is seen most clearly in the undermining of the purpose of the Safe Harbor provisions. These provisions are intended to provide a means to acknowledge substantial improvement that falls short of yearly achievement goals. Reducing the percentage of students who are not proficient by 10 percentage points can hold a school harmless from the

---

[7] In states where dropouts are concentrated in a small number of high-poverty high schools, however, reaching even these apparently low goals can still be a challenge for low-performing high schools.

sanctions associated with not making AYP. The rationale is that if a school makes substantial improvement but falls a little short of ambitious improvement goals, it should not be penalized.

In low-performing high schools, with existing proficiency levels a great distance from their states' AYP levels (such as the 25 percent of high schools in our sample with mathematics proficiency levels of 20 percent or less), reaching Safe Harbor becomes the only feasible yearly achievement goal. When this is combined with the fact that high school students are typically only tested in one grade for AYP, a perverse situation occurs. The most logical course for the low-performing high school is to focus all its available resources and reform efforts on a very small number of students—those students who are close to proficient in the tested grade.

Consider the following example. In one high school in our sample from Pennsylvania, only 5 percent of the students are proficient in mathematics. The current state achievement target is 45 percent. To reach this target in one year is tantamount to running a marathon in sixty seconds. But to make Safe Harbor the school needs to see only a 10 percentage point reduction in the number of eleventh graders who are not proficient. This school has a nearly 50 percent dropout rate and as a result many fewer eleventh and twelfth graders than ninth and tenth graders. Thus while there are 1,500 students in the school, there are only 250 eleventh graders, 10 percent of which is 25 students. NCLB in this particular application is not prodding the school to improve the education of its 1,500 students, but rather to focus all its efforts on those 25 eleventh graders.

NCLB "NEEDS IMPROVEMENT"

State differences in how NCLB is being implemented at the high school level make it difficult to identify which high schools are truly low-performing, and virtually impossible to determine if the nation's low-performing high schools are getting better or which schools are making the greatest strides toward fulfilling the intent of the law. In addition, the examples cited previously show how some features of current implementations of NCLB actually provide incentives or means to evade or even operate counter to the law's intent. These examples illustrate how low baseline requirements or minimal improvement targets for graduation rates may offer incentives for schools to improve achievement scores and reach AYP by pushing students out in the ninth or tenth grade. They also show how low-performing schools that are making meaningful improvements in both achievement and graduation measures can fail to make AYP (and invite sanctions) while similar schools that demonstrate far less improvement make AYP in other states. Equally troubling is the incentive produced through the Safe Harbor provision to target only a small number of students for instructional improvement, enabling schools with high concentrations of needy students to avoid more comprehensive reforms that could reach all students.

Based on these findings, we offer three proposals for improving NCLB in light of its pending reauthorization.

Proposal 1: Reconceptualize Safe Harbor So It Focuses Low-Performing High Schools on the Key Points Where Students Fall off the Graduation Path and Encourages Them to Implement Strategic Schoolwide Reforms.

At its core, the NCLB accountability framework is an ambitious attempt to use incentives and sanctions to change behavior. But as any economist or parent will tell you, getting the signals right is very tricky business. Carrots and sticks can work but they need to be the right ones for the situation and involve a shared understanding of the desired outcome between the two parties involved.

Safe Harbor as it is currently conceptualized is sending the wrong signals. It is encouraging low-performing high schools to focus their reform efforts on a very few students rather than on improving the whole school. Moreover, improvements in academic achievement and graduation rates in practice do not tend to happen in steady yearly increments. Nor should we really want them to in low-performing high schools. In a high school, where less than 10 percent of students are proficient in mathematics and reading and less than 50 percent are graduating, do we really want to spend five years establishing that it needs a major transformation or longer if it manages to make incremental improvements in a few of those years?

An alternative might be to base Safe Harbor around significant yearly improvements in the percentage of students earning promotion from one grade to the next and taking a rigorous sequence of high school courses. The high school course sequence promoted by the U.S. Department of Education State Scholars program might be a good starting point, along with giving students the option to include a coherent sequence of high-quality career and technical education courses in the mix. Chris Swanson's (2004) Cumulative Promotion Index (CPI) might provide one model of how progress from grade to grade could be measured using existing enrollment data already collected by the education department. The CPI measures high school graduation through a stepwise process composed of three grade-to-grade promotion transitions (grade nine to ten, ten to eleven, and eleven to twelve) in addition to the ultimate graduation event (grade twelve to diploma; Swanson, 2005). Basing Safe Harbor on significant increases in the percentage of students earning on-time promotion from grade to grade and taking a rigorous sequence of high school courses would focus low-performing schools on improving the education of every student in every grade. It would also direct their reform efforts toward two of the major school-level variables that affect both graduation rates and achievement levels (Allensworth & Eaton, 2005).

Proposal 2: Use NCLB Reform as an Opportunity to Solve the Conundrum of Title I Funding for High Schools and Acknowledge That Different High Schools Face Greatly Different Degrees of Educational Difficulty.

NCLB aims to provide both sanctions and supports. Yet, to date, the supports have been underdeveloped and largely focused on governance issues, as opposed to the comprehensive organizational, instructional, and professional development/teacher support reforms that many low-performing high schools need. Equally significant is the fact that NCLB sanctions and supports are supposed to be directed at schools that receive Title I funding. Yet, most of the nation's lowest-performing high schools do not receive Title I funds, even though they educate primarily high-poverty students. In our random sample of low-performing high schools, for example, only 47 percent were receiving Title I funds, even though 73 percent had 40 percent or more of the student body receiving free or reduced-price lunch. This means that *the* federal program for providing supplemental support to schools that face the challenge of educating students impacted by the ill effects of poverty is not reaching many of the nation's high schools with the greatest need for additional support.

One way to resolve both problems would be to establish a separate stream of Title I funding for high-poverty high schools. Funds would be distributed by a formula that factors in both the poverty rate and the degree of educational difficulty faced by the high school. Educational difficulty would be defined in part by the number of entering students who are overage for grade, have failed courses in the middle grades, have below-grade-level skills, and/or have weak attendance habits. Finally, continuation of funding should be contingent on high schools implementing comprehensive, evidence-based reforms that address student attendance, behavior, and engagement, provide intensive and sustained extra help to those with below-grade-level skills, increase available social supports, and enable teachers and students to develop and use the skills needed to teach and learn rigorous academic material.

Proposal 3: Act Now to Transform or Replace the Lowest-Performing High Schools.

Our data indicate that a significant number of low-performing schools will not be improved through accountability systems and the standards movement alone. Our experience indicates that they lack the sufficient human, organizational, instructional, and financial resources to reform themselves, regardless of the amount of reform pressure put on them. Nor do we need an improved accountability system to identify these high schools. We know today which ones they are and where they are located (Balfanz & Legters, 2004). What is needed is a coordinated federal, state, and local effort to provide the vision, resources, tools, training, and technical assistance required to transform or replace the approximately 15 percent of high schools that produce most of the nation's dropouts. Thus, part of revising NCLB should involve providing the means and methods to do so. This could involve state and districts working together to provide struggling high schools with technical assistance teams either directly or by contracting with established third-party school reform organizations with proven track records. It will involve making sure that the technical assistance teams and high schools have the necessary human and financial resources to implement, institutionalize, and sustain comprehensive reforms (for information on effective reforms and costs, see Balfanz, 2005; Kemple, Herlihy, & Smith, 2005; Legters, Balfanz, Jordan, & McPartland, 2002; Quint, Bloom, Black, & Stephens, 2005). It will also involve ensuring that states, districts, and technical assistance teams are backed with necessary statutory power to enact needed reforms that challenge existing staffing, scheduling, and other regulatory structures.

CONCLUSION

There are about 2,000 high schools in the United States where graduation is not the norm. These are high schools in which the senior class routinely shrinks to 60 percent or less, often much less, of the freshman class that entered four years earlier. High schools with weak promoting power are the engines driving the low national graduation rate for minority students and the growing number of dispossessed young adults who are neither employed nor in school. These high schools must be specifically targeted for reform if the American high school is to fulfill its pivotal role as the means by which children who grow up in poverty can become adults who lead the nation. Transforming the nation's dropout factories into high schools that prepare all their students for postsecondary schooling or training and successful adulthood should thus be an urgent national priority.

Providing all students with access to a high-quality, standards-based education is the primary intent of NCLB. We fully embrace the spirit of NCLB, yet our research shows that this landmark legislation is falling short of its intentions at the high school level. This is due to weakness in NCLB's core accountability measure (AYP) and substantial variation across states in how NCLB is being implemented at the high school level. Rather than identifying low-performing high schools effectively and consistently, AYP has created a confusing landscape in which improving low-performing high schools are sanctioned, while similar schools showing less improvement are not. As implemented, AYP can work against the spirit of NCLB by creating incentives for low-performing high schools to push out students and forgo costly, but ultimately more effective, comprehensive reforms in favor of test preparation for a targeted few.

We offer several proposals to address these shortcomings—reconceptualizing Safe Harbor for high schools so it focuses low-performing high schools on the strategic schoolwide reforms, taking a hard look at how Title I funding is distributed to low-performing high schools, and making focused efforts to provide comprehensive reforms to the most challenged high schools. These proposals attempt to strike a balance between the need for uniform standards designed to ensure that all students graduate from high school prepared for success in college, career, and civic life and the high degree of educational challenge faced by low-performing high schools. Such changes would increase the effectiveness of NCLB and more closely align implementation of the law with its stated purpose of ensuring equal access to a high standard of education for all.

13

Can NCLB Improve High School Graduation Rates?

Russell W. Rumberger

Over the last decade, many state governments have implemented performance-based accountability systems as a strategy for improving their public schools (Fuhrman & Elmore, 2004). Accountability systems mandate improvements in student and school performance and provide rewards and sanctions that carry high stakes for both students and schools. Although test scores are the primary indicator of student and school performance, increasingly accountability systems are requiring improvements in high school graduation rates.

The federal No Child Left Behind (NCLB) Act of 2001 imposed a federal accountability system on states as a condition for receiving Title I funds. Although NCLB shares many features of state accountability systems, it also has some unique provisions such as mandating that 100 percent of all students and students from major subgroups reach academic proficiency by the year 2013–2014. NCLB also mandates improvements in high school graduation rates.

I would like to thank Dan Losen, Gail Sunderman, Jill Morningstar, and Lorraine McDonnell for their helpful comments on earlier versions of this paper.

This chapter examines NCLB and performance-based accountability systems as a strategy for improving school performance and raising high school graduation rates. The first section examines the extent to which schools contribute to dropout rates. The second section reviews research on effective strategies for reducing high school dropout rates. The third section examines the research literature on reforming high schools. The fourth section analyzes the shortcoming of performance-based accountability systems for improving school performance including the weak accountability provisions of NCLB for improving graduation rates. The final section suggests ways to address these shortcomings.

HIGH SCHOOLS AND DROPOUT RATES

One of the most important and fundamental issues in educational research and policy is the extent to which schools contribute to student achievement. The reason is that many educational policies including NCLB are predicated on the belief that differences in student achievement are largely due to differences in schools, so improving schools—particularly low-performing schools—will raise overall student achievement and reduce differences in achievement between high-performing advantaged students and low-performing disadvantaged students.

While researchers and policymakers from all political persuasions agree that schools contribute to student achievement, the extent of that contribution is much less clear. Famed sociologist James Coleman (1990) sparked widespread debate with the publication of his report in 1966, which concluded that schools had relatively little impact on student achievement compared to the background of the students who attend them: "family background differences account for much more variation than do school differences" (p. 124). More specifically, Coleman found that schools only accounted for 5 percent to 38 percent of the variation in achievement among different grade levels, ethnic groups, and regions of the country (p. 77). And although Coleman's analysis was subjected to considerable scrutiny and debate, more recent research studies using more refined statistical techniques continue to find that no more than one-third of the variation in student achievement lies between different schools (Organization for Economic Cooperation and Development, 2001, p. 60; Raudenbush & Bryk, 2002; Rumberger & Palardy, 2004). This has important implications for policies designed to improve student achievement that focus on schools as the sole arena for change, a topic I revisit (Coleman, 1990; Rothstein, 2004).

Coleman (1990) found not only that differences in schools account for relatively modest differences in student achievement but also that "the social composition of the student body is more highly related to achievement, independent of the student's own social background, than is any school factor " (p. 119) including school facilities and attributes of teachers. Recent studies have also confirmed these findings (Organization for Economic Cooperation and Development, 2001, p. 199; Rumberger & Palardy, 2005a). These findings, too, have implications for school reform strategies.

To what extent do schools contribute to dropout and graduation rates? This question is more difficult to answer than a similar question concerning student achievement, but there is little reason to suggest that it is much different from student achievement. Research from one recent study found that more than half of the differences in dropout rates among a sample of 912 high schools from across the United States was due to differences in the background characteristics of students who attended the schools rather than to differences in the characteristics of schools themselves (Rumberger & Palardy, 2005b). Yet even controlling for differences in student background characteristics, there remain substantial differences in dropout rates of U.S. high schools: a student with average background characteristics is less than half as likely to drop out from a high-performing high school than from a low-performing high school (Rumberger & Palardy, 2005b, Table 1). At the same time, a recent analysis of school dropout rates estimates that nearly half of the nation's dropouts come from about 12 percent of all high schools in which only 60 percent or less of the entering freshman class reaches senior year four years later (Balfanz & Legters, this volume).

Existing research suggests the potential and limitations of schools as a vehicle for improving the nation's high school graduation rate. Even if all the existing differences between high schools in the United States were eliminated, substantial differences in dropout rates among students would remain. Yet improving the nation's high schools can substantially improve students' prospects for graduating

EFFECTIVE STRATEGIES FOR REDUCING DROPOUT RATES IN HIGH SCHOOLS

There are two basic approaches for reducing dropout rates in high school. The first approach focuses on *programmatic interventions* that either provide supplemental academic and social supports to students within an existing school program, or provide an alternative school program in an existing school (school within a school) or in a separate facility (alternative school).

This approach attempts to alter the values, attitudes, and behaviors of targeted, at-risk students without attempting to alter the characteristics of the larger families, schools, and communities that may contribute to those individual characteristics. The second approach focuses on *systemic interventions* that attempt fundamentally to transform the way families, schools, and communities serve all youth.

Both approaches have strengths and weaknesses. Programmatic interventions are easier to develop, evaluate, and disseminate widely than systemic interventions, but they can be costly and impact relatively few students. And despite the large number of dropout prevention programs in the United States, and the relative ease in evaluating them, few dropout intervention programs have been evaluated using scientifically rigorous, random-assignment evaluations. For example, the U.S. General Accounting Office (1987) surveyed more than 1,000 dropout programs in the fall of 1986, yet it found only twenty rigorous evaluations of the 479 programs that responded to the survey. A more recent review of more than 100 federally funded dropout prevention programs found that only 30 programs had rigorous evaluations, and only three significantly reduced high school dropout rates (Dynarski, 2004). Although most dropout prevention programs focus on students at risk of dropping out in middle and high school, a number of preschool programs designed to improve the cognitive and social development of disadvantaged children have been shown to significantly reduce high school dropout rates (Barnett, 1995).

Systemic interventions have the potential to reduce dropping out in a much large number of students by improving some of the environmental factors in families, schools, and communities that contribute to dropout behavior (National Research Council Panel on High-Risk Youth, 1993). Systemic solutions may be particularly appropriate in schools and communities where the concentration of students at risk of dropping out is high.

Although the promise of systemic solutions to the dropout problem is great, the reality is not. The reason is simply that systemic changes are extremely difficult to achieve because they involve making fundamental changes in the way institutions work individually and within the larger system of which they are a part. In addition, systemic interventions are difficult to evaluate with rigorous, scientific methods involving random assignment (Cook, 2005).

To date, most systemic intervention strategies in education have relied on externally developed comprehensive school reform (CSR) models that transform the entire operation of schools through a series of coherent and reinforcing strategies (U.S. Department of Education, 2002). Hundreds of schools in the United States have adopted these models with financial support from the federal government through the Comprehensive School

Reform Program and NCLB (Desimone, 2002). However, there is little evidence that CSR models have been effective in reducing high school dropout rates. A recent evaluation of twenty-nine of the most widely adopted CSR models found that most models focus on elementary schools, and those that focus on high schools have been evaluated primarily in terms of their effects on student achievement (test scores) and not dropout rates (Borman, Hewes, Overman, & Brown, 2003). Another study of eighteen middle and high school reform models found sparse research evidence on nonachievement outcomes, including graduation rates (Comprehensive School Reform Center, 2006).

There is at least some evidence that reforming high schools to reduce dropout rates may be particularly challenging. In their study of 207 urban high schools that were attempting major school reform programs based on the effective schools literature, Louis and Miles (1990) found widespread improvement in a number of areas such as student behavior and student and staff morale, but even among programs that had implemented these changes for several years and enjoyed improvements in student achievement, improvement in dropout rates were "rarely achieved no matter how long a program had been in operation" (Louis & Miles, 1990, p. 49). Another review of five school restructuring efforts supported by large, multi-million dollar grants from the federal dropout prevention program found that none of these restructured schools significantly reduced dropout rates in relation to comparable schools (Dynarski & Gleason, 1998).

Features of Effective Schools

One approach for creating effective schools is to identify the critical features that contribute to school performance. Since the publication of the Coleman report in 1966, countless studies have been undertaken to identify the characteristics of effective schools. These studies have ranged from large-scale statistical studies of national data sets (as Coleman did) to small-scale case studies of particular schools (Purkey & Smith, 1983). Although a number of specific features have been identified in these studies, they essentially address two basic features of schools: *school inputs* or the material conditions of schools, which include school resources and school structure and the characteristics of students and teachers; and *school processes*, which include the attitudes, behaviors, and practices of students, teachers, and administrators as well as the policies, practices, and culture (or climate) of the school as a whole.

There is considerable disagreement on the requisite inputs needed to develop and support effective schools. That is, what resources, teacher characteristics, student characteristics, and structural features are necessary to create an effective school? For example, there is ongoing debate on whether school resources make a difference (Hanushek, 1986; Hedges, Laine, & Greenwald, 1994). There are similar debates about the extent to which other school inputs matter: (1) teacher characteristics such as credentials and training (Wayne & Youngs, 2003); (2) the racial or socioeconomic composition of students in the school (Kahlenberg, 2001; Orfield & Lee, 2005) ; and (3) certain structural features of schools such as school size (Luyten, 1994; National Research Council, Committee on Increasing High School Students' Engagement and Motivation to Learn, 2004) and the type of organizational control such as private, public, charter, and magnet schools (Bettinger, 2005; Bryk, Lee, & Holland, 1993; Coleman, Hoffer, & Kilgore, 1982; Gamoran, 1996).

One reason for the lack of consistent findings on the relationship between school inputs and student outcomes is that school inputs may be necessary to create effective schools, but not sufficient. What is equally important is how the inputs are allocated and used, which, in turn, depends on what goes on within schools. Consequently, many researchers have sought to identify the policies, practices, and climate within effective schools (Edmonds, 1979; Purkey & Smith, 1983; Teddlie & Reynolds, 2000).

Other researchers have looked beyond these discernable features of the effective schools and tried to identify the requisite "building blocks" necessary to create effective schools and effectively utilize school inputs. These building blocks have to do with the characteristics of both individuals and the school as a whole. For example, Cohen, Raudenbush, and Ball (2003) argued that conventional school resources such as teachers' formal qualifications, books, facilities, and time offer only the capacity to improve teaching and learning, but to do so requires the teachers' *personal resources*, which they define as their will, skills, and knowledge. Similarly, Newmann (1993) argued that new organizational structures such as site-based management or team teaching may do little if teachers and administrators do not have the requisite commitment and competencies. Finally, Bryk and Schneider (2002) argued that a requisite building block for school improvement is a *social resource* known as relational trust, which they define as the social relationships at work in a school: "[W]e view relational trust as creating the fertile social ground for core technical resources (such as standards, assessments, and new curricula) to take root and develop into something of value" (p. 135). In their simplest form, the two essential building blocks of school reform are *will* and *capacity* that characterize both individuals and schools as institutions.

One fundamental question is whether will and capacity constitute prerequisites for developing effective schools or whether schools—with the proper incentives, resources, and support—can develop the requisite will and capacity. Some research suggests they are prerequisites. For example, many comprehensive school reform models require that teachers display the necessary will to reform by first voting on whether to adopt the model (Borman et al., 2003). A comprehensive review of efforts to scale-up comprehensive school reform models found that a lack of teacher capacity led to weak implementation of the reforms (Berends, Bodilly, & Kirby, 2002). Bryk and Schneider (2002) argued that relationship trust is easier to build in schools that both students and teachers have chosen to attend, thereby assuring a shared commitment (p. 142). This literature suggests that it may be necessary to recruit and select teachers with at least some preexisting level of will and capacity before undertaking school reform. Yet other research suggests that teacher beliefs and commitment can be altered through mandated or coerced involvement in reform that is demonstrated to be successful (Guskey, 1989; McLaughlin, 1990). In addition, certain organizational features such as smaller school size and shared decision making may be necessary to develop and support teachers' will and capacity (Ancess, 2000; Newmann, 1993).

THE CHALLENGE OF REFORMING HIGH SCHOOLS

The challenge of reforming high schools to reduce dropout rates is formidable. The challenge is less formidable in the relatively large proportion of high schools where students at risk of dropping out of school comprise a small proportion of the student population. In those schools, programmatic interventions should be sufficient to provide the additional academic and social supports that at-risk students need to stay in school. The challenge is much more formidable in the relatively small proportion of high schools where a large proportion of students drop out, many of which are large, urban high schools with high rates of poverty. In those schools, systemic interventions that address the needs of the entire student body will be required to transform the entire school.

What role can state and federal policies play, including NCLB, in bringing about such reforms? There is extensive research literature examining the implementation and impact of past federal and state policies designed to bring about widespread reform of public schools. This literature provides a very sobering assessment of the prospect for reforming schools (McLaughlin, 1987). A recent evaluation of the ten-year effort of the New American Schools (NAS) to develop, implement, and scale-up research-based comprehensive school reform models reached a similar conclusion: "The causal chain of events leading to strong implementation and outcomes have proven to be more complex than originally considered by NAS and one that remained largely outside of its control and influence...[which is] in keeping with the literature on implementation indicating the complexity of the change process" (Berends et al., 2002, p. 147). Not only is reform difficult, it is also uneven, varying widely across schools and districts (McLaughlin, 1990). The difficulty and unevenness of reform efforts can be traced to a number of factors, some of which have to do with the features of the reform itself, but others that have to do with local contexts and conditions that are largely outside the control of the reform itself (Desimone, 2002). Thus, even with sufficient incentives and support, local conditions and contexts remain formidable obstacles that must be addressed if widespread reforms are to be successful (Berends et al., 2002, Desimone, 2002).

Beyond simply identifying factors that promote or impede reform, it is important to identify a *theory of action* to explain the underlying causal process of how reform is supposed to bring about improved student and school performance. Policymakers have a limited number of mechanisms or policy instruments at their disposal to effect change in public schools, and they often lack an explicit understanding of how the mechanisms they employ are supposed to work (McDonnell, 2004; McDonnell & Elmore, 1987).

To elaborate, policymakers can use five basic instruments to effect change in schools: (1) mandates, (2) inducements, (3) capacity building, (4) system changing, and (5) hortatory. Each policy instrument employs specific mechanisms that are suited for particular types of educational problems, and each is based on assumptions about the existing will (behavior) and capacity of policy targets—individuals and institutions—and the ability to alter them (McDonnell, 2004, Table 2.1). For example, mandates impose rules on policy targets in order to get them to produce desired outcomes under the assumption that the policy targets have the capacity to comply. Inducements provide money to institutions to produce more desired outcomes under the assumption that the capacity exists or that it can easily be acquired. In contrast, capacity-building instruments provide money for investment under the assumption that the policy targets lack the current capacity to produce the desired outcome. System-changing instruments go one step further by supporting new entrants (e.g., private service providers or private schools) under the assumption that existing institutions, even with more rules and money, are incapable of producing the directed outcomes. Finally, hortatory instruments attempt to alter behavior of individuals and institutions by providing relevant information that appeals to their values to produce the desired outcomes under the assumption that they will act on the information.

Policymakers often utilize more than one policy instrument, especially when they wish to achieve multiple policy goals and when the problems they are addressing are complex. This is often the case in education. State performance-based accountability systems, for example, often use mandates, inducements, capacity building, and persuasion to bring about school reform.

Policymakers' choice of policy instruments depends upon (1) how they define the educational problem they are trying to solve and (2) a range of resources and constraints they face including governmental capacity, fiscal resources, policy support and opposition, and available information (McDonnell & Elmore, 1987). These choices and actions are not just based on technical considerations and available information but are also based on policymakers' values: "[P]olicymakers also interpret this information using their own pre-existing values about how the system actually works and how it is supposed to work...[and they] prefer policy instruments consistent with their own values" (McDonnell & Elmore, 1987, pp. 145–146). Because of the complexity of both the educational problems policymakers address and the policymaking process, the theory of action underlying a policy may be wrong or at least incomplete. This problem plagues current education policies including NCLB.

For example, the NAS had a theory of action based on the idea that by developing "break-the-mold" comprehensive school designs and by getting local schools to adopt them, student performance would increase. That is, NAS was premised on a belief that capacity building alone would be sufficient to bring about school reform. But an evaluation of this effort concluded that this theory of action "was largely under-developed and underspecified" (Berends et al., 2002, p. 147).

Performance-based accountability systems such as NCLB also have a theory of action underlying them. They attempt to improve student and school performance by:

- developing content standards that specify what all students are expected to know and do;
- developing assessments to measure whether students are meeting those standards;
- specifying performance standards that students and schools are expected to reach and a timetable for reaching them;
- providing a series of rewards and sanctions—high stakes—for both students and schools to meet the performance standards.

According to Elmore (2004a), "Performance-based accountability systems operate on the theory that measuring performance, when coupled with rewards and sanctions. . .will cause schools and individuals who work in them, including students, teachers, and administrators, to work harder and perform at higher levels" (p. 277). Elmore argued that this theory, too, is "underspecified" (p. 278) because it remains unknown how schools and the individuals in them are supposed to respond to these rewards and sanctions in order to produce the desired outcomes. He goes on to argue that how schools respond is largely determined by the degree of the alignment between the requirements of the external accountability system and the school's internal accountability mechanisms that reflect the coherence and agreement around individual responsibility and collective expectations for teaching practice and student learning (Elmore, 2004b, Chapter 4). In addition to an underspecified theory of action, performance-based accountability systems suffer from a number of other, technical shortcomings, including a lack of valid, reliable, and accurate assessments of student and school performance (Furhman & Elmore, 2004).

Performance-based accountability systems rely on high-stakes incentives as the primary mechanism for reforming schools and improving student achievement, rather than providing resources and support to increase capacity. This assumes that the primary impediment to improved student outcomes is a lack of will rather than a lack of capacity, an assumption that some observers question (Elmore, 2004a, p. 280). While past research on policy implementation clearly recognizes the importance of incentives (Hanushek & Jorgenson, 1996), it also clearly demonstrates that students, educators, and schools require resources and support to improve their capacity (Elmore, 2004b; McLaughlin, 1987, 1990). Moreover, improving capacity may also lead to improvements in will (Guskey, 1989).

THE SHORTCOMINGS OF NCLB

While the limitations of all performance-based accountability systems discussed previously apply to NCLB, several other shortcomings afflict NCLB as a strategy for improving schools in general and for increasing high school graduation rates.

One of the general limitations that afflict all federal policy initiatives in education is the fragmented educational system in the United States. The constitutional authority for education in the United States resides in states that, in turn, have delegated substantial authority to the more than 15,000 local education agencies. This fragmentation of authority and power makes it difficult for the federal government to effect widespread and meaningful change in educational practice at the local level (Cohen & Spillane, 1992).

NCLB suffers from this problem. Many of the key provisions of the law specify ambitious federal policy goals, but allow states considerable authority in how they respond to those provisions. For example, while NLCB sets a federal policy goal that all students in the United States should be proficient in key academic subjects by the year 2014, states have the authority to set content and achievement standards. Similarly, NCLB mandates that schools receiving Title I funds show adequate yearly progress (AYP) toward reaching the performance target for all identifiable subgroups of students (e.g., racial and ethnic minority, poor, English language learner, and disabled students), but states have the authority to determine how AYP is calculated and the size of the identifiable subgroups. As a result, there is considerable unevenness among states in how many schools are meeting AYP goals and for which students (Sunderman, 2006). There are also inconsistencies and conflicts between NCLB as a federal accountability system and state accountability systems that have different policy goals and performance measures (Sunderman & Kim, 2007).

Another shortcoming of NCLB is the mix of policy instruments it employs. NCLB draws on all five of the policy instruments described earlier in order to achieve its ambitious goals, but the mix of instruments is problematic. In particular, NCLB is heavy on mandates and short on inducements and capacity building. NCLB has been criticized, for example, because it fails to provide sufficient financial support for its mandates, such as annual testing, resulting in a claim of it being an "unfunded mandate" (Kim & Sunderman, 2004). More fundamental is the heavy reliance on mandates and inducements, which evoke short-term responses, and less reliance on capacity building, which relies on long-term investment to improve capacity. The immediate need to meet the short-term mandates of the NLCB performance goals undermines the ability to provide the investment needed to improve the long-term capacity of individuals and institutions to improve schools (Elmore, 2004b). For example, under NCLB, failure of schools to meet AYP goals for two years invokes the provision that allows students to transfer to another public school in the district, and failure to meet goals for three years invokes a provision that low-income students be offered supplemental educational services. Both actions drain resources and effort away from improving the long-term capacity of low-performing schools. Moreover, the capacity-building provisions of NCLB are focused on improving the individual capacity of teachers through professional development, not on improving the organizational capacity of schools so they can provide ongoing, collaborative professional development that will yield sustained improvements in teaching and learning (Ancess, 2000; Elmore, 2004b, Chapter 3; Malen & Rice, 2004).

In addition to suffering from the fundamental shortcomings of all performance-based accountability systems, NCLB suffers from a number of shortcomings as a policy for reducing high school dropout rates. These shortcomings have to do with the weak accountability provisions concerning dropout rates:

1. Whereas NCLB mandates a common performance goal—100 percent proficiency on state exams by the year 2014—NCLB allows states to set their own performance goals with respect to dropout rates. As a result, some states have set high performance goals and others have set low performance goals.

2. Whereas NCLB gives states little leeway to document yearly progress toward meeting the performance goals for student achievement, NCLB allows states incredible leeway in meeting performance goals for graduation rates. As a result, some districts could take up to 300 years to reach their performance goals for graduation rates.

3. Whereas NCLB requires that schools, districts, and states report and demonstrate performance of seven subgroups of students with meeting achievement goals, NCLB does not require any breakdowns with respect to meeting graduation goals (Orfield, Losen, Wald & Swanson, 2004, pp. 10–14).

Strong accountability for test score performance coupled with weak accountability for graduation rate performance provides perverse incentives to districts. One way to raise test score performance is to remove or discharge low-performing students (Bowditch, 1993; Riehl, 1999; Rumberger & Larson, 1998). For example, both the New York City and Houston school systems have been investigated over the past years for "pushing out" their low-performing students into alternative, nondiploma programs or classifying them as transfers so they would also not be counted as dropouts (Archer, 2003; Gotham, 2002; Lewin & Medina, 2003).

RECOMMENDATIONS FOR STRENGTHENING NCLB

NCLB can be strengthened in such a way as to foster meaningful reform in high schools that would help reduce dropout rates, but the task would be formidable. It would involve not just strengthening the provisions of the law that focus specifically on high school graduation but also altering some fundamental provisions of the law designed to improve public schools more generally.

Changes in the law involving high school graduation rates would be relatively easy. One recommended change is to strengthen the accountability provisions for high school graduation rates to make them consistent with those for student achievement provisions so that schools have more incentive to address this aspect of student performance. These changes should include:

1. Requiring states to use a common method for calculating graduation rates, such as the method endorsed by all fifty governors in 2005 (National Governors Association, 2006).

2. Setting national performance goals for school dropout rates.

3. Establishing more rigid annual progress goals.

4. Requiring performance goals for the same demographic subgroups required for student achievement.

Of course, as suggested earlier, simply altering incentives alone will do little to improve graduation rates without also improving the capacity of schools to respond. This would require a substantial investment in both programmatic and systematic reforms. More resources should be provided to fund proven dropout prevention and recovery programs in schools where programmatic reforms may be sufficient to address the dropout problem. The federal government's *What Works Clearinghouse*, which was established by the U.S. Department of Education in 2002 to provide scientific evidence on what works in education, has begun to evaluate scientifically validated dropout prevention programs. Together, these actions would help schools to focus on the problem of school dropout and would provide some resources for them to undertake useful, programmatic changes.

But to improve high school graduation rates in the schools where the problem is endemic will require major revisions to NCLB to address some of the underlying flaws in this approach to high school reform. Elmore (2004a) identified five design principles for accountability systems that would bring about meaningful and sustained reform in schools:

1. Individual and collective stakes should be based on defensible, empirically based theories about what it is possible to accomplish on measured performance within a given period of time.

2. Stakes should be based on valid, reliable, and accurate information about student and school performance.

3. Students should not be accountable for learning content they have not been taught.

4. Schools should be accountable for the value they add to student learning, not the effects of prior instruction; school systems should be accountable for the cumulative learning of students over their career in the system.

5. Reciprocity of accountability and capacity—for each increment in performance I require of you, I have an equal and reciprocal

responsibility to provide you with the capacity to produce that performance (pp. 290–294).

Adopting these principles would require time, research, and resources and, more importantly, a political will to reexamine the premises underlying this reform strategy. In essence, it would require a complete rethinking of virtually all the current provisions of NCLB.

CONCLUSIONS

Improving the nation's high school graduation rate remains a formidable challenge. Performance-based accountability systems such as NCLB attempt to improve graduation rates by improving public schools. However, these systems lack a sound and tested theory of action as to how students and schools are supposed to improve. In particular, they rely on high-stakes sanctions designed to motivate students, educators, and schools to improve without providing sufficient resources and supports to develop the capacity to improve. The research literature suggests that such a strategy is unlikely to yield sustained and meaningful improvements in teaching and learning, or to improve graduation rates. To make this strategy effective will require a better balance of incentives, resources, and support based on valid, comprehensive measures of student and school performance and a tested theory of action. In other words, it will require a complete rethinking of NCLB and state-level, performance-based accountability systems.

Yet even with substantial revisions, school-based strategies are limited because schools alone cannot be the sole arena for the improvement of student performance. To improve student outcomes and close the achievement gap will require addressing the pervasive inequalities found in family and community resources (Armor, 2003; Rothstein, 2004).

Conclusion

Accountability After Five Years

Since 1965, the federal government has committed itself to improving the educational opportunities of low-income and minority students. With No Child Left Behind (NCLB), Congress promised to continue that commitment, but impatient with the pace of change, adopted stringent new accountability requirements. Based on the assumption that test-based accountability would lead to improved student achievement, NCLB expanded federal authority over core educational functions and combined specific educational goals for students with timelines for achieving those goals. It placed considerable reliance on state education agencies to implement the law and to intervene in low-performing schools, but when it came to the developing the infrastructure or providing resources to support implementation, the focus was on compliance rather than on capacity building. Federal policymakers apparently believed that states would have the capacity and resources to implement the law's requirements and intervene in low-performing schools and districts. They were wrong.

Presenting a range of perspectives, the contributors to this book raise important questions about the law's effects and ways to improve it: How do we develop assessment and accountability systems that assist rather than interfere with educational progress? How do we press for change without being counterproductive and undermining the good that is happening in our nation's schools? How do we create a viable educational agenda that is mindful of state and local capacity? These questions reflect both the nuance of the debate we need to have on NCLB and underscore the challenges of designing workable accountability systems that lead to coherent efforts to improve schools.

At stake are the educational opportunities available to our nation's poor and minority students and whether they will gain the skills they need to be contributing members of society. Current socioeconomic conditions underscore the importance of focusing on improving the achievement of all students, but particularly that of low-income students. Orfield and Lee (2007) report that, among school-aged children, poverty has increased substantially over the past six years. This poverty cuts across racial and ethnic groups, with the largest increase in poverty among white students. In central cities where poverty is concentrated, nearly two-thirds of black and Latino students attend schools where free and reduced lunch eligibility reaches 75 percent or higher. One of the causes of the growing poverty is the increase in low-income Latino students, the most rapidly growing segment of the school-aged population.

These demographic changes and the relationship between educational outcomes and economic success suggest that we need to intensify our efforts to educate students who traditionally have not performed well in our educational system. Since the Reagan administration's excellence movement, our reform policies have focused on raising standards and putting pressure on schools, teachers, and students to improve performance and narrow the achievement gap, with minimal success. NCLB raises of the stakes of this strategy by putting real teeth into the enforcement of these accountability policies, and, unfortunately, the largest consequences fall on schools serving the nation's most disadvantaged students. The findings and analyses presented here suggest that improving NCLB will require rethinking our approaches to measuring and supporting school performance so that we can achieve both accountability goals and a narrowing of the racial achievement gap.

The contributors here identify a number of things that can be done to accomplish these goals. First, more needs to be done to develop an accountability system that is fair, yields information that informs and advances student learning goals, and contributes to improving instruction. There are some concrete steps that can make NCLB accountability better by altering some of its provisions. The unrealistic goal of 100 percent proficiency should be replaced with a goal that is still ambitious, but also realistic and obtainable. Adopting multiple measures of student progress that reflect improvement across a range of performance indicators will help to reduce incentives to ignore some groups of students or push them out in order to boost test scores. These should include such factors as attendance, course passage, and graduation and grade retention rates. For example, requiring states and districts to report grade enrollment and grade retention rates would allow easy examination of the progression of students through the grades. Including mechanisms that track growth in student performance rather than simply identifying a fixed performance level can improve the way adequate yearly progress is determined and allow us to evaluate schools on their contribution to student learning. To lessen the narrowing of the curriculum and instruction that accompanies high-stakes testing, we need to routinely evaluate the performance of accountability systems and audit state reported gains on high stakes tests. This can be accomplished in part by continuing to use the National Assessment of Educational Progress as an independent measure of student performance. But equally important to revising and improving the current system, the nation needs to begin the work of research and development required for creating better accountability systems.

Second, there needs to be greater investment in capacity building in the nation's lowest-performing schools and districts. The high expectations written into NCLB must be paired with adequate support and investment in school reform if low-performing schools and districts are to improve. This includes requiring schools to use resources more productively, but also federal investment in programmatic and systemic reforms and recognition that schools need help. Reform initiatives must be coupled with realistic timetables for school improvement and incentives for recruiting and retaining high quality teachers in places where they are needed most. Because it is unrealistic to expect improvements in the educational system to fully offset the disadvantages faced by historically lower performing groups of students, we need to complement these programmatic and systemic reforms with out-of-school interventions, such as high quality preschool services, and programs that address nonschool conditions such as housing, poverty, health care, and safety. States also must receive adequate funding if they are to accomplish the additional tasks that are placed on them by NCLB. This should include resources for both administrative tasks and school improvement activities, but it might also include adopting Title I funding reforms that would compensate for interstate disparities in fiscal capacity. At the same time, an independent, federally funded analysis of what it takes in administrative and financial resources for states to have a reasonable chance of turning around low-performing schools is needed that takes into account the enormous variation in states' political, administrative, and educational structures.

Finally, we need to reexamine the premises underlying this reform strategy. Research presented in this book suggests that the lofty goals of NCLB—to improve student achievement and narrow the achievement gap—are not being accomplished, and careful analysis concludes that schools will not reach the 100 percent proficiency goals by 2014. For educational systems to move in directions that will ensure high levels of learning for all students, we need to engage in a serious reassessment of whether an external, test-driven accountability policy will ultimately lead us in that direction.

References

INTRODUCTION

Kantor, H., & Lowe, R. (2006). From new deal to no deal: No Child Left Behind and the devolution of responsibility for equal opportunity. *Harvard Educational Review, 76*(4), 474–502.

Rothstein, R. (2004). *Class and schools: Using social, economic, and educational reform to close the black-white achievement gap.* New York: Teachers College Press.

Sunderman, G. L., Kim, J. S., & Orfield, G. (2005). *NCLB meets school realities: Lessons from the field.* Thousand Oaks, CA: Corwin Press.

CHAPTER 1

Beaton, A. E., Mullis, I. V. S., Martin, M. O., Gonzalez, E. J., Kelly, D. L., & Smith, T. A. (1996). *Mathematics achievement in the middle school years: IEA's Third International Mathematics and Science Study (TIMSS), Appendix E.* Chestnut Hill, MA: Boston College, TIMSS International Study Center.

Cushman, J. H. (1998, February 11). Makers of diesel truck engines are under pollution inquiry. *The New York Times.* Retrieved August 15, 2007, from http://query.nytimes.com/gst/fullpage.html?sec=technology&res=9405E5D8173CF932A25751C0A96E958260

Farhi, P. (1996, November 17). Television's 'sweeps' stakes: Season of the sensational called a context out of control. *The Washington Post,* p. A01.

Fuller, B., Gesicki, K., Kang, E., & Wright, J. (2006). *Is the No Child Left Behind Act working? The reliability of how states track achievement.* Berkeley: Policy Analysis for California Education.

Fuller, B., Wright, J., Gesiucki, K., & Kang, E. (2007). Gauging growth: How to judge No Child Left Behind? *Educational Researcher, 36*(5), 268–278.

Hambleton, R. K., Jaeger, R. M., Koretz, D., Linn, R. L., Millman, J., & Phillips, S. E. (1995). *Review of the measurement quality of the Kentucky instructional results information system, 1991–1994.* Frankfort: Kentucky General Assembly, Office of Education Accountability.

Hickman, A., Levin, C., Rupley, S., & Willmott, D. (1997, January 6). Did Sun cheat? *PC Magazine.*

Ho, A. D., & Haertel, E. H. (2006). *Metric-free measures of test score trends and gaps with policy-relevant examples.* (CSE Tech. Rep. No. 665). Los Angeles: University of California, Center for the Study of Evaluation.

Jacob, B. (2002). *Accountability, incentives and behavior: The impact of high-stakes testing in the Chicago public schools* (Working paper W8968). Cambridge, MA: National Bureau of Economic Research.

Klein, S. P., Hamilton, L. S., McCaffrey, D. F., & Stecher, B. M. (2000). *What do test scores in Texas tell us?* (Issue paper IP-202). Santa Monica, CA: RAND. Retrieved January 12, 2004, from http://www.rand.org/publications/IP/IP202/

Koretz, D. (2003, April). Attempting to discern the effects of the NCLB accountability provisions on learning. In K. Ercikan (Chair), *Effects of accountability on learning.* Presidential invited session, annual meeting of the American Educational Research Association, Chicago.

Koretz, D., & Barron, S. I. (1998). *The validity of gains on the Kentucky Instructional Results Information System (KIRIS).* MR-1014-EDU, Santa Monica, CA: RAND.

Koretz, D., & Hamilton, L. S. (2006). Testing for accountability in K–12. In R. L. Brennan (Ed.), *Educational measurement* (4th ed., pp. 531-578). Westport, CT: American Council on Education.

Koretz, D., Linn, R. L., Dunbar, S. B., & Shepard, L. A. (1991, April). The effects of high-stakes testing: Preliminary evidence about generalization across tests. In R. L. Linn (Chair), *The effects of high stakes testing.* Symposium conducted at the annual meetings of the American Educational Research Association and the National Council on Measurement in Education, Chicago.

Koretz, D., McCaffrey, D., & Hamilton, L. (2001). *Toward a framework for validating gains under high-stakes conditions* (Tech. Rep. No. 551). Los Angeles: University of California, Center for the Study of Evaluation.

Lee, J. (2006). *Tracking achievement gaps and assessing the impact of NCLB on the gaps: An in-depth look into national and state reading and math outcome trends.* Cambridge, MA: The Civil Rights Project at Harvard University.

Lewis, P. H. (1998, September 10). How fast is your system? That depends on the test. *The New York Times*, p. E1.

Linn, R. L. (2000). Assessments and accountability. *Educational Researcher, 29*(2), 4–16.

Linn, R. L. (2003). Performance standards: Utility for different uses of assessments. *Education Policy Analysis Archives, 11*(3). Retrieved January 26, 2007, from http://epaa.asu.edu/epaa/v11n31/

Linn, R. L. (2005, June 28). Conflicting demands of No Child Left Behind and state systems: Mixed messages about school performance. *Educational Policy Analysis Archives, 13*(33). Retrieved January 26, 2007, from http://epaa.asu.edu/epaa/v13n33/

Linn, R. L., & Dunbar, S. B. (1990). The Nation's report card goes home: Good news and bad about trends in achievement. *Phi Delta Kappan, 72*(2), 127–133.

Markoff, J. (2002, August 27). Chip maker takes issue with a test for speed. *The New York Times*, p. C3.

McAllister, A. (1998, January 10). 'Special' delivery in W. Virginia: Postal employees cheat to beat rating system. *The Washington Post*, p. A1.

McCaffrey, D. F., Lockwood, J. R., Koretz, D. M., & Hamilton, L. S. (2003). *Evaluating value-added models for teacher accountability.* Santa Monica, CA: RAND. Retrieved August 15, 2007, from http://www.rand.org/publications/MG/MG158/

Rothstein, R., & Jacobsen, R. (2006). The goals of education. *The Phi Delta Kappan, 88*(4), 264-272.

Narins, C. R., Dozier, A. M., Ling, F. S., & Zareba, W. (2005). The influence of public reporting of outcome data on medical decision making by physicians. *Archives of Internal Medicine, 165,* 83–87.

Schemo, D. J., & Fessenden, F. (2003, December 3). Gains in Houston schools: How real are they? *The New York Times.* Retrieved December 3, 2003, from http://www.nytimes.com

Stecher, B. (2002) Consequences of large-scale, high-stakes testing on school and classroom practice. In L. Hamilton, B. Stecher, & S. P. Klein (Eds.), *Test-based accountability: A guide for practitioners and policymakers* (pp. 79–100). Santa Monica, CA: RAND. Retrieved August 15, 2007 from http://www.rand.org/publications/MR/MR1554/MR1554.ch4.pdf

Sunderman, G. L., Tracey, C., Kim, J., & Orfield, G. (2004). *Listening to teachers: Classroom realities and No Child Left Behind.* Cambridge, MA: The Civil Rights Project at Harvard University.

Zuckerman, L. (2000, December 26). In airline math, an early arrival doesn't mean you won't be late. *The New York Times.* Retrieved on August 15, 2007, from http://select.nytimes.com/search/restricted/article?res=F3071FFF385C0C75 8EDDAB0994D8404482

CHAPTER 2

Braswell, J. S., Dion, G. S., Daane, M. C., & Jin, Y. (2005). *The nation's report card: Mathematics 2003.* (NCES 2005-451). Washington, DC: U.S. Government Printing Office.

Center on Education Policy. (2006). *From the capitol to the classroom: Year 4 of the No Child Left Behind Act.* Washington, DC: Author. Retrieved October 1, 2006, from http://www.ctredpol.org/

Chudowski, N., & Chudowski, V. (2005). *States test limits of AYP flexibility.* Washington, DC: Center on Education Policy.

Donahue, P. L., Daane, M. C., & Jin, Y. (2005). *The nation's report card: Reading 2003* (NCES 2005-453). Washington, DC: U.S. Government Printing Office.

Elementary and Secondary Act of 1965, Public Law No. 89-10.

Glass, G. V. (1978). Standards and criteria. *Journal of Educational Measurement, 15,* 237–261.

Hess, F. M., & Petrilli, M. J. (2006). *No Child Left Behind primer.* New York: Peter Lang.

Improving America's Schools Act of 1994, Public Law No. 103-382.

Jaeger, R. M. (1989). Certification of student competence. In R. L. Linn (Ed.), *Educational measurement* (3rd ed., pp. 485–514). New York: Macmillan.

Kim, J. S., & Sunderman, G. L. (2005). Measuring academic proficiency under the No Child Left Behind Act: Implications for educational equity. *Educational Researcher, 34*(8), 3–13.

Koretz, D. (2005). Alignment, high stakes, and the inflation of test scores. In J. L. Herman & E. H. Haertel (Eds.), *Uses and misuses of data in accountability testing. Yearbook of the National Society for the Study of Education* (Vol. 104, Part I, pp. 99–118). Malden, MA: Blackwell.

Lee, J. (2006). *Tracking achievement gaps and assessing impact of NCLB on the gaps: An in-depth look into national and state reading and math outcome trends.* Cambridge, MA: The Civil Rights Project at Harvard University.

Linn, R. L. (2003a). Accountability: Responsibility and reasonable expectations. *Educational Researcher, 32*(7), 3–13.

Linn, R. L. (2003b, September 1). Performance standards: Utility for different uses of assessments. *Education Policy Analysis Archives, 11*(31).

Linn, R. L. (2005). Conflicting demands of No Child Left Behind and state systems: Mixed messages about school performance. *Educational Policy Analysis Archives, 13*(33), 1–17.

Linn, R. L. (in press). Performance standards: What is proficient performance? In C. E. Sleeter (Ed.), *Educating for democracy and equity in an era of accountability.* New York: Teachers College Press.

Marion, S. T., White, C., Carlson, D., Erpenbach, W. J., Rabinowitz, A., & Sheinker, J. (2002). *Making valid and reliable decisions in determining adequate yearly progress.* A paper series: Implementing the state accountability requirements under the No Child Left Behind Act of 2001. Washington, DC: Council of Chief State School Officers.

Mullis, I. V. S., Martin, M. O., & Foy, P. (2005). *IEA's TIMSS 2003 international report on achievement in the mathematics cognitive domains. Findings from a developmental project.* Newton, MA: TIMSS & PIRLS International Study Center, Lynch School of Education, Boston College.

No Child Left Behind Act of 2001, Public Law No. 107-110.

Novak, J. R., & Fuller, B. (2003, December 3/4). Penalizing diverse schools? Similar test scores, but different students, bring federal sanctions. *Policy Brief,* Berkeley: University of California. Retrieved October 25, 2006, from http://pace.berkeley.edu

Olson, L. (2005). Room to maneuver. A progress report on the No Child Left Behind Act [Special section]. *Education Week,* S1–S6.

Olson, L. (2006). As AYP bar rises, more schools fail: Percent missing NCLB climbs amid greater testing. *Education Week, 2*(4), 1, 20.

Perie, M., Grigg, W., & Dion, G. (2005). *The nation's report card: Mathematics 2005* (NCES 2006-453). Washington, DC: U.S. Government Printing Office.

Perie, M., Grigg, W., & Donahue, P. (2005). *The nation's report card: Reading 2005* (NCES 2006-451). Washington, DC: U.S. Government Printing Office.

Public Education Network. (2007). Open to the public: How communities, parents and students assess the impact of the No Child Left Behind Act 2004-2007: The realities left behind. Washington, DC.

Spellings, M. (2005, November 21). Letter to Chief State School Officers, announcing growth model pilot program, with enclosures. Retrieved September 15, 2006, from http://www.ed.gov/nclb/landing.jhtml

Spellings, M. (2006, May 17). Secretary Spellings approves Tennessee and North Carolina growth model pilots for 2005–2006 [Press release]. Retrieved September 15, 2006, from http://www.ed.gov/news/pressreleases/2006/05/05172006a.html

Sunderman, G. L. (2006). *The unraveling of No Child Left Behind: How negotiated changes transform the law*. Cambridge, MA: The Civil Rights Project at Harvard University.

Sunderman, G. L., Tracey, C. A., Kim, J., & Orfield, G. (2004). *Listening to teachers: Classroom realities and No Child Left Behind*. Cambridge, MA: The Civil Rights Project at Harvard University.

Zieky, M. J. (1995). A historical perspective on setting standards. In *Proceedings of the Joint Conference on Standard Setting for Large-Scale Assessments in Statistics*. (pp. 1–38). Washington, DC: National Assessment Governing Board and National Center for Education Statistics.

CHAPTER 3

American Educational Research Association, American Psychological Association, & National Council on Measurement in Education. (1999). *Standards for educational and psychological testing*. Washington, DC.

Axtman, K. (2005, January 11). When tests' cheaters are the teachers. *Christian Science Monitor, online*. Retrieved October 1, 2006, from http://www.csmonitor.com/2005/0111/p01s03-ussc.htm

Bandalos, M. M. (2004). Can a teacher-led state assessment system work? *Educational Measurement, Issues and Practice, 23*(2), 33–40.

Black, P., & Wiliam, D. (1998a). Assessment and classroom learning. *Educational Assessment: Principles, Policy and Practice, 5*(1), 7–74.

Black, P., & Wiliam, D. (1998b). Inside the black box: Raising standards through classroom assessment. *Phi Delta Kappan, 80*(2), 139–148.

Bolton, E. (1998). HMI—The Thatcher years. *Oxford Review of Education, 24*(1), 45–55.

Booher-Jennings, J. (2005). Below the bubble: "Educational triage" and the Texas accountability system. *American Educational Research Journal, 42*(2), 231–268.

Center on Education Policy (2005). *NCLB policy brief 3: Is NCLB narrowing the curriculum?* Washington, DC: Center on Education Policy. Retrieved November 10, 2005, from http://www.cep-dc.org/nclb/NCLBPolicyBriefs2005/CEPPB3web.pdf

Center on Education Policy. (2006). *From the Capitol to the classroom: Year 4 of the No Child Left Behind Act*. Washington, DC. Retrieved October 1, 2006, from http://www.cep-dc.org

Chappius, S., & Stiggins, R. J. (2002). Classroom assessment for learning. *Educational leadership, 60*, 40–43.

Crooks, T. J. (1988). The impact of classroom evaluation on students. *Review of Educational Research, 58*(4), 438–481.

Darling-Hammond, L. (2000). New standards and old inequalities: School reform and the education of African American students. *The Journal of Negro Education, 69*(4), 263–287.

Darling-Hammond, L. (2004). Inequality and the right to learn: Access to qualified teachers in California's public schools. *Teachers College Record, 106*(10), 1936–1966.

Fuller, B., Gesicki, K., Kang, E., & Wright, J. (2006) *Is the No Child Left Behind Act working? The reliability of how states track achievement* (Working paper 06-1). Berkeley: Policy Analysis for California Education. Retrieved October 5, 2006, from http://pace.berkeley.edu/reports/WP.06-1.pdf

GI Forum, *Image de Tejas* v. *Texas Education Agency*, 87 F. Supp. 667 (W.D. Tex. 2000).

Hauser, R. M. (2001). Should we end social promotion? Truth and consequences. In G. Orfield & M. L. Kornhaber (Eds.), *Raising standards or raising barriers? Inequality and high-stakes testing in public education* (pp. 151–178). New York: Century Foundation Press.

Heubert, J., & Hauser, R. M. (Eds.). (1999), *High stakes: Testing for tracking, promotion, and graduation.* Washington, DC: National Academy Press.

Hoffman, L. M. (2003). *Overview of public elementary and secondary schools and districts: School year 2001–02 statistical analysis report.* (NCES 2003–41). Washington, DC: U.S. Department of Education Institute of Education Sciences.

Holmes, C. T. (1989). Grade level retention effects: A meta-analysis of research studies. In L. Shepard & M. L. Smith (Eds.), *Flunking grades: Research and policies on retention* (pp. 16–33). London: Falmer Press.

Kim, J. S., & Sunderman, G. L. (2005). Measuring academic proficiency under the No Child Left Behind Act: Implications for educational equity. *Educational Researcher, 34*(8), 3–13.

Klein, S. P., Hamilton, L. S., McCaffrey, D. F., & Stecher, B. M. (2000). *What do test scores in Texas tell us?* Santa Monica, CA: RAND.

Koretz, D. (1998). Large scale portfolio assessments in the US: Evidence pertaining to the quality of measurement. *Assessment in Education: Principles, Policy & Practice, 5*(3), 309–334.

Koretz, D. (2003). Using multiple measures to address perverse incentives and score inflation. *Educational Measurement: Issues and Practice, 22*(2), 18–26.

Koretz, D., & Barron, S. (1998). *The validity of gains in scores on the Kentucky Instructional Results Information System (KIRIS).* Santa Monica, CA: RAND.

Kornhaber, M. L. (1998). A roundtable: The black-white test score gap. *The American Prospect, 41,* 64, 66.

Lee, J. (2006). *Tracking achievement gaps and assessing the impact of NCLB on the gaps: An in-depth look into national and state reading and math outcomes trends.* Retrieved November 1, 2006, from http://www.civilrightsproject.harvard.edu/news/press-releases/nclb_report06.php

Lee, J., & Wong, K. K. (2004). The impact of accountability on racial and socioeconomic equity: Considering both school resources and achievement outcomes. *American Educational Research Journal, 41*(4), 797–832.

Linn, R. L., & Baker, E. L. (1996). Can performance-based student assessments be psychometrically sound? In J. B. Baron & D. P. Wolf (Eds.), *Performance-based student assessment: Challenges and possibilities. Ninety-fifth Yearbook of the National*

Society for the Study of Education, Part I (pp. 84–103). Chicago: University of Chicago Press.

Losen, D. J. (2004). Graduation rate accountability under the No Child Left Behind Act and the disparate impact on students of color. In G. Orfield (Ed.), *Dropouts in America: Confronting the graduation rate crisis.* Cambridge, MA: Harvard Education Publishing Group.

McDonnell, L. M., McLaughlin, M. J., & Morison, P. (1997). *Educating one and all: Students with disabilities and standards-based reform.* Commission on Behavioral and Social Sciences and Education. Washington, DC: National Academy Press.

McNeil, L. M. (1988). *Contradictions of control: School structure and school knowledge.* New York: Routledge.

McNeil, L. M., & Valenzuela, A. (2001). The harmful impact of the TAAS system of testing in Texas: Beneath the accountability rhetoric. In G. Orfield & M. L. Kornhaber (Eds.), *Raising standards or raising barriers? Inequality and high-stakes testing in public education* (pp. 127–150). New York: Century Foundation Press.

Natriello, G., & Pallas, A. M. (2001). The development and impact of high-stakes testing. In G. Orfield & M. L. Kornhaber (Eds.), *Raising standards or raising barriers? Inequality and high-stakes testing in public education* (pp. 19–38). New York: Century Foundation Press.

Nichols, S. L., & Berliner, D. C. (2007). *Collateral damage: How high-stakes testing corrupts America's schools.* Cambridge, MA: Harvard Education Publishing Group.

No Child Left Behind Act of 2001, Public Law No. 107–110.

Olson, L. (2005, December 14). Room to maneuver. A progress report on the No Child Left Behind Act. *Education Week*, pp. S1–S6.

Pellegrino, J. W., Chudowsky, N., & Glaser, R. (Eds.). (2001). *Knowing what students know.* Committee on the Foundations of Assessment. Washington, DC: National Academy Press.

Popham, W. J. (2004, July). *Ruminations regarding NCLB's most malignant provision: Adequate yearly progress.* Paper prepared for a forum on No Child Left Behind sponsored by the Center on Education Policy, Washington, DC.

Shepard, L. A. (2000). The role of assessment in a learning culture. *Educational Researcher, 29*(7), 4–14.

Smith, G. (2000). Research and inspection: HMI and Ofsted, 1981–1996: A commentary. *Oxford Review of Education, 26*(3/4) 333–352.

Stake, R. (1998). Some comments on assessment in U.S. education. *Education Policy Analysis Archives, 6*(14). Retrieved September 30, 2006, from http://epaa.asu.edu/epaa/v6n14.html

Stecher, B. (1998). The local benefits and burdens of large-scale portfolio assessment. *Assessment in Education: Principles, Policy & Practice, 5*(3), 335–352.

Stiggins, R. J. (2001). The unfulfilled promise of classroom assessment. *Educational Measurement, Issues and Practice, 20*(3), 5–15.

Suen, H. K., & Yu, L. (2006). Chronic consequences of high-stakes testing: Lessons from the Chinese civil service exam. *Comparative Education Review, 58*(1), 46–65.

Sunderman, G. (2006) *The unraveling of No Child Left Behind: How negotiated changes transform the law.* Cambridge, MA: The Civil Rights Project at Harvard University.

Swanson, C. B. (2004). Sketching a portrait of public high school graduation: Who graduates? Who doesn't? In G. Orfield (Ed.), *Dropouts in America: Confronting the graduation rate crisis.* Cambridge, MA: Harvard Education Publishing Group.

Thurlow, M. L., Thompson, S. J., & Lazarus, S. S. (2006). Considerations for the administration of tests to special needs students: Accommodations, modifications, and more. In S. M. Downing & T. M. Haldyna (Eds.), *Handbook of test development* (pp. 653–673). Mahwah, NJ: Lawrence Erlbaum.

von Zastrow, C. (2004). Academic atrophy: The condition of the liberal arts in America's public schools. Washington, DC: Council for Basic Education. Retrieved December 5, 2004, from http://www.ecs.org/html/offsite.asp?document=http%3A%2F%2Fdownloads%2Encss%2Eorg%2Flegislative%2FAcademic Atrophy%2Epdf

Wiggins, G. (1998). *Educative assessment: Designing assessments to inform and improve student performance.* San Francisco: Jossey-Bass.

Wiliam, D. (2001). An overview of the relationship between assessment and the curriculum. In D. Scott (Ed.), *Curriculum and assessment* (pp. 165–181). Greenwich, CT: JAI Press.

Wiliam, D. (2004, June). *Keeping learning on track: Integrating assessment with instruction.* Invited address to the 30th annual conference of the International Association for Educational Assessment, Philadelphia.

CHAPTER 4

Abedi, J. (2003). *Impact of student language background on content-based performance: Analysis of extant data.* Los Angeles: Center for Research on Evaluation, Standards, and Student Testing.

Abedi, J. (2005, April). *Content alignment of existing and new English language proficiency tests: A research perspective.* Paper presented at the annual meeting of the American Educational Research Association, Montreal, Canada.

Abedi, J., Courtney, M., & Leon, S. (2003). *Effectiveness and validity of accommodations for English language learners in large-scale assessments.* Los Angeles: Center for Research on Evaluation, Standards, and Student Testing.

Abedi, J., Courtney, M., Mirocha, J., Leon, S., & Goldberg, J. (2005). *Language accommodations for English language learners in large-scale assessments: Bilingual dictionaries and linguistic modification.* Los Angeles: Center for Research on Evaluation, Standards, and Student Testing.

Abedi, J., Hofstetter, C., Baker, E., & Lord, C. (2001). *NAEP math performance test accommodations: Interaction with student language background.* Los Angeles: Center for Research on Evaluation, Standards, and Student Testing.

Abedi, J., Lord, C., & Hofstetter, C. (1998). *Impact of selected background variables on students' NAEP math performance.* Los Angeles: Center for Research on Evaluation, Standards, and Student Testing.

August, D., & Hakuta, K. E. (1997). *Improving schooling for language-minority children: A research agenda.* Washington, DC: National Academy Press.

August, D., & Shanahan, T. (2006). *Understanding literacy development in a second language: The report of the national literacy panel.* Mahwah, NJ: Lawrence Erlbaum Associates.

Bailey, A. L., & Butler, F. A. (2003). *An evidentiary framework for operationalizing academic language for broad application to K–12 education: A design document.* Los Angeles: Center for Research on Evaluation, Standards, and Student Testing.

Burt, M. K., Dulay, H. C., & Hernández-Chávez, E. (1976). *Bilingual syntax measure.* San Antonio, TX: Harcourt, Brace, Jovanovich.

Carlo, M. S., August, D., McLaughlin, B., Snow, C. E., Dressler, C., Lippman, D. N., et al. (2004). Closing the gap: Addressing the vocabulary needs of English-language learners in bilingual and mainstream classrooms. *Reading Research Quarterly, 39,* 188–215.

Cazden, C. (1986). Classroom discourse. In M.C. Wittrock (Ed.), *Handbook of research on teaching* (3rd ed., pp. 432–463). New York: MacMillan.

Cuevas, G. J. (1984). Mathematics learning in English as a second language. *Journal for Research in Mathematics Education, 15*(2), 134–144.

Del Vecchio, A., & Guerrero, M. (1995). *Handbook of English language proficiency tests.* Albuquerque, NM: Evaluation Assistance Center.

Development Associates. (2003). *Descriptive study of services to LEP students and LEP students with disabilities. Volume 1: Research report.* Arlington, VA: Author.

de Avila, E. A., & Duncan, S. E. (2005). *Language assessment scales, English.* Monterey, CA: CTB MacMillan McGraw-Hill.

de Jong, E. J. (2004). After exit: Academic achievement patterns of former English language learners. *Education Policy Analysis Archives, 12*(50), 1–18. Retrieved November 3, 2006, from http://epaa.asu.edu/epaa/v12n50/

Ferrara, S. (2006, April). *Design, psychometric, and instructional considerations in several states of the speaking proficiency component of the English Development Language Assessment.* Paper presented at the annual meeting of the American Educational Research Association, San Francisco.

Francis, D. J. (2006). *Bridging Title I and Title III assessment and accountability.* Unpublished manuscript.

Francis, D. J., Snow, C. E., August, D., Carlson, C. D., Miller, J., & Iglesias, A. (2006). Measures of reading comprehension: A latent variable analysis of the Diagnostic Assessment of Reading Comprehension. *Scientific Studies of Reading, 10*(3), 301–322.

Francis, D. J., Lesaux, N., Rivera, M., Kieffer, M., & Rivera, H. (2006). *Research-based recommendations for the use of accommodations in large-scale assessments.* Portsmouth, NH: Center on Instruction.

Gándara, P., Rumberger, R., Maxwell-Jolly, J., & Callahan, R. (2003). English learners in California schools: Unequal resources, unequal outcomes. *Education Policy Analysis Archives, 11*(36), 1–52. Retrieved November 3, 2006, from http://epaa.asu.edu/epaa/v11n36/

Kieffer, M. J., & Lesaux, N. K. (2008). Breaking down words to build meaning: Morphology, vocabulary, and reading comprehension in the urban classroom. *The Reading Teacher, 61,* 134-144.

Lager, C. A. (2006). Types of mathematics-language reading interactions that unnecessarily hinder algebra learning and assessment. *Reading Psychology, 27,* 165–204.

Linquanti, R. (2001). *The redesignation dilemma: Challenges and choices in fostering meaningful accountability for English learners* [Policy report]. Santa Barbara, CA: University of California Linguistic Minority Research Institute.

Pray, L. (2005). How well do commonly used language instruments measure English oral-language proficiency? *Bilingual Research Journal, 29*(2), 387–409.

Proctor, C. P., Carlo, M., August, D., & Snow, C. E. (2005). Native Spanish-speaking children reading in English: Toward a model of comprehension. *Journal of Educational Psychology, 97*(2), 246–256.

Ragan, A., & Lesaux, N. (2006). Federal, state, and district level English language learner program entry and exit requirements: Effects on the education of language minority learners. *Education Policy Analysis Archives, 14*(20). Retrieved November 3, 2006, from http://epaa.asu.edu/epaa/v14n20/

Rivera, C., & Collum, E. (2006). *State assessment policy and practice for English language learners: A national perspective* (pp. 1–173). Mahwah, NJ: Lawrence Erlbaum Associates.

Sattler, J. (2001). *Assessment of children: Cognitive applications* (4th ed.) La Mesa, CA: Sattler Publishing.

Scarcella, R. (2003). *Academic English: A conceptual framework.* Los Angeles: Linguistic Minority Research Institute.

Tabors, P., Páez, M., & Lopez, L. (2003). Dual language abilities of bilingual four-year-olds: Initial findings from the Early Childhood Study of language and literacy development of Spanish-speaking children. *NABE Journal of Research and Practice, 1*(1), 70–91.

U.S. Department of Education. (2004). Fact sheet: NCLB provisions ensure flexibility and accountability for limited English proficient students. Retrieved on November 3, 2006, from http://ed.gov

CHAPTER 5

Center on Education Policy. (2006). *From the capital to the classroom: Year 4 of the No Child Left Behind Act.* Retrieved May 15, 2006, from http://www.cep-dc.org

Education Trust. (2004). *Measured progress: Achievement rises and gaps narrow, but too slowly.* Washington, DC: Author.

Education Trust. (2006). *Primary progress, secondary challenge: A state-by-state look at student achievement patterns.* Washington, DC: Author.

FairTest. (2005, October 19). *Flatline NAEP scores show failure of test-driven school reform: "No Child Left Behind" has not improved academic performance.* Retrieved May 15, 2006, from http://www.fairtest.org

Fuller, B., Gesicki, K., Kang, E., & Wright, J. (2006). *Is the No Child Left Behind Act working? The reliability of how states track achievement* (PACE Working Paper 06-1). Berkeley: University of California.

Klein, S. P., Hamilton, L. S., McCaffrey, D. F., & Stecher, B. M. (2000). *What do test scores in Texas tell us?* Santa Monica, CA: RAND.

Koretz, D., & Barron, S. I. (1998). *The validity of gains on the Kentucky instructional results information system (KIRIS)* (MR-792-PCT/FF). Santa Monica, CA: RAND.

Lee, J. (2006). *Tracking achievement gaps and assessing the impact of NCLB on the gaps: An in-depth look into national and state reading and math outcome trends.* Cambridge, MA: The Civil Rights Project at Harvard University.

Lee, J. (2007). Do national and state assessments converge for educational accountability? A meta-analytic synthesis of multiple measures in Maine and Kentucky. *Applied Measurement in Education, 20*(2), 1–33.

Linn, R. L. (2000). Assessments and accountability. *Educational Researcher, 2*(29), 4–16.

Linn, R. L., Baker, E. L., & Betebenner, D. W. (2002). Accountability systems: Implications of requirements of the No Child Left Behind Act of 2001. *Educational Researcher, 31*(6), 3–16.

Loveless, T. (2006). *How well are American students learning? Brown Center Report on American Education* (Vol. 2, No. 1). Washington, DC: Brookings Institution.

National Education Goals Panel. (1996). *Profile of 1994–95 state assessment systems and reported results.* Washington, DC: Author.

Olson, L. (2007, January 11). New bills would prod states to take national view on standards. *Education Week.* Retrieved January 29, 2007, from www.edweek.org

Perie, M., Grigg, W., & Dion, G. (2005). *The nation's report card: Mathematics 2005* (NCES 2006-453). Washington, DC: U.S. Government Printing Office.

Perie, M., Grigg, W., & Donahue, P. (2005). *The nation's report card: Reading 2005* (NCES 2006-451). Washington, DC: U.S. Government Printing Office.

Resnick, L. (1999). *Reflections on the future of NAEP: Instrument for monitoring or for accountability?* Los Angeles: Center for the Study of Evaluation. (ERIC Document Reproduction Service No. ED429108).

U.S. Department of Education. (2005, November/December). Nation's report card. *The Achiever, 4*(12), 2.

CHAPTER 6

Abrams, L. & Haney, W. (2004). Accountability and the grade 9 to 10 transition: The impact on attrition and retention rates. In G. Orfield (Ed.), *Dropouts in America: Confronting the graduation rate crisis* (pp. 181–205). Cambridge, MA: Harvard Education Press.

Arrow, K. J. (1950). A difficulty in the concept of social welfare. *Journal of Political Economy, 58,* 328–346.

Ayres, L. (1909). *Laggards in our schools: A study of retardation and elimination in city school systems.* New York: Charities Publication Committee.

Braswell, J. S., Dion, G. S., Daane, M. C., & Yin, J. (2005). *The nation's report card: Mathematics 2003* (NCES 2005-451). Washington, DC: U.S. Government Printing Office.

Bush, J., & Bloomberg, M. (2006, August 13). How to help our students: Building on the "No Child" law. *The Washington Post,* p. B7.

Cohen, J. (1977). *Statistical power analysis for the behavioral sciences.* (Rev. ed.). New York: Academic Press.

Cooper, H., & Hedges, L. V. (1994). *The handbook of research synthesis*. New York: Russell Sage.

Edley, C., Jr., & Wald, J. (2002, December 16). The grade retention fallacy. *The Boston Globe*, A19.

Greene, J. P. (2002a). *High school graduation rates in the United States: Revised.* New York: Manhattan Institute for Policy Research. Retrieved May 28, 2003, from http://www.manhattan-institute.org/pdf/cr_baeo.pdf

Greene, J. P. (2002b). *Public school graduation rates in the United States* (Civic Report No.31). New York, NY: Manhattan Institute for Policy Research. Retrieved May 28, 2003, from Document1 http://www.manhattan-institute.org/pdf/cr_31.pdf

Greene, J. P., & Foster, G. (2003). *Public high school graduation and college readiness rates in the United States.* New York: Manhattan Institute for Policy Research. Retrieved September 25, 2003, from http://www.manhattan-institute.org/htm/ewp_o3.htm.

Haney, W. (2000). The myth of the Texas miracle in education. *Education Policy Analysis Archives*, 8(41). Retrieved September 27, 2000, from http://epaa.asu.edu/epaa/v8n41

Haney, W. (2001, January). *Revisiting the myth of the Texas miracle in education: Lessons about dropout research and dropout prevention.* Paper presented at the conference, Dropouts in America: How severe is the problem? What do we know about intervention and prevention?, Cambridge, MA. Retrieved June 11, 2003, from http://www.civilrightsproject.harvard.edu/research/dropouts/haney.pdf

Haney, W., Madaus, G., Abrams, L., Wheelock, A., Miao, J., & Gruia, I. (2004). *The education pipeline in the United States, 1970–2000.* Chestnut Hill, MA: The National Board on Educational Testing and Public Policy. Retrieved February 17, 2004, from http://www.bc.edu/research/nbetpp/statements/nbr3.pdf

Heubert, J., & Hauser, R. (Eds.). (1999). *High stakes: Testing for tracking, promotion, and graduation. A Report of the National Research Council.* Washington, DC: National Academy Press.

Honawar, V. (2006, July 12). NEA opens campaign to rewrite federal education law. *Education Week, 25*: (42), 8.

Jimerson, S. R. (2001). Meta-analysis of grade retention research: Implications for practice in the 21st century. *School Psychology Review, 30*(3), 420–437.

Jimerson, S. R., Anderson, G. E., & Whipple, A. D. (2002). Winning the battle and losing the war: Examining the relation between grade retention and dropping out of high school. *Psychology in the Schools, 39*(4), 441–457.

Linn, R., & Baker, E. L. (2002). *Accountability systems: Implications of requirements of the No Child Left Behind Act of 2001.* University of California, Los Angeles, Center for the Study of Evaluation. Retrieved October 3, 2003, from http://www.cse.edu/products/Reports/TR567.pdf

Miao, J., & Haney W. (2004, October 15). High school graduation rates: Alternative methods and implications. *Education Policy Analysis Archives*, 12(55). Retrieved October 16, 2006, from http://epaa.asu.edu/epaa/v12n55/

Mishel, L., & Roy, J. (2006). *Rethinking high school graduation rates and trends.* Washington, DC: Economic Policy Institute. Retrieved January 7, 2007, from http://www.epi.org/content.cfm/index_pubs_books_studies

Perie, M., Grigg, W., & Dion, G. (2005). *The nation's report card: Mathematics 2005* (NCES 2006–453). Washington, DC: U.S. Government Printing Office.

Schumpeter, J. A. (1954). *History of Economic Analysis.* New York, NY: Oxford.

Shepard, L. A., & Smith, M. L. (Eds.) (1989). *Flunking grades: Research and policies on retention.* New York, NY: The Falmer Press.

Swanson, C. B. (2003). *NCLB implementation report: State approaches for calculating high school graduation rates.* Washington, D.C.: The Urban Institute. Retrieved October 10, 2003, from http://www.urban.org/UploadedPDF/410848_NCLB_Implementation.pdf

Swanson, C. B. (2004). *Who graduates? Who doesn't? A statistical portrait of public high school graduation, class of 2001.* Washington, DC: The Urban Institute. Retrieved February 25, 2004, from http://www.urban.org/UploadedPDF/410934_WhoGraduates.pdf

Swanson, C. B., & Chaplin, D. (2003). *Counting high school graduates when graduates count: Measuring graduation gates under the high stakes of NCLB.* Washington, DC: The Urban Institute. Retrieved May 23, 2003, from http://www.urban.org/UploadedPDF/410641_NCLB.pdf

Warren, J. R. (2003, August). *State-level high school graduation rates in the 1990s: Concepts, measures, and trends.* Paper presented at the annual meeting of the American Sociological Association, Atlanta, GA.

Wolf, F. M. (1986). *Meta-analysis: Quantitative methods for research synthesis.* Newbury Park, CA: Sage.

Young, B. (2002). *Public high school dropouts and completers from the Common Core of Data: School year 1998–99 and 1999–2000* (NCES 2002–382). Washington, DC: US. Department of Education. Retrieved May 28, 2003, from http://nces.ed.gov/pubs2002/2002382.pdf

CHAPTER 7

Card, D., & Payne, A. A. (2002). School finance reform, the distribution of school spending, and the distribution of student test scores. *Journal of Public Economics, 83,* 49–82.

Common Core of Data. (2006). Local education agency (school district) finance survey (F-33) data. Retrieved January 31, 2007, from http://nces.ed.gov/ccd/f33agency.asp

Driscoll, W., & Fleeter, H. (2003). *Projected costs of implementing the federal "No Child Left Behind Act" in Ohio.* Columbus, OH: Levin, Driscoll & Fleeter.

Education Finance Statistics Center. (2006). Comparable wage index data files. Retrieved January 31, 2007, from http://nces.ed.gov/edfin/prodsurv/data.asp

Evans, W. N., Murray, S. E., & Schwab, R. M. (1999). The impact of court-mandated school finance reform. In H. F. Ladd, R. Chalk, & J. S. Hansen (Eds.), *Equity and adequacy in education finance: Issues and perspectives* (pp. 72–98). Washington, DC: National Academy Press.

Ferguson, R. F., & Ladd, H. F. (1996). How and why money matters: An analysis of Alabama schools. In H. F. Ladd (Ed.), *Holding schools accountable: Performance-based reform in education* (pp. 265–298). Washington, DC: Brookings Institution.

Finn, Jr., C. E., Julian, L., & Petrilli, M. J. (2006). *To dream the impossible dream: Four approaches to national standards and tests for America's schools.* Washington, DC: Thomas B. Fordham Foundation.

Finn, J. D., & Achilles, C. M. (1999). Tennessee's class size study: Findings, implications, misconceptions. *Educational Evaluation and Policy Analysis, 21,* 97–109.

Gordon, R. (2006, March 15). The federalism debate: Why the idea of national education standards is crossing party lines. *Education Week,* p. 48.

Greenwald, R., Hedges, L. V., & Laine, R. D. (1996). The effect of school resources on student achievement. *Review of Educational Research, 66,* 361–396.

Grissmer, D., Flanagan, A., Kawata, J., & Williamson, S. (2000). *Improving student achievement: What state NAEP test scores tell us.* Santa Monica, CA: RAND.

Grissmer, D., Flanagan, A., & Williamson, S. (1998). Why did the black-white score gap narrow in the 1970s and 1980s? In C. Jencks & M. Phillips (Eds.), *The black-white test score gap* (pp. 182–226). Washington, DC: Brookings Institution.

Guryan, J. (2003). *Does money matter? Estimates from education finance reform in Massachusetts.* Retrieved January 31, 2007, http://faculty.chicagogsb.edu/jonathan.guryan/research/GuryanDoesMoneyMatter.pdf

Hanushek, E. (1996). School resources and student performance. In G. Burtless (Ed.), *Does money matter? The effect of school resources on student achievement and adult success* (pp. 43–73). Washington, DC: Brookings Institution.

Hedges, L. V., & Nowell, A. (1998). Black-white test score convergence since 1965. In C. Jencks & M. Phillips (Eds.), *The black-white test score gap* (pp. 149–181). Washington, DC: Brookings Institution.

Imazeki, J., & Reschovsky, A. (2004). Is No Child Left Behind an un (or under) funded federal mandate? Evidence from Texas. *National Tax Journal, 57,* 571–588.

Joondeph, B. W. (1995). The good, the bad, and the ugly: An empirical analysis of litigation-prompted school reform. *Santa Clara Law Review, 35,* 763–824.

Krueger, A. B. (1999). Experimental estimates of education production functions. *Quarterly Journal of Economics, 114,* 497–532.

Levin, H., Belfield, C., Muennig, P., & Rouse, C. (2007). *The costs and benefits of an excellent education for all of America's children.* New York: Teachers College, Columbia University.

Liu, G. (2006). Interstate inequality in educational opportunity. *New York University Law Review, 81,* 2044–2128.

Mathis, W. J. (2003). No Child Left Behind: Costs and benefits, *Phi Delta Kappan, 84,* 679–686.

Murray, S. E., Evans, W. N., & Schwab, R. M. (1998). Education-finance reform and the distribution of education resources. *American Economic Review, 88,* 789–812.

National Assessment of Educational Progress. (2006). *State profiles.* Retrieved January 31, 2007, from http://nces.ed.gov/nationsreportcard/states/

National Center for Education Statistics. (2006). *State education data profiles.* Retrieved January 31, 2007, from http://nces.ed.gov/programs/stateprofiles/

National Clearinghouse for English Language Acquisition and Language Instruction Educational Programs. (2006). *ELL demographics by states.* Retrieved January 31, 2007, from http://www.ncela.gwu.edu/stats/3_bystate.htm

No Child Left Behind Act of 2001. Public Law No. 107.110.

Odden, A. R., & Kim, L. (1992). Reducing disparities across the states: A new federal role in school finance. In A. R. Odden (Ed.), *Rethinking school finance: An agenda for the 1990s* (pp. 260–297). San Francisco: Jossey-Bass.

Parrish, T., Harr, J., Wolman, J., Anthony, J., Merickel, A., & Esra, P. (2004). *State special education finance systems, 1999–2000, Part II: Special education revenues and expenditures.* Palo Alto, CA: American Institutes for Research, Center for Special Education Finance.

Parrish, T. B. (1994). A cost analysis of alternative instructional models for limited English proficient students in California. *Journal of Education Finance, 19,* 256–278.

Quality counts at 10: A decade of standards-based education. (2006, January 5). *Education Week.*

Ravitch, D. (1995). *National standards in American education: A citizen's guide.* Washington, DC: Brookings Institution.

Riddle, W., & Apling, R. (2000). *Education for the disadvantaged: Allocation formula issues in ESEA Title I reauthorization legislation.* Washington, DC: Congressional Research Service.

Rubinfeld, D. L. (1995). California fiscal federalism: A school finance perspective. In B. E. Cain & R. G. Noll (Eds.), *Constitutional reform in California: Making state government more effective and responsive* (pp. 431–453). Berkeley: University of California.

Taylor, L. L., & Fowler, W. J., Jr. (2006). *A comparable wage approach to geographic cost adjustment.* Washington, DC: National Center for Education Statistics.

U.S. Census Bureau. (2006a). *Public education finances 2004.* Washington, DC.

U.S. Census Bureau. (2006b). *Small area income and poverty estimates.* Retrieved January 31, 2007, from http://www.census.gov/hhes/www/saipe/tables.html

U.S. Department of Commerce. (2006). Regional economic accounts. Retrieved January 31, 2007, from http://bea.gov/bea/regional/data.htm

U.S. Department of Education. (2006). *Fiscal year 2001–2007 state tables for the U.S. Department of Education.* Retrieved January 31, 2007, from http://www.ed.gov/about/overview/budget/statetables/index.html

U.S. Department of the Treasury. (2002). *Treasury methodology for estimating total taxable resources.* Retrieved January 31, 2007, from http://www.treasury.gov/offices/economic-policy/resources/nmpubsum.pdf

U.S. Department of the Treasury. (2006). *TTR estimates.* Retrieved January 31, 2007, from http://www.treasury.gov/offices/economic-policy/resources/estimates.shtml

U.S. General Accounting Office. (1998). *School finance: State and federal efforts to target poor students.* Washington, DC: Author.

CHAPTER 8

Arizona State Board of Education. (2004, March 29). *Minutes.* Retrieved August 31, 2005, from http://www.ade.state.az.us/stateboard/minutes/default.asp

Center for Education Policy. (2005). *Title I funds—Who's gaining and who's losing: School year 2005–06 update.* Washington, DC: Author.

Education Commission of the States. (2004). *State takeovers and reconstitutions.* Retrieved March 28, 2006, from http://ecs.org/clearinghouse/51/67/5167.htm

Education Commission of the States. (2006). *Accountability—Sanctions: Takeovers.* Retrieved March 27, 2006, from http://www.ecs.org/html/issue.asp?issueid=222&subIssueID=158

Elmore, R. F., & Fuhrman, S. H. (1995). Opportunity-to-learn standards and the state role in education. *Teachers College Record, 96*(3), 432–457.

Government Accountability Office. (2003). *Title I: Characteristics of tests will influence expenses; information sharing may help states realize efficiencies* (No. GAO-03-389). Washington, DC: Author.

Hunter, R. C. (1997). The mayor versus the school superintendent: Political incursions into metropolitan school politics. *Education and Urban Society, 29*(2), 217–232.

Illinois State Board of Education. (2005). *Proposed FY 2006 budget.* Retrieved April 29, 2005, from http://www.isbe.net/budget/FY06/06_Budget_Book.pdf

Mathews, J. (2000, September 18). State to end takeover of Compton schools. *Los Angeles Times.*

McDermott, K. A. (2004). Incentives, capacity, and implementation: Evidence from Massachusetts education reform. *Journal of Public Administration Research and Theory, 16,* 45–65.

Mintrop, H., & Trujillo, T. (2005). Corrective action in low performing schools: Lessons for NCLB implementation from first-generation accountability systems. *Education Policy Analysis Archives, 13*(48). Retrieved December 3, 2005, from http://epaa.asu.edu/epaa/v13n48/

New York State Education Department Office of Human Resources Management. (2004). *1999-2004 State Education Department work force study.* Albany, NY: Author.

O'Day, J., & Bitter, C. (2003). *Evaluation study of the Immediate Intervention/Underperforming Schools Program and the High Achieving/Improving Schools Program of the Public Schools Accountability Act of 1999.* Sacramento, CA: American Institutes of Research.

Strauss, V., & Loeb, V. (1998, March 27). A general's strategy backfires. *Washington Post,* p. B1.

U.S. Census Bureau. (2006). *Statistical abstract of the United States.* Washington DC: Author.

U.S. Department of Education. (2005, April 15). *Statewide longitudinal data system grants.* Retrieved March 28, 2006, from http://www.ed.gov/programs/slds/applicant.html

Weizel, R. (1997, April 16). Hartford public schools face state takeover. *Boston Globe,* p. C16.

Wirt, F. M., & Kirst, M. W. (1982). *The politics of education: Schools in conflict.* Berkeley, CA: McCutchan Publishing Corporation.

Wyatt, E. (2000, July 13). Little improvement despite an overhaul, L.I. school district is at a crossroads. *New York Times,* p. B1.

CHAPTER 9

Blanc, S. (2003, Summer). Supports and challenges in the multiple provider model: Principals offer mixed perspectives on first year of takeover. *Philadelphia Public School Notebook.*

Bracey, G. (2002). *The market in theory meets the market in practice: The case of Edison Schools.* Tempe: Arizona State University, College of Education, Education Policy Studies Laboratory, Education Policy Research Unit. Retrieved November 2, 2005, from http://www.asu.edu/educ/epsl/EPRU/documents/EPRU% 202002-107/EPSL-0202-107-EPRU.htm

Brady, R. (2003). *Can failing schools be fixed?* Washington, DC: Thomas B. Fordham Foundation.

Brown Center. (2003). *Charter schools: Achievement, accountability, and the role of expertise.* Washington, DC: Brookings Institution.

Bulkley, K., & Wohlstetter, P. (2003). *Taking account of charter schools: What's happened and what's next?* New York: Teachers College Press.

California Department of Education. (2001). *Public school accountability (1999-2000): Immediate Intervention/Underperforming Schools Program (II/USP): How low performing schools in California are facing the challenge of improving student achievement.* Sacramento, CA: Author.

Cibulka, J., & Lindle, J. (2001). *The politics of accountability for school improvement in Kentucky and Maryland* (Tech. Rep. Vol. 4). Washington, DC: U.S. Department of Education, Office of Educational Research and Improvement.

Council of Chief State School Officers. (2003). *State support to low-performing schools.* Washington DC: Author.

Consortium for Policy Research in Education. (2001). U.S. Department of Education regional forum on turning around low performing schools: Implications for policy (Policy Bulletin pb-01-01). Philadelphia: Author.

Creemers, B. (1994). *The effective classroom.* New York: Cassell.

David, J., Coe, P., & Kannapel, P. (2003). *Improving low-performing schools: A study of Kentucky's Highly Skilled Educator Program.* Lexington: Partnership for Kentucky Schools.

Education Commission of the States. (2002). *State interventions in low performing schools and school districts.* Denver, CO: Author.

Elmore, R. (2006). *School reform from the inside out.* Cambridge, MA: Harvard Education Press.

Ferguson, C. (2000). *The progress of education in Texas.* Austin, TX: Southwest Educational Development Laboratory.

Fullan, M. (2003). *Change forces with a vengeance.* London: RoutledgeFalmer.

Garland, L. (2003). Navigating treacherous waters: A state takeover handbook. Lanham, MD: Scarecrow Press.

Goe, L. (2001, April). *Implementation of California's Immediate Intervention/Underperforming Schools Program: Preliminary findings.* Paper presented at the annual meeting of the American Educational Research Association, Seattle, WA.

Hess, G. A. (2003). Reconstitution—three years later: Monitoring the effect of sanctions on Chicago high schools. *Education and Urban Society, 35*(3), 300–327.

Holdzkom, D. (2001). *Low-performing schools: So you've identified them—now what?* Charleston, WV: AEL.

Kannapel, P., & Coe, P. (2000). Improving schools and school leaders. In R. Pankratz & J. Petrosko (Eds.), *All children can learn: Lessons from the Kentucky reform experience* (pp. 159–176). San Francisco: Jossey Bass.

Kentucky Department of Education. (2000a). *Assistance for schools: Guidelines for scholastic audit.* Frankfort, KY: Author.

Kentucky Department of Education. (2000b). *Commonwealth Accountability Testing System: Interim accountability cycle briefing packet (1996–1997 to 1999–2000).* Frankfort, KY: Author.

Ladd, H. F., & Zelli, A. (2001). *School-based accountability in North Carolina: The responses of school principals.* Durham, NC: Duke University, Terry Sanford Institute of Public Policy.

Malen, B., Croninger, R., Muncey, D., & Jones, D. (2002). Reconstituting schools: "Testing" the "theory of action." *Educational Evaluation and Policy Analysis, 24*(2), 113–132.

Mintrop, H. (2002). *State oversight and the improvement of low-performing schools in California, expert witness report for* Eliezer Williams et al. v. State of California. Los Angeles: University of California. Retrieved November 2, 2005, from http://128.121.78.24/decentschools/expert_reports/mintrop_report.pdf

Mintrop, H. (2003). The limits of sanctions in low-performing schools: A study of Maryland and Kentucky schools on probation. *Education Policy Analysis Archives, 11*(3). Retrieved November 2, 2005, from http://epaa.asu.edu/epaa/v11n3.html

Mintrop, H. (2004). *Schools on probation: How accountability works (and doesn't work).* New York: Teachers College Press.

Mintrop, H., & Papazian, R. (2003, December). *Systemic strategies to improve low-performing schools—Lessons from first-generation accountability systems* (CSE Tech. Rep. No. 617). Los Angeles: National Center for Research on Evaluation, Standards, and Student Testing.

Mintrop, H., & Trujillo, T. (2006). Corrective action in low-performing schools: Lessons for NCLB implementation from state and district strategies in first-generation accountability systems. *Educational Policy Analysis Archives, 13*(48). Retrieved August 28, 2007, from http://epaa.asu.edu/epaa/v13n48.html

Molnar, A. (2005). *School commercialism.* New York: Routledge.

Murphy, J., & Datnow, A. (2002). *Leadership lessons from comprehensive school reforms.* Thousand Oaks, CA: Corwin Press.

New York State Education Department, Office of New York City School Improvement and Community Services. (2003). *2002-03 Registration Review Initiative: A summary of the Registration Review report findings.* New York: Author.

O'Day, J., & Bitter, C. (2003). *Evaluation study of the Immediate Intervention/Underperforming Schools Program and the High Achieving/Improving Schools Program of the Public Schools Accountability Act of 1999.* Sacramento, CA: American Institutes of Research.

O'Day, J., & Finnigan, K. (with Wakelyn, D.). (2003). *External support to schools on probation: Getting a leg up?* Chicago: Consortium on Chicago School Research.

Peterson, P., & Hess, F. (2006). *Keeping an eye on state standards: A race to the bottom?* Retrieved March 20, 2006, from http://media.hoover.org/documents/ednext20063_28.pdf

Phenix, D., Siegel, D., Zaltsman, A., & Fruchter, N. (2005). A forced march for failing schools: Lessons from the New York City Chancellor's District. *Education Policy Analysis Archives, 13*(40). Retrieved November 2, 2005, from http://epaa.asu.edu/epaa/v13n40/

Porter, A., & Chester, M. (2002). Building a high-quality assessment and accountability program: The Philadelphia example. *Brookings Papers on Education Policy*, 285–337.

Posnick-Goodwin, S. (2003, September). Under close scrutiny. *CTA California Educator, 8*.

Ravitch, D. (1974). *The great school wars*. New York: Basic Books.

Rudo, Z. (2001). *Corrective action in low-performing schools and school districts*. Austin, TX: Southwest Educational Development Laboratory.

Scheerens, J., & Bosker, R. (1997). *The foundations of educational effectiveness*. New York: Elsevier.

Snipes, J., Doolittle, F., & Herlihy, C. (2002). *Foundations for success: Case studies of how urban school systems improve student achievement*. Washington, DC: MDRC for the Council of Great City Schools.

Teddlie, C., & Reynolds, D. (Eds.). (2000). *The international handbook of school effectiveness research*. New York: Falmer.

Texas Education Agency. (2002). *2002 comprehensive annual report on Texas public schools: A report to the 78th legislature*. Austin, TX: Author.

Travers, E. (2003). *Characteristics of schools under diverse providers 2002–2003*. Philadelphia: Research for Action.

Useem, E. (2005). *Learning from Philadelphia's school reform: What do the research findings show so far?* Philadelphia: Research for Action.

Ziebarth, T. (2002). *State takeovers and reconstitutions* (Rev. ed.). Denver, CO: Education Commission of the States.

CHAPTER 10

Advocates for Children. (2002). *Pushing out at-risk students: An analysis of high school discharge figures—a joint report by AFC and the Public Advocate*. Retrieved October 3, 2007, from http://www.advocatesforchildren.org/pubs/pushout-11-20-02.html

Barker, R. G., & Gump, P. V. (1964). *Big school, small school: High school size and student behavior*. Stanford, CA: Stanford University Press.

Boyd, D., Grossman, P., Lankford, H., Loeb, S., & Wyckoff, J. (2006). How changes in entry requirements alter the teacher workforce and affect student achievement. *Education Finance and Policy, 1*, 176–216.

Clotfelter, C., Ladd, H., Vigdor, J., & Diaz, R. (2003, February). *Do school accountability systems make it more difficult for low performing schools to attract and retain high quality teachers?* Paper prepared for the annual meeting of the American Economic Association, Washington, DC.

Darling-Hammond, L. (2000). Teacher quality and student achievement. *Educational Policy Analysis Archives, 8*(1). Retrieved August 21, 2007, from http://epaa.asu.edu/epaa/v8n1

Darling-Hammond, L. (2004). From "separate but equal" to "No Child Left Behind": The collision of new standards and old inequalities. In D. Meier & G. Wood (Eds.), *Many children left behind* (pp. 3–32). New York: Beacon Press.

Darling-Hammond, L. (2005). Teaching as a profession: International lessons in teacher preparation and professional development. *Phi Delta Kappan, 87*(3), 237–240.

Darling-Hammond, L., Ancess, J., & Ort, S. (2002). Reinventing high school: Outcomes of the Coalition Campus School Project. *American Educational Research Journal, 39*(3), 639–673.

Darling-Hammond, L., & Bransford, J. (2005). *Preparing teachers for a changing world: What teachers should learn and be able to do.* San Francisco: Jossey-Bass.

Darling-Hammond, L., Holtzman, D., Gatlin, S., & Heilig, J. (2005). Does teacher preparation matter? Evidence about teacher certification, Teach for America, and teacher effectiveness. *Education Policy Analysis Archives, 13*(42). Retrieved August 21, 2007, from http://epaa.asu.edu/epaa/v13n42

Darling-Hammond, L., Ross, P., & Milliken, M. (in press). *High school size, organization, and content: What matters for student success?* Washington, DC: Brookings Institution Press.

Darling-Hammond, L., & Rustique-Forrester, E. (2005). The consequences of student testing for teaching and teacher quality. In J. Herman and E. Haertel (Eds.), *The uses and misuses of data in accountability testing. The 104th yearbook of the National Society for the Study of Education, part II* (pp. 289–319). Malden, MA: Blackwell.

Darling-Hammond, L., & Sykes, G. (2003, September). Wanted: A national teacher supply policy for education: The right way to meet the "highly qualified teacher" challenge. *Educational Policy Analysis Archives, 11*(33). Retrieved August 21, 2007, from http://epaa.asu.edu/epaa/v11n33/

DeVise, D. (1999, November 5). A+ plan prompts teacher exodus in Broward County. *Miami Herald.*

Erpenpach, W. J., Forte-Fast, E., & Potts, A. (2003). *Statewide educational accountability under NCLB.* Washington DC: Council for Chief State School Officers.

Fuller, B. (2004, February 1). Only the politicking gets an "A." *The Washington Post,* p. B04.

Goodlad, J. I. (1984). *A place called school.* New York: McGraw-Hill.

Gottfredson, G. D., & Daiger, D. C. (1979). *Disruption in 600 schools.* Baltimore: The Johns Hopkins University, Center for Social Organization of Schools.

Haney, W. (2002). Lake Woebeguaranteed: Misuse of test scores in Massachusetts, part I. *Educational Policy Analysis Archives, 10*(24). Retrieved August 21, 2007, from http://epaa.asu.edu/epaa/v10n24/

Heilig, J. V. (2005). *An analysis of accountability system outcomes.* Palo Alto, CA: Stanford University Press.

Jacob, B. A. (2001). Getting tough? The impact of high school graduation exams. *Education and Evaluation and Policy Analysis, 23*(2), 99–122.

Kim, J. S., & Sunderman, G. L. (2005). Measuring academic performance under NCLB: Implications for educational equity. *Educational Researcher, 34*(8) 2–13.

Lee, V. E., Bryk, A. S., & Smith, J. B. (1993). The organization of effective secondary schools. In L. Darling-Hammond (Ed.), *Review of research in education*, (Vol. 19, pp. 171–268). Washington, DC: American Educational Research Association.

Lee, V. E., & Smith, J. B. (1993). Effects of school restructuring on the achievement and engagement of middle-grade students. *Sociology of Education, 66*(3), 164–187.

Lee, V. E., & Smith, J. B. (1995). Effects of high school restructuring and size on early gains in achievement and engagement. *Sociology of Education, 68*(4), 241–270.

Lee, V. E., Smith, J. B., & Croninger, R.G. (1995, Fall). Another look at high school restructuring. *Issues in Restructuring Schools*, 9, 1–10.

Lilliard, D., & DeCicca, P. (2001). Higher standards, more dropouts? Evidence within and across time. *Economics of Education Review, 20*(5), 459–473.

Linn, R. L. (2003). Accountability: responsibility and reasonable expectations. *Educational Researcher, 32*(7), 3–13.

National Academy of Education (2005). *A good teacher in every classroom: Preparing the highly qualified teachers our children deserve.* San Francisco: Jossey-Bass.

Newmann, F. M., Marks, H. M., & Gamoran, A. (1996). Authentic pedagogy and student performance. *American Journal of Education, 104*(4), 280–312.

Novak, J., & Fuller, B. (2003). *Penalizing diverse schools? Similar test scores but different students bring federal sanctions.* Berkeley, CA: Policy Analysis for California Education.

Orfield, G., & Ashkinaze, C. (1991). *The closing door: Conservative policy and black opportunity.* Chicago: University of Chicago Press.

Packer, J. (2004, July). *No Child Left Behind and adequate yearly progress fundamental flaws: A forecast for failure.* Paper presented at the Center for Education Policy Forum on Ideas to Improve the Accountability Provisions, Washington, DC.

Roderick, M., Bryk, A. S., Jacob, B. A., Easton, J. Q., & Allensworth, E. (1999). *Ending social promotion: Results from the first two years.* Chicago: Consortium on Chicago School Research.

Sunderman, G. L., Kim, J. S., & Orfield, G. (2005). *NCLB meets school realities: Lessons from the field.* Thousand Oaks, CA: Corwin Press.

Tracey, C. (2005). Listening to teachers: Classroom realities and NCLB. In G. L. Sunderman, J. S. Kim, & G. Orfield (Eds.), *NCLB meets school realities: Lessons from the field* (pp. 81–104). Thousand Oaks, CA: Corwin Press.

Wald, M., & Losen, D. (2003). *Deconstructing the school to prison pipeline.* San Francisco: Jossey-Bass.

Wheelock, A. (2003). *School awards programs and accountability in Massachusetts: Misusing MCAS scores to assess school quality.* Retrieved February 12, 2004, from http://www.fairtest.org/arn/Alert%20June02/Alert%20Full%20Report.html

Wiley, E. W., Mathis, W. J., & Garcia, D. R. (2005). *The impact of the adequate yearly progress requirement of the federal "No Child Left Behind" Act on schools in the Great Lakes region.* Tempe: Educational Policy Studies Laboratory, Arizona State University.

Wood, G. (2004). A view from the field: NCLB's effects on classrooms and schools. In D. Meier & G. Wood (Eds.), *Many children left behind* (pp. 33–52). New York: Beacon Press.

CHAPTER 11

American Institutes for Research. (2006). CSRQ Center report on education service providers. Washington, DC: Author.

Belfield, C .R., & d'Entremont, C. (2005). Will disadvantaged students benefit from a free market in educational services? *American School Board Journal, 7*, 28–31.

Betts, J. R., Zau, A. C., & Rice, L. A. (2003). *New insights into school and classroom factors affecting student achievement* (Research Brief No. 76). San Francisco: Policy Institute of California.

Booher-Jennings, J. (2005). Below the bubble: "Educational triage" and the Texas accountability system. *American Educational Research Journal, 42*(2), 231–268.

Carey, K. (2006). Hot air: How states inflate their educational progress under NCLB. Washington, DC: Education Sector.

Center on Education Policy. (2006a). *From the capital to the classroom: Year 4 of the No Child Left Behind Act.* Washington, DC: Author.

Center on Education Policy. (2006b). Wrestling the devil in the details: An early look at restructuring in California. Washington, DC: Author.

Cuban, L. (2001). *How can I fix it? Finding solutions and managing dilemmas: An educator's roadmap.* New York: Teachers College Press.

Downs, A. (1966). *Inside bureaucracy.* Boston: Little Brown & Company.

Elmore, R. F. (2003). A plea for strong practice. *Educational Leadership, 61*(3), 6–11.

Fullan, M. (2001). *The new meaning of educational change* (3rd ed.). New York: Teachers College Press.

Fullan, M. (2005). *Leadership and sustainability: Systems thinkers in action.* Thousand Oaks, CA: Corwin Press.

Gill, B. P., Hamilton, L. S., Lockwood, J. R., Marsh, J. A., Zimmer, R. W., & Hill, D. (2005). *Inspiration, perspiration and time: Operations and achievement in Edison schools.* Santa Monica, CA: RAND.

Glennan, T., Bodilly, S., Galeher, J., & Kerr, K. A. (2004). Expanding the reach of educational reforms: What we have learned about scaling up educational interventions. Santa Monica, CA: RAND.

Goertz, M.E. (2005). Implementing the No Child Left Behind Act: Challenges for states. *Peabody Journal of Education, 80*(2), 73–89.

Gunn, J. H., & King, M. B. (2003). Trouble in paradise: Power, conflict and community in an interdisciplinary teaching team. *Urban Education, 38*(2), 173–195.

Hargreaves, A., & Fink, D. (2004). Sustaining leadership. *Phi Delta Kappan, 83*(9), 693–700.

Hawley, W. D., (1976). Horses before carts: Developing adaptive schools and the limits of innovation. In S. K. Gove & F. E. Wirt (Eds.), *Political science and school politics* (pp. 1–22). Lexington, MA: Lexington Books.

Hawley, W. D., & Sykes, G. (2007). Continuous school improvement. In W. D. Hawley & D. Rollie (Eds.), *The keys to effective schools: Educational reform as continuous improvement* (2nd ed., pp. 153–172). Thousand Oaks, CA: Corwin Press.

Hirschman, A. O. (1970). *Exit, voice, and loyalty.* Cambridge, MA: MIT Press.

Hoxby, C. M. (2003). Peer effects in the classroom: Learning from gender and race variation (Working Paper No. 7867). Cambridge, MA: National Bureau of Economic Research.

Hoxby, C. M., (2005). Adequate yearly progress: Refining the heart of the No Child Left Behind Act. In J. Chubb (Ed.), *Within our reach: How America can educate every child* (pp. 79–94). Stanford, CA: Stanford University, The Hoover Institution.

Kennedy, M. (2005). *Inside teaching: How classroom life undermines reform.* Cambridge, MA: Harvard University Press.

Kim, J. S., & Sunderman, G. L. (2005). Measuring academic proficiency under the No Child Left Behind Act: Implications of educational equity. *Educational Researcher, 34*(8), 2–13.

Lawler, E. E., III. (1994). Motivation in work organizations. San Francisco: Jossey-Bass.

Lee, J. (2006). *Tracking achievement gaps and assessing the impact of NCLB on the gaps: An in-depth look into national and state reading and math outcomes.* Cambridge, MA: The Harvard Civil Rights Project.

Leithwood, K., & Louis, K. (Eds.). (1998). *Organizational learning in schools.* Lisse, Netherlands: Swets & Zeitlinger.

Levin, H. (2005, November). *Why is educational entrepreneurship so difficult?* Paper presented at the American Enterprise Institute Conference, "Educational Entrepreneurship: Why It Matters, What Risks It Poses, and How to Make the Most of It," Washington, DC.

Linn, R. L. (2005). Issues in the design of accountability systems. In J. L. Herman & E. H. Haertel (Eds.), *Uses and misuses of data for educational accountability and improvement* (pp. 78-98). Chicago: National Society for the Study of Education.

Lissitz, R. (Ed.). (2005). Value-added models in education: Theory and practice. Maple Grove, MN: JAM Press.

Loeb, S., Darling-Hammond, L., & Luczak, J. (2005). How teaching conditions predict teacher turnover in California schools. *Peabody Journal of Education, 80*(3), 44–70.

Louis, K., Toole, J., & Hargreaves, A., (1999). Rethinking school improvement. In J. Murphy & K. Louis (Eds.), *Handbook of research on educational administration* (pp. 251–276). San Francisco: Jossey-Bass..

Manna, P. (2006, November). *State implementation of No Child Left Behind's remedies for troubled schools and districts.* Paper presented at the American Enterprise Institute/Thomas B. Fordham Foundation Conference, Washington, DC.

Maranto, R., & Maranto, A.G. (2005, November). *From markets to clans: The short term limits and long term promise of new education providers.* Paper presented at the American Enterprise Institute Conference, Washington, DC.

McClure, P. (2005). *School improvement under No Child Left Behind.* Washington, DC: Center for American Progress.

National Research Council and National Institute of Medicine, Board on Children, Youth, and Families. (2004). *Engaging schools: Fostering high school students' motivation to learn.* Washington, DC: The National Academies Press.

New Commission on the Skills of the American Workforce. (2007). *Tough choices: Tough times.* San Francisco: Jossey-Bass.

Nichols, S. L., & Berliner, D. C. (2005). *The inevitable corruption of indicators and educators through high stakes testing.* Tempe: Arizona State University, Educational Policy Studies Laboratory.

Popham, W. J. (2005). The age of compliance. *Educational Leadership, 63*(2), 84–85.

Popham, W. J. (2006). A test is a test—not. *Educational Leadership, 64*(4), 88–89.

Reville, S. P. (2005). Reinventing high school accountability: Authenticity, pressure, and support. *Voices in Urban Education, 8*. Providence, RI: Annenberg Institute for School Reform. Retrieved December 16, 2005, from http://www.annenberginstitute.org/VUE/summer05

Rice, J. K., (2003). *Teacher quality: Understanding the effectiveness of teacher attributes.* Washington, DC: Economic Policy Institute.

Shepard, L. A., (2000). The role of assessment in a learning culture. *Educational Researcher, 29*(7), 4–14.

Smrekar, C., & Goldring, E. (1999). *School choice in urban America: Magnet schools and the pursuit of equity.* New York: Teachers College Press.

Spillane, J. P. (2005). *Standards deviation: How schools misunderstand education policy.* Philadelphia: University of Pennsylvania, Center for Policy Research in Education.

Stecher, B., & Kirby, S. N. (2004). *Organizational improvement and accountability: Lesson for education from other sectors.* Santa Monica, CA: RAND.

Stringfield, S. (1998). Organizational learning and current reform efforts from exploitation to exploration. In K. Leithwood & K. Louis (Eds.), *Organizational learning in schools* (pp. 261–274). Lisse, Netherlands: Swets & Zeitlinger.

Stullich, S., Eisner, E., McCrary, J., & Roney, C. (2006). *National assessment of Title I interim report: Implementation of Title I.* Washington, DC: U.S. Department of Education, Institute of Education Sciences.

Sunderman, G. L., Tracey, C. A., Kim, J. S., & Orfield, G. (2004). *Listening to teachers: Classroom realities and No Child Left Behind.* Cambridge, MA: The Civil Rights Project at Harvard University.

Sunderman, G. L., Kim, J. S., & Orfield, G. (2005). *NCLB meets school realities: Lessons from the field.* Thousand Oaks, CA: Corwin Press.

Toch, T. (2006). *Margins of error: The education testing industry in the No Child Left Behind era.* Washington, DC: The Education Sector.

Vernez, G., Karam, R., Mariano, L. T., & Demartini, C. (2006). *Evaluating comprehensive school reform models at scale: Focus on implementation.* Santa Monica, CA: RAND.

Waters, J. T., Marzano, R. J., & McNulty, B. (2004). Leadership that sparks learning. *Educational Leadership, 61*(7), 48–51.

Wiley, E. W., Mathis, W. J., & Garcia, D. R. (2005*). The impact of the adequate yearly progress requirement of the federal "No Child Left Behind Act" on schools in the Great Lakes region.* East Lansing, MI: The Great Lakes Center for Educational Research and Practice.

CHAPTER 12

Allensworth, E., & Eaton, J. (2005). *The on-track indicator as predictor of high school graduation.* Chicago: Consortium of Chicago School Research.

Alliance for Excellent Education. (2006). *Graduation rates.* Washington, DC: Author. Retrieved February 28, 2007, from http://www.all4ed.org/publications/GraduationRates_FactSheet.pdf

Balfanz, R. (2005). *What does it cost to operate a high school organized into small learning communities?* Paper presented at Office of Vocational and Adult Education, Washington, DC.

Balfanz, R., & Legters, N. (2004). Locating the dropout crisis: Which high schools produce the nation's dropouts? In G. Orfield (Ed.), *Dropouts in America: Confronting the graduation rate crisis* (pp. 57–84). Cambridge, MA: Harvard Education Press.

Greene, J. P., & Winters, M. A. (2006). *Leaving boys behind: Public high school graduation rates.* New York: Manhattan Institute for Policy Research.

Hall, D. (2005). *Getting honest about grad rates.* Washington, DC: The Education Trust.

Hecker, D. (2005). Occupational employment projections to 2014. *Monthly Labor Review, 128*(11), 75.

High School Survey of Student Engagement. (2005). *HSSSE 2004 overview.* Bloomington: Indiana University.

Kemple, J., Herlihy, C., & Smith T. (2005). *Making progress towards graduation: Evidence from the talent development high school model.* New York: MDRC.

Legters, N., Balfanz R., Jordan, W., & McPartland J. (2002). *Comprehensive reform for urban high schools: A talent development approach.* New York: Teachers College Press.

Levin, H., Belfield, C., Muennig, P., & Rouse, C. (2007). *The costs and benefits of an excellent education for all of America's children.* New York: Teachers College.

Quint, J., Bloom, H., Black, R., & Stephens, L. (2005). *The challenge of scaling up educational reform: Findings and lessons from first things first.* New York: MDRC.

Swanson, C. (2004). *Who graduates? Who doesn't? A statistical portrait of public high schools graduation, class of 2001.* Washington, DC: Education Policy Center, the Urban Institute.

Swanson, C. (2005). *Projections of 2003–04 high school graduates: Supplemental analyses based on findings from Who graduates? Who doesn't?* Washington, DC: Education Policy Center, the Urban Institute.

Ziedenberg, J., & Schiraldi, V. (2002). *Cellblocks or classrooms? The funding of higher education and corrections and its impact on African American men.* Washington, DC: Justice Policy Institute.

CHAPTER 13

Ancess, J. (2000). The reciprocal influence of teacher learning, teaching practice, school restructuring, and student learning outcomes. *Teachers College Record, 102,* 590–619.

Archer, J. (2003, September 24) Houston case offers lessons on dropouts. *Education Week.* Retrieved March 7, 2007, from http://www.edweek.org/ew/articles/2003/09/24/04houston.h23.html

Armor, D. (2003). *Maximizing intelligence.* Somerset, NJ: Transaction Publishers.

Barnett, W. S. (1995). Long-term effects of early childhood programs on cognitive and school outcomes. *The Future of Children, 5,* 25–50.

Berends, M., Bodilly, S. J., & Kirby, S. N. (2002). *Facing the challenges of whole-school reform: New American schools after a decade.* Santa Monica, CA: RAND.

Bettinger, E. P. (2005). The effect of charter schools on charter students and public schools. *Economics of Education Review, 24,* 133–147.

Borman, G. D., Hewes, G. M., Overman, L. T., & Brown, S. (2003). Comprehensive school reform and achievement: A meta-analysis. *Review of Educational Research, 73,* 125–230.

Bowditch, C. (1993). Getting rid of troublemakers: High school disciplinary procedures and the production of dropouts. *Social Problems, 40,* 493–509.

Bryk, A. S., Lee, V. E., & Holland, P. B. (1993). *Catholic schools and the common good.* Cambridge, MA: Harvard University Press.

Bryk, A. S., & Schneider, B. (2002). *Trust in schools: A core resource for improvement.* New York: Russell Sage.

Cohen, D. K., Raudenbush, S. W., & Ball, D. L. (2003). Resources, instruction, and research. *Educational Evaluation and Policy Analysis, 25,* 119–142.

Cohen, D. K., & Spillane, J. P. (1992). Policy and practice: The relations between governance and instruction. *Review of Research in Education, 18,* 3–49.

Coleman, J. S., Hoffer, T., & Kilgore, S. B. (1982). *High school achievement: Public, Catholic, and private schools compared* . New York: Basic Books.

Coleman, J. S. (1990). *Equality and achievement in education.* San Francisco: Westview Press.

Comprehensive School Reform Quality Center. (2006). *CSRQ center report on middle and high school comprehensive school reform models.* Washington, DC: American Institutes for Research. Retrieved March 7, 2007, from http://www.csrq.org/documents/MSHS2006Report_FinalFullVersion01-02-07.pdf

Cook, T. D. (2005). Emergent principles for the design, implementation, and analysis of cluster-based experiments in social science. *Annals of the American Academy of Political and Social Science, 599,* 176–198.

Desimone, L. (2002). How can comprehensive school reform models be successfully implemented? *Review of Educational Research, 72,* 433–479.

Dynarski, M. (2004). Interpreting the evidence from recent federal evaluations of dropout-prevention programs: The state of scientific evidence. In G. Orfield (Ed.), *Dropouts in America: Confronting the graduation rate crisis* (pp. 255–267). Cambridge, MA: Harvard Education Press.

Dynarski, M., & Gleason, P. (1998). *How can we help? What we have learned from federal dropout-prevention programs.* Princeton, NJ: Mathematica Policy Research.

Edmonds, R. R. (1979). Effective schools for the urban poor. *Educational Leadership, 37,* 15–27.

Elmore, R. F. (2004a). Conclusion: The problem of stakes in performance-based accountability systems. In S. H. Furhman & R. F. Elmore (Eds.), *Redesigning accountability systems for education* (pp. 274–296). New York: Teachers College Press.

Elmore, R. F. (2004b). *School reform from the inside out.* Cambridge, MA: Harvard Education Press.

Furhman, S. H., & Elmore, R. F. (Eds.). (2004). *Redesigning accountability systems for education.* New York: Teachers College Press.

Gamoran, A. (1996). Student achievement in public magnet, public comprehensive, and private city high schools. *Educational Evaluation and Policy Analysis, 18,* 1–18.

Gotham, B. (2002). *Pushing out at-risk students: An analysis of high school discharge figures.* New York: The Public Advocate for the City of New York and Advocates for Children.

Guskey, T. R. (1989). Attitude and perceptual change in teachers. *International Journal of Educational Research, 13,* 439–453.

Hanushek, E. A. (1986). The economics of schooling: Production and efficiency in public schools. *Journal of Economic Literature, 24,* 1141–1177.

Hanushek, E. A., & Jorgenson, D. W. (Eds.). (1996). *Improving America's schools: The role of incentives.* Washington, DC: National Academy Press.

Hedges, L. V., Laine, R. D., & Greenwald, R. (1994). Does money matter? A meta-analysis of studies of the effects of differential school inputs on student outcomes. *Educational Researcher, 23,* 5–14.

Kahlenberg, R. D. (2001). *All together now: Creating middle-class schools through public school choice.* Washington, DC: Brookings Institution.

Kim, J. S., & Sunderman, G. L. (2004). *Large mandates and limited resources: State response to the No Child Left Behind Act and implications for accountability.* Cambridge, MA: Civil Rights Project at Harvard University.

Lewin, T., & Medina, J. (2003, July 31). To cut failure rate, schools shed students. *New York Times,* p. A1.

Louis, K. S., & Miles, M. B. (1990). *Improving the urban high school: What works and why.* New York: Teachers College Press.

Luyten, H. (1994). School size effects on achievement in secondary-education: Evidence from the Netherlands, Sweden, and the USA. *School Effectiveness and School Improvement, 5,* 75–99.

Malen, B. & Rice, J. K. (2004). A framework for assessing the impact of education reforms on school capacity: Insights from studies of high-stakes accountability initiatives. *Educational Policy, 18,* 631–660.

McDonnell, L. M. (2004). *Politics, persuasion, and educational testing.* Cambridge, MA: Harvard University Press.

McDonnell, L. M., & Elmore, R. F. (1987). Getting the job done: Alternative policy instruments. *Educational Evaluation and Policy Analysis, 9,* 133–152.

McLaughlin, M. W. (1987). Learning from experience: Lessons from policy implementation. *Educational Evaluation and Policy Analysis, 9,* 171–178.

McLaughlin, M. W. (1990). The RAND change agent study revisited: Macro perspectives and micro realities. *Educational Researcher, 19,* 11–16.

National Governors Association. (2006). Implementing graduation counts: State progress to date. Washington, DC: NGA. Retrieved September 7, 2007, from http://www.nga.org/Files/pdf/0608GRADPROGRESS.PDF

National Research Council, Committee on Increasing High School Students' Engagement and Motivation to Learn. (2004). *Engaging schools: Fostering high school students' motivation to learn.* Washington, DC: National Academies Press.

National Research Council, Panel on High-Risk Youth. (1993). *Losing generations: Adolescents in high-risk settings.* Washington, DC: National Academies Press.

Newmann, F. M. (1993). Beyond common sense in educational restructuring. *Educational Researcher, 22,* 4–13, 22.

Orfield, G., & Lee, C. (2005). *Why segregation matters: Poverty and educational inequality.* Cambridge, MA: The Civil Rights Project, Harvard University.

Orfield, G., Losen, D., Wald, J., & Swanson, C. B. (2004). *Losing our future: How minority youth are being left behind by the graduation rate crisis*. Cambridge, MA: The Civil Rights Project at Harvard University.

Organization for Economic Cooperation and Development. (2001). *Knowledge and skills for life: First results from the OECD programme for international student assessment (PISA) 2000*. Paris: OECD.

Purkey, S. C., & Smith, M. S. (1983). Effective schools: A review. *The Elementary School Journal, 83*, 426–452.

Raudenbush, S. W., & Bryk, A. S. (2002). *Hierarchical linear models: Applications and data analysis methods* (2nd ed.). Thousand Oaks, CA: SAGE.

Riehl, C. (1999). Labeling and letting go: An organizational analysis of how high school students are discharged as dropouts. In A. M. Pallas (Ed.), *Research in sociology of education and socialization* (pp. 231–268). New York: JAI Press.

Rothstein, R. (2004). *Class and schools: Using social, economic, and educational reform to close the black-white achievement gap*. Washington, DC: Economic Policy Institute.

Rumberger, R. W., & Larson, K. A. (1998). Student mobility and the increased risk of high school drop out. *American Journal of Education, 107*, 1–35.

Rumberger, R. W., & Palardy, G. J. (2004). Multilevel models for school effectiveness research. In D. Kaplan (Ed.), *Handbook of quantitative methodology for the social sciences* (pp. 235–258). Thousand Oaks, CA: SAGE.

Rumberger, R. W., & Palardy, G. J. (2005a). Does segregation still matter? The impact of student composition on academic achievement in high school. *Teachers College Record, 107*, 1999–2045.

Rumberger, R. W., & Palardy, G. J. (2005b). Test scores, dropout rates, and transfer rates as alternative indicators of school performance. *American Educational Research Journal, 41*, 3–42.

Sunderman, G. L. (2006). *The unraveling of No Child Left Behind: How negotiated changes transform the law*. Cambridge, MA: Civil Rights Project at Harvard University.

Sunderman, G. L. & Kim, J. S. (2007). The expansion of federal power and the politics of implementing the No Child Left Behind Act. *Teachers College Record, 109*, 1057–1085.

Teddlie, C., & Reynolds, D. (Eds.). (2000). *The international handbook of school effectiveness research*. New York: Falmer Press.

U.S. General Accounting Office. (1987). *School dropouts: Survey of local programs* (Publication No. GAO/HRD-87-108). Washington, DC: U.S. Government Printing Office.

U.S. General Accounting Office. (2004). *Unfunded mandates: Analysis of Reform Act coverage* (Publication No. GAO-04-637. Washington, DC: U.S. Government Printing Office.

Wayne, A. J., & Youngs, P. (2003). Teacher characteristics and student achievement gains: A review. *Review of Educational Research, 73*, 89–122.

CONCLUSION

Orfield, G. & Lee, C. (2007). *Historic reversals, accelerating resegregation, and the need for new integration strategies*. Los Angeles: The Civil Rights Project.

Index

CORWIN PRESS